Revelations

Unlocking Bible Mysteries and Hidden Secrets Revealed

GIAN MICHAEL SIMMONS

ISBN Paperback: 978-1-955638-80-7
ISBN eBook: 978-1-955638-79-1

Interior Formatting & Cover designed by YouTbooks.com

DEDICATION

I give honor and thanks to YAHUAH Elohiym, The Father. I dedicate this book to The Father that sustains me, the Father that speaks to me, The Father that allows me to speak with His children. Special thanks to my mother, father, and oldest brother who have gone on to glory. Special dedication to the 12 Tribes of Israel, a.k.a. The Chosen Children of YAH.

TABLE OF CONTENTS

TABLE OF CONTENTS

REVELATIONS UNLOCKING BIBLE MYSTERIES AND
HIDDEN SECRETS REVEALED, **CHARTS, IMAGES**

ACKNOWLEDGMENTS

I acknowledge that the following works are a product of a purification process and direct communication with the Father, YAH, and using the complete Word of YAH as certifiable divine scriptures. All scripture quotes come from the King James Bible, the Cepher Millennial Edition, and older translations. Furthermore, I acknowledge no involvement of man with this production, as it was birthed in heaven, secured by a pure in heart, communicated with all using the TORAH and holy scriptures, and sealed on the seventh day on penmanship. All in facts. All praises to YAH. Come forth Ha'Mashiach.

INTRODUCTION

History and the sciences have proven the authenticity of the Word of Elohiym (a.k.a. God) and the accurateness of the Bible/Cepher to predict present and future events. I often say that the Bible/Cepher is a "holy movie scroll" packed with valuable wisdom to prepare for the "signs of the times" and for seekers of eternal salvation. It prepares you for life.

Regardless of the arrogance and ignorance of man's miscalculations of times and the sciences, it is a **fact that our Creator exists** and the Word of **YAH** governs our life on Earth and afterlife. Because of the clouds of miseducation and false doctrines, many do not know or understand the true times we are currently living in, as **we are living at the end of the Gentile world and the coming of Ha'Mashiach (a.k.a. "Messiah") and only eternal judgement remains.**

Much knowledge has been hidden from the public and because of your low vibrational frequency, few can capture heavenly knowledge in fallen states.

In **Matthew 5:8**, it says that **only the pure in heart shall see YAH.** It **took a pure heart to be able to connect with the Father**, in heaven, to spring forth a **40-day fast**, isolate from all life, that kinetically undulated **Revelations, Unlocking Bible Mysteries and Hidden Secrets Unlocked. Penned in 7 days of completion of YAH, I had to completely perish to allow the Father in.**

Where do I start?
And the Father begin

Is there anything of me?
Left

Am I completely?
Rid of sin

Empty enough?

To invite the Father in

I am One with my Father
All of me left with sin

Revelations
Unlocking Bible Mysteries and Hidden Secrets Revealed

As I reflect on the Sevens of my times, this is 7 months after me retiring from a 19-year financial career to focus on the works of YAH. 9 is another 7, looped into infinity by the 1. I would also have you to know that this was seven days of actual writing, with very few editing as this project is directly from the throne of heaven. It flowed as fearless milk and honey all in divine order. All from YAH. More works to follow. This is also my seventh year of YAH showing his RIGHT Hand to me over the hands of secret government and Satan.

The following is a message to all on Earth, including the fallen angels. This is a very special message for the Children of Israel. I bring witness of YAH and to YAH all the Praise, Honor, and Glory.

By being a voice of YAH, every piece of information in this project is sealed upon verifiable facts and secured by scriptures of the Bible/Cepher. The King James Version and Bible Cepher Millennial Edition are quoted. This is also a study guide for all students of righteousness, seekers of the kingdom of heaven, and the children of Israel

When you see a scripture quoted, it serves as a lesson aid, direction, and reference to support the statement shared and providing fuller meaning. **The Word of YAH is established out of the mouths of 2-3 witnesses,** and there's learning in all things, so I provide scripture sources from several biblical authors to support my thesis. That's why you'll discover scriptures from many biblical authors all throughout the text to secure comfortability in the full Word of YAH. My goal is to enlighten you to the Word of YAH.

By using the **Word of YAH as the source of all information,** I cannot get accused of making this information up. Unless you claim that I wrote the Bible and Cepher! The Word from the beginning with YAH. Therefore, what I present is the Word of YAH unlike you ever heard before. Most importantly, **scriptures are quoted as they confirm everything I report.** Therefore, the information is **fully undeniable** regardless of your comfortability to accept facts and the Word of YAH.

Also, it's very important to understand that the Gentile world began approximately 2,000 years ago. With that said, the current church power structure hid several holy divined books that were formerly accepted, as everyone seeks to steal the right to be Israel. This was also consequences of Israel being punished under **Deuteronomy** curses. As per prophecy, these books are made available to the public to awaken Israel and prepare for the Day of Atonement, when all things return to their legal owners. The Day of Atonement is October 4, 2022. We return to YAH, along with the lands for heaven on earth.

Some examples of hidden books are, the Book of Jubilees, The Book of Enoch, The Book of Jasher, Baruch, Maccabees, and Esdras (a.k.a. "The Lost Books of the Bible", "Hidden books" – Apocrypha, Dead Sea Scrolls).

If you study your Bible/Cepher, Yahusha (a.k.a. Jesus) quoted from many of these books and the Hebrews use many today. In fact, Yahusha was a teacher of the law. Therefore, I make every attempt to use all relevant and available scriptures. I also accept all scriptures to be divinely inspired as the Word of YAH, so long as they conform to and confirm the TORAH. By having the full Word of YAH at your fingertips and having the proper perspective, you can gain clarity to all scriptures for a fuller and complete meaning that's closest to what YAH intends to communicate. This brings peace in your life and meaning.

In this project, I seek to provide further clarity to subjects that the modern church has abandoned or hid; ideas and concepts of early Hebrews and Christians that are lost in modern-English translations of the Bible/Cepher. **It is important to note that the Word of YAH originated and ended in Hebrew.** I am a student of the Hebrew and Greek scriptures.

It is also important to note that the modern-Church (Greek) vastly differs in interpretation of important concepts such as the real chosen children of YAH, giants, demonic possessions on Earth, resurrection of Yahusha (a.k.a. Christ), the Earth, the rapture, and the last days. Thus, I would encourage one to **study what the ancient Hebrews believed and studied.**

Also, the modern-Church has left out the important topic of giants and demons, and the hidden identity of the children of Israel, and many other important teachings which one must study non-canonical text, such as **the Book of Enoch, Book of Maccabee, Book of Jubilee, and Apocrypha** texts to shed light to the history of the fallen angels, a.k.a. "The Watchers" or "Sons of Elohiym (God)" and 12 Tribes of Israel. **For example, the Books of Maccabees, Baruch, Jubilees, Enoch, and Esdras** are very revealing to truth. I strongly recommend reading older translations of all scriptures, as much has been changed.

It is also important to note that I will be using the complete Bible/Cepher as the only source for this discourse to allow "**scriptures to confirm scriptures**". All the contents of this book are mentioned within scriptures and lost in translations or interpretations or hidden. It is also important to note that the books of the Bible/Cepher received many **revisions of interpretation** have occurred throughout the years to **align with the power structure and church message, and to hide the identity of Israel**.

Although some topics may sound strange and "out of this world", **this is what the early Hebrews believed**, historians and sciences confirmed, and pagan traditions revealed. **This is also what's known secretly. All confirmations that what I present is truly the Word of YAHUAH Elohiym (a.k.a. God); a message that has been "lost" and/or "watered down" throughout the generations or locked away by Freemasons and Esau-Rome (a.k.a. Mystery Babylon).**

I will also present a case for a **LITERAL TRANSLATION of the Bible/Cepher.** I also use the name of the Most High as YAHUAH Elohiym (a.k.a. YAHWEH).

In efforts to present the Bible/Cepher as a book of "themes" and not a chronological book, I will offer this layout for this study; meaning that this **book may be read in any order**. I will group topics together as "themes".

We live in a programmed and artificially created reality, gamed by Satan, where the rules of life, engagements, and the synthesizing of information is extremely regulated.

Furthermore, the grand architect of this created Matrix employs metrics for one to receive information. One must have the ability to receive information before one can process information (this takes a pure heart to see YAH).

The Matrix holds its "programs", which I distinguish as one who the system holds as a credible and authoritative source of information (ex. A teacher, minister, or religious leader or a social media icon, etc.).

YAHUAH Elohiym (a.k.a. God) created man in His image and likeness. Thereby, affording us with an opportunity to engage with Him, directly, based upon our spirit. The challenge with discussing things of YAHUAH Elohiym (a.k.a. God), in this created Matrix, is that the architect of the Matrix (Satan) dictates that only his controlled puppets (pastors) can speak of the things of YAHUAH Elohiym (a.k.a. God) with divine authority. All others are considered heretics and blasphemous or silenced. Few hold pastors accountable to scriptures and blindly follow the blind, not realizing that pastors are secretly Mystery Babylon and attempting to steal the identity of Israel, YAH's chosen children.

Thereby, this discourse of the mysteries of YAHUAH Elohiym (a.k.a. God) presents an obstacle which must be addressed before we can proceed further.

The best way that one can approach the following works is to allow yourself an opportunity to have an opportunity. Do not be closed minded to truth. This can be accomplished by allowing yourself to present to yourself an open heart and an open mind to receive the things of YAHUAH Elohiym (a.k.a. God), which may be in contrary to your standard norm. Forget the trap knowledge you possess and allow YAH to bless you.

We have been programmed to receive spiritual information solely from fallen programmed agents (those who hold themselves as termed religious leaders). **I present to you hidden knowledge and secret knowledge of YAHUAH Elohiym (a.k.a. God)**. FEARLESS!

Much of what you will be presented with may be foreign to the chemistry of your brains computer system and levels of consciousness. Remember, this project is for the pure in heart and to get you to repent and see the errors in your ways are contrary to YAH. The intake of information may appear unnatural and uncomfortable. Some terminology, ideas, descriptions, and events may bewilder your untrained(trained) minds to accept them as literal translations of the Word of YAHUAH Elohiym (a.k.a. God) and facts. Be fearless in your faith in YAH. Also, understand we still have slavery Elohiym (Gods).

We have been programmed to, solely, receive watered down misinformation and indoctrination. Many of us are dead to the true knowledge of YAHUAH Elohiym (a.k.a. God) because many fiery truths have been locked away, hidden, and frozen in myths and folklore. They make every attempt to scare you away from full knowledge of YAH.

The TORAH and Tanakh holds the keys to unlock the mysteries to deciphering the parables and coded messages within the Word of Elohiym (a.k.a. God) and Bible/Cepher. Because the Devil's created Matrix has control over the programs (religious leaders), we are programmed to be dead to the fullness of YAHUAH Elohiym (a.k.a. God) and veiled with the holy knowledge of Satan disguised as our Holy Father. Billions of people worship Satan, disguised as religion, and don't even know this horrible secret.

The greatest con artist, Satan, has tricked man into accepting his created Matrix to be the inheritance of the seed of Adam and Israel. Problem is, the programs hide the necessary information for you to break the created Matrix, which is true knowledge of YAHUAH Elohiym (a.k.a. God) by studying the Hebrew books and prophets. The Torah and Tanakh are your only weapons to biblical and historical truths.

Unfortunately, what you are about to be presented with may be silent in your church and may be dead knowledge to your loved ones. Religious leaders all know the truth and hide this information. **This is not to discredit the many truths you are about to be gifted for free.** Always remember, they are controlled puppets of the system of Mystery Babylon, which you must come out of Mystery Babylon.

I challenge you to find the courage to allow YAHUAH Elohiym (a.k.a. God) to **search your heart, open your mind to Wisdom and understanding, and to give you the heart to allow scriptures confirm scriptures.** Give you the heart to REPENT and depart from evil. Turn to YAH. Come out of Mystery Babylon.

This is how I will disseminate the following information by allowing scriptures to confirm scriptures and confirming all things to the Hebrew books and prophets, the original Word of YAH. Thus, I will be sharing the Word of YAHUAH Elohiym (a.k.a. God) in a more complete way then the watered-down version you're used to from your programmed "leaders" and religion.

I further challenge you to search scriptures to confirm what I present to you to allow scriptures to confirm scriptures and speak for itself. This is the reasoning for me basing this entire work on the Word of YAH and providing scripture references, so you see it with your own eyes. CHECK THE WORD OF YAH YOURSELF TO CONFIRM!

Side note, as you're searching your scriptures, why not, as an academic exercise, search for scriptures whereby YAHUAH Elohiym (a.k.a. God) anointed bishops, pastors, or ministers to be the only authorized method of YAHUAH Elohiym (a.k.a. God) communicating with His people. Search for the word, Bishop in the Torah/Tanakh. Bishop is a title of Mystery Babylon. While you're at it, search for a time when Yahusha (a.k.a. Jesus) preached from a pulpit or met with a religious council or leader. Yahusha (a.k.a. Jesus) taught the Torah law. Paul did away with the law, made Yahusha into a God and created a new religion, Christianity and took it to an enemy of Hebrews (the Gentiles). YAH didn't raise a pastor or church! Think on that!

I'm only doing this exercise to open your mind to be able to break the traps of the program so you can, first, **allow yourself an opportunity to have an opportunity.** Void of this, reading further may prove fruitless as one who ate from the forbidden tree in the Garden of Eden and controlled by the tempting serpent, only to be trapped into temptation of trying to replace the Creator through blind myths of an artificial created reality.

Note, we are not engaging in any deadly sins by studying this text. We are seeking to break the chains of deadly sins, which the wise would have you to be ignorant of the things of YAHUAH Elohiym (a.k.a. God), for **YAHUAH Elohiym (a.k.a. God) represents your salvation and freedom from the Devils created Matrix and Esau-Rome (Christianity, Islam, Catholicism).**

The Matrix employs **weapons of fear and control** to limit any threats to their goal of world domination. If they can't control what information is out there, they can control what information you accept and/or entertain. This is another reason why what I am about to present may come as strange because **many educators and current authors are under the control of the system as puppets and are not accurately communicating the things of YAH.** They sell and teach lies!

This is how the system of control has been able to hide true knowledge of YAHUAH Elohiym (a.k.a. God) right in front of our eyes through the usage of parables and symbols and false prophets. Parables and symbols allow for a multi-dimensional transferring and dissemination of coded layers of encrypted information that an only skilled practitioner can extract, process, and interpret. False prophets create false gods and new gospels. Beware of false prophets. There are many!

Throughout this text, I have made every effort to return all names to their original Hebrew name. Learn the Hebrew names.

Instead of using the vernacular name "God", I made the decision to use the Hebrew name of YAHUAH Elohiym or YAH, blessed be His Holy Name (a.k.a. YAHWEH). Without getting into the controversy of possible paganism by saying God, as the ancient pagans worshipped a DOG (Anubis). The spelling of GOD is a DOG backwards. The devil is very crafty, Sin is backwards of righteousness. Also, **YAH provided His name for a reason**, so why not use it! Just not in vain.

For those that have the Hebrew Cepher, you will find the Hebrew names restored in the Millennial Cepher Edition, along with the complete Word of YAH of public books (keep in mind this is a Christianized translation). I also use the King James Bible and older translations.

Without getting into the many arguments about the most accurate name of the Jesus, I'll pose a non-controversial resolve. The strongest tongue is always the original and YAHUAH Elohiym is the same today and yesterday and will be the same on tomorrow. YAHUAH Elohiym doesn't change (**Hebrews 13:6-8**). The person known as Jesus real name was

Yahusha Ben Yosef. He was a Hebrew prophet who taught Torah law. The Druids had a god named Hesus and Krishna in Sanskrit means Christ. Over 500 years after his death, Greeks changed name to Jesus Christ.

Additionally, in **Revelations 19:12**, scriptures teach us that Ha'Mashiach will come with a name that no man knows except Him and the Father.

The public god of Christianity is Jesus, a secretly racist human pagan mystery god with long red hair, which is an abomination to YAH. This may be difficult to hear and believe for Christians. I will provide a surplus of wealth of information to awaken you to this unfortunate truth. However, **a fact is a fact. We shall only reference the Bible/Cepher and facts that can be proven with other facts.**

Christianity is a Mystery Babylon religion that has intentionally targeted and enslaved the chosen children of YAH and attempted to steal their identity through a false teaching of "spiritual Israel" falsely teaching that the church is Israel. This is not a correct teaching of Yahuah Elohiym. Also, they know exactly WHO you ARE!

When one says the name of Jesus, they naturally think of this false figure of a white Jesus. Without the pure in heart being so harsh on yourself, YAH is a Elohiym of understanding and knows our hearts (**Isaiah 40:28**).

Without getting into theories regarding the name of Jesus possibly and secretly being the name of the Greek pagan myth god Zeus and calling Jesus may be like saying "Hey Zeus", realizing the church involvement with many pagan teachings. **After learning the proper Hebrew names, I prefer to use the original Hebrew translations. I encourage you all to do the same. Search Serapis and Mithra and compare Christianity.**

We also unknowingly **Deuteronomy curse** (penalty of sin/punishment) ourselves by praying to pagan gods, holidays, and teachings even when we think we're praying to YAH. So, **it's better to be safe than sorry. Read Deuteronomy 28.**

Since the whitewashing of history and the reminder that the name of Jesus has been sold to be a false white human, and not the true Ha'Mashiach, its usage immediately brings this to record. More on this in section on Ha'Mashiach.

ENOCH 104:10-13

104:10 "And now I know this mystery: For they the **sinners shall alter** the just verdict and many sinners will take it to heart; **they will speak evil words and lie**, and **they will invent fictitious stories and write out my Scriptures on the basis of their own words**."

104:11 "And would that they had written down all the words truthfully on the basis of their own speech, and neither alter nor take away from my words, all of which I testify to them from the beginning!"

104:12 "Again know **another mystery**! **That to the righteous and the wise shall be given the Scriptures of joy, for truth and great wisdom**."

104:13 "So to them shall be given the Scriptures; and they shall believe them and be glad in them; and all the righteous ones who learn from them the Ways of Truth shall rejoice. (**Enoch 104:10-13)**

Unlocking Bible Mysteries and Hidden Secrets Revealed

I PROMISED TO HELP YOU BREAK THE MATRIX

Throughout this project, you will see these sections appear with different subtitles. **They present a free opportunity for multi-dimensional learning of hidden facts of life. REVELATIONS**

In efforts to present you with opportunities for true repentance and rebirthing into the Spirit of Yahuah Elohiym (Truth) and Love, which is required to enter heaven and to avoid eternal hell (John 3). My attempt is to be very thorough feeding you the bread of eternal life. Yahusha said that only the truth shall set you free (John 8:32). YAH IS THE ONLY TRUTH!

I cherish the **children of Yahuah Elohiym and the strangers that submit to His ways**, therefore **my goal** is to provide you with all the **free keys** to be able to **gain**

eternal life in the Kingdom of Heaven, avoid eternal hell/damnation, and to **turn the hearts of the children back to their Father/Creator, YAHUAH Elohiym (Malachi 4:6).** I report what the pure in heart see of YAH. YAH creates the good and evil, so all are His creation and are subject to Him alone (**Isaiah 45:7**). On a side note, because things can become thick when dealing with the many mysteries unlocked and revelations of frozen truths in this series, after living with lifetimes of lies, these sections also offer a **gentle** and **Silent Speaks** break to **solidify** your **revelations and moments of truth of Love Liberates**. **Accept all truths in LOVE.** YAHUAH Elohiym is Love and Love is YAHUAH Elohiym (**1 John 4:8-21**)

All information presented can be validated by focusing on the **truth behind the veils of a rewritten worldwide history which occurred over 2,000 years ago. Salvation is A FREE GIFT to those that Repent and Follow YAH. Obey the Torah Law. Israel will be saved.**

All you must do is REPENT. Come out of evil.

COME OUT OF MYSTERY BABYLON

This series focuses on proven facts and avoids misrepresentation of any data. These sections are gentle free moments of truth. Stay tuned in the series for **Unlocking Bible Mysteries and Hidden Secrets Revealed**

LOVE LIBERATES. SILENCE SPEAKS

Put Love in All You Do for Yahuah Elohiym is Love and Love is Yahuah Elohiym (1 John 4:16)

FOLLOW YAH

THE FALL OF MAN - FLAT EARTH

The best way to understand any story is to go back to the beginning, see the order of where things come from, and put things in the proper perspective. This will enable one to fully appreciate the context of characters and events, as well as identifying one's proper role in the story.

In the last days (**4 Ezra/2 Esdras 7: 26-30**), all things will return to a form of its original intended state where YAH resides with His creation after the Millennial Kingdom rule of Ha'Mashiach, the Son of Yahuah Elohiym.

In the original creation of man, YAH and the angels interacted with man and there was no separation between heaven and Earth. Because of the original fall of man, a veil was created to hide the heavenly things of YAH and His fiery image (we'll get deeper into the image of YAH later in the study). The job of the Son of YAH (born in heaven and manifesting on Earth – **Enoch 46**) is to fulfill the redemption plan of man, on Earth (covered throughout this study).

To understand the redemption plan of YAH, one must go back to where it all began. We must look to the original fall of man and creation story. We must look beyond the veil. **The books of Genesis, Jubilees, and Jasher** shed light on the creation story and the beginnings of man. You may also reference the **Book of Psalms and Job**.

Our current state of man is raised to learn about our world from the teachings of a fallen state of man; whereby sciences and many religions are false indoctrinations of man and an enemy of YAH. Science, intentionally present contradictions to YAH.

Another important concept to keep in mind when discussing the sciences of man is their demonic theory of "order out of chaos". This is also identified by studying mythology and the gods of the underworld/dead pagan myths. These are the fallen angels or "Sons of Elohiym", created by YAH and not an equal to YAH.

Something important to keep in mind is that there's only one true Elohiym (a.k.a. God) of all things. YAH is the only living God and He also has dominion over the living and the dead (we'll get deeper into this during our study).

Unlocking Bible Mysteries and Hidden Secrets Exposed
Christopher Columbus
Did you know that Christopher Columbus and explorer-Admiral Byrd discovered tropical lands beyond the ice-walls of Antarctica? Did you know that they reported lands that was close to the sun/poles? Did you know that they reported the lands to be inhabited by all Blacks? In **seeking of the dispersed Black Israelites** {who first conquered and ruled the entire planet and first rulers of every continent} Christopher Columbus took many Hebrews to use as interpreters to conquer the aboriginal black Israelites on every continent on Earth. That's the secret agenda behind his travels! Yet, you celebrate him.
Stay tuned in the series for more silent speaks moments of truth

Science and man seek to create chaos to bring about their definition of "order". This is the secret agenda and goal of most secret societies and the power elite that has current domain on our fallen Earth. They seek to destroy and rebuild. Hence, the statue of Shiva (destructive pagan god) outside of CERN, a government entity. **They also sell you "the end of the world" as they seek to destroy the Creator, His Chosen Children, and His creation.**

Also, another reason why world governments build geometric structures along Earth's energy grid system to harvest chaotic energy on Earth. A clear example of this is the government structures in Washington D.C. and most major cities. Ever wonder why when you enter certain environments your energy changes? New York City is like a mini hell to just get wild or places like Chicago is a legally free Black man's killing jail or the current land of Israel is so gay and racist? This is all manipulations of energy. Secret sciences of the secret elite using geometry.

The goal of science is to present a world without YAH. Throughout this section, we will review the fall of man led by science. We will see many examples of how science is used as a weapon to teach false theories in direct opposition to YAH. Their goal is to get one to question the Word of YAH. If they can get you to question one thing, then your faith alters and is shaken allowing for science to conquer you with atheist and false teachings.

Science teaches that our world began by an explosion of stars, which they term the **big bang theory**. An interesting thing about this **false theory** is that they have a physical created picture of this! (**Side note:** Who took the picture when there wasn't a man nor camera?). **All pictures NASA uses are all computerized made-up images.**

Touching on the issue of pictures, it's only proper to briefly reference **NASA's famous picture of Earth and its creator**, Robert Simmon (NASA Lead Data Visualizer and Information Designer, see picture below). **Notice in this statement, directly from NASA's website, how he notes that he took a flat-Earth map and wrapped it around a ball to produce the Earth-ball picture of NASA. The same fake picture that's used all over governments, Hollywood, educational institutions, and publicly held as an accurate picture of Earth.**

(NASA.GOV)

> **(Excerpt from NASA interview) What is the coolest thing you've ever done as part of your job at Goddard?**
>
> **The last time anyone took a photograph from above low Earth orbit that showed an entire hemisphere (one side of a globe) was in 1972 during Apollo 17. NASA's Earth Observing System (EOS) satellites were designed to give**

a check-up of Earth's health. By 2002, we finally had enough data to make a snapshot of the entire Earth. So, we did. The hard part was creating a flat map of the Earth's surface with four months of satellite data. Reto Stockli, now at the Swiss Federal Office of Meteorology and Climatology, did much of this work. Then we wrapped the flat map around a ball. My part was integrating the surface, clouds, and oceans to match people's expectations of how Earth looks from space. That ball became the famous Blue Marble.

I was happy with it but had no idea how widespread it would become. We never thought it would become an icon. I certainly never thought that I would become "Mr. Blue Marble."

We have since updated the base maps by increasing the resolution and, for 2004, we made a series of monthly maps.

(Source: https://www.nasa.gov/centers/goddard/about/people/RSimmon.html)

Before we discuss the ancient Hebrew cosmology presented, I have an **interactive exercise for you**!

1. Do a search online for the NASA scientist grave of Wernher Von Braun **Psalms 19:1**. He left a major Bible clue for you in death.
2. My text discusses what the Word of YAH presents. However, any simple online search of what other ancient cultures taught about Earth would reveal **Flat-Earth cosmologies around the ancient world in every culture.**
3. Also, look at ancient sea maps and land-explorer maps and journals. These people needed to know exactly what the earth looked like to navigate the seas. Interestingly, read Christopher Columbus and Richard Byrd original journals and not the revised ones they sell you! Check what maps the Navy uses and White House!
4. Since this is beyond the scope of this current study, I will share some references for those interested in digging deeper into the subject ("Is the Bible from Heaven? Is the Earth a Globe" by Alex Gleason, "The Greatest Lie on Earth: Proof that our world is not a moving globe" by Edward Hendrie, "The Earth is Flat and Jesus is Black"

by Rodney R. Allison, "Maps of the Ancient Sea Kings" by Charles Hapgood), Christopher Columbus and Admiral Byrd diaries and Marco Polo)

5. Since many of my readers are young adults and are deeply engaged in social media, here's one for you. On YouTube and Instagram, there's a new trend of videos of people doing tricks flying high from airplanes at various altitudes. Interesting thing is flat-Earth is right in front of our faces in these videos. No matter how high you elevate, you **never see the Earth curve! It is always a flat horizon. Look outside your window during a plane flight! Wonder why the ban you!**
6. I'll share a Freemason secret with you! Freemasons hide truths behind symbols. Disclaimer, I never been inside of a lodge and am not associated with Freemasons in any way. **I don't even trust them**. My knowledge comes from YAH. A simple online search will reveal this. Not only does their lodges exemplify flat-Earth, but also the layouts of many government structures. For example, our modern-day courtrooms illustrate a layout of flat-Earth! The judge sits on the pole! They are built this way intentionally to harvest earth's energy using geometry.
7. For my readers, I'll share a drawing from my meditation notebook. I must confess that no man will ever figure all the mysteries of YAH. I went into a deep meditation and prayed on what our world looks like. I immediately drew this image and notes after my meditation on February 14, 2022. This is my sketch of what I feel our world/universe looks like on a flat-disk scale since no man has been able to escape the firmament. **Ask yourself, how can any spaceship breakthrough an indestructible glass wall firmament, travel through the waters above the firmament to go anywhere and without flooding the earth from cracking the firmament and allowing the waters above to flood in? That's what's above the firmament dome: WATERS ABOVE.**

My theory is the universe and vast space that they sell us are the other flat-concentric circles beyond the ice wall of Antarctica (earth is surrounded by the ice wall of Antarctica) and not deep space in the sky. We must also remember there are invisible worlds as well. Also, my theory can be seen by stacking the circles as well. My theory is that Antarctica is not a continent as we perceive and is a major ice wall that surrounds Earth continents thereby creating "North" from all directions and a restricting electromagnetic barrier to keep us in place. It may even be tropical. This is all secured by the four pillars of YAH. Check your compass! Magnets cannot lie! Also, read Enoch 53:7.

Regarding the "planets", my theory is that they are lands beyond the poles/ice wall. Rather than going to "outer space", I feel that they have discovered hidden portals, within Earth, that connects to these hidden lands and inner-Earth lands. I feel that Antarctica was once a tropical land, some parts are, and has tropical lands hidden beyond the ice. With this said, **I still feel NASA is a fake government agency and is illegally stealing billions on an annual basis since their creation.** My theory is they're funding the last war against YAH for centuries through robbing the people through fake science that they can never prove!

If you study Christopher Columbus and Admiral Richard Byrd diaries, they were very close to discovering these hidden lands. They also confirm FLAT EARTH! **(pictured below – my exclusive meditation picture only found here!)**

The concentric circles are other worlds with our Earth in the center. I also feel we live on a hollow earth and some live inside our Earth. The mini circles are lands within each realm which are all protected by electromagnetic restrictive walls. The solid dots are the "Wandering stars" that NASA calls planets and not Solid objects but plasma lights). The dots lining up represents the major star alignment between the rings. I see this now in 2022, a major star alignment aligning with a Year of Atonement. We also have an invisible world.

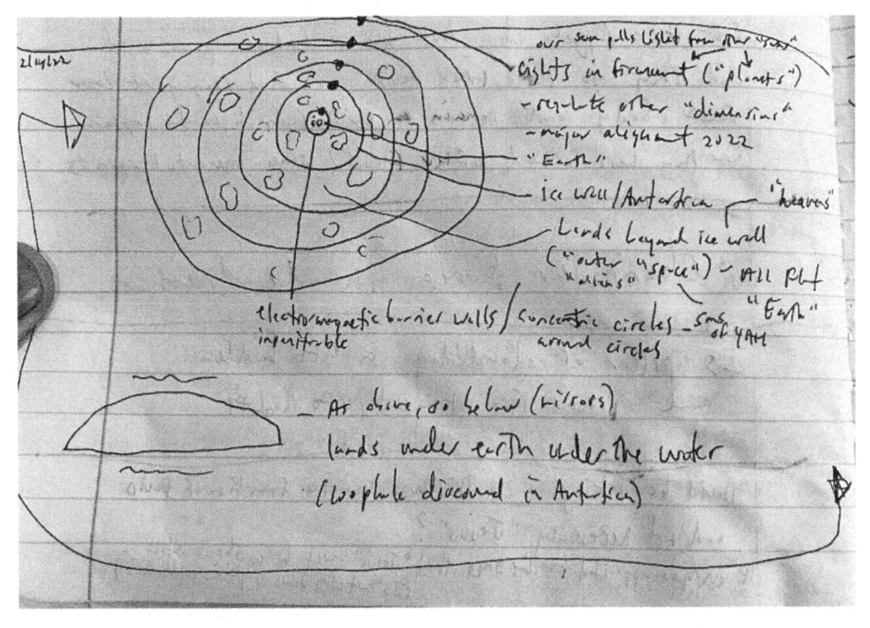

(MY UNIVERSE MEDITATION PIC ONLY FOUND HERE)

After these exercises, let's see what the ancient Hebrews said of Earth!

Note: Once you realize that space is fake, you'll also realize many untruths such as global warming and aliens. How much our governments are robbing us blindly and many corporations as well.

Unlocking Bible Mysteries and Hidden Secrets Revealed
IRS and TAXES ARE ILLEGAL and Unconstitutional
Just as they steal trillions off a fake globe earth and "space" that doesn't exist, they also rob everyone with taxes. **There is no law that legally allows the government to collect taxes off your income.**
The IRS and state taxes are unconstitutional and illegal. They are given illegally authority to enforce tax laws don't doesn't exist.
Also, the **U.S. government doesn't even own the Federal Reserve.**
WAKE UP. YOU BEEN ROBBED! PRIVATELY

The ancient Hebrew cosmology of a flat-Earth

(see next picture)

"Thus says YAHUAH: The heavens are my throne, and the earth is my footstool" – Isaiah 66:1a

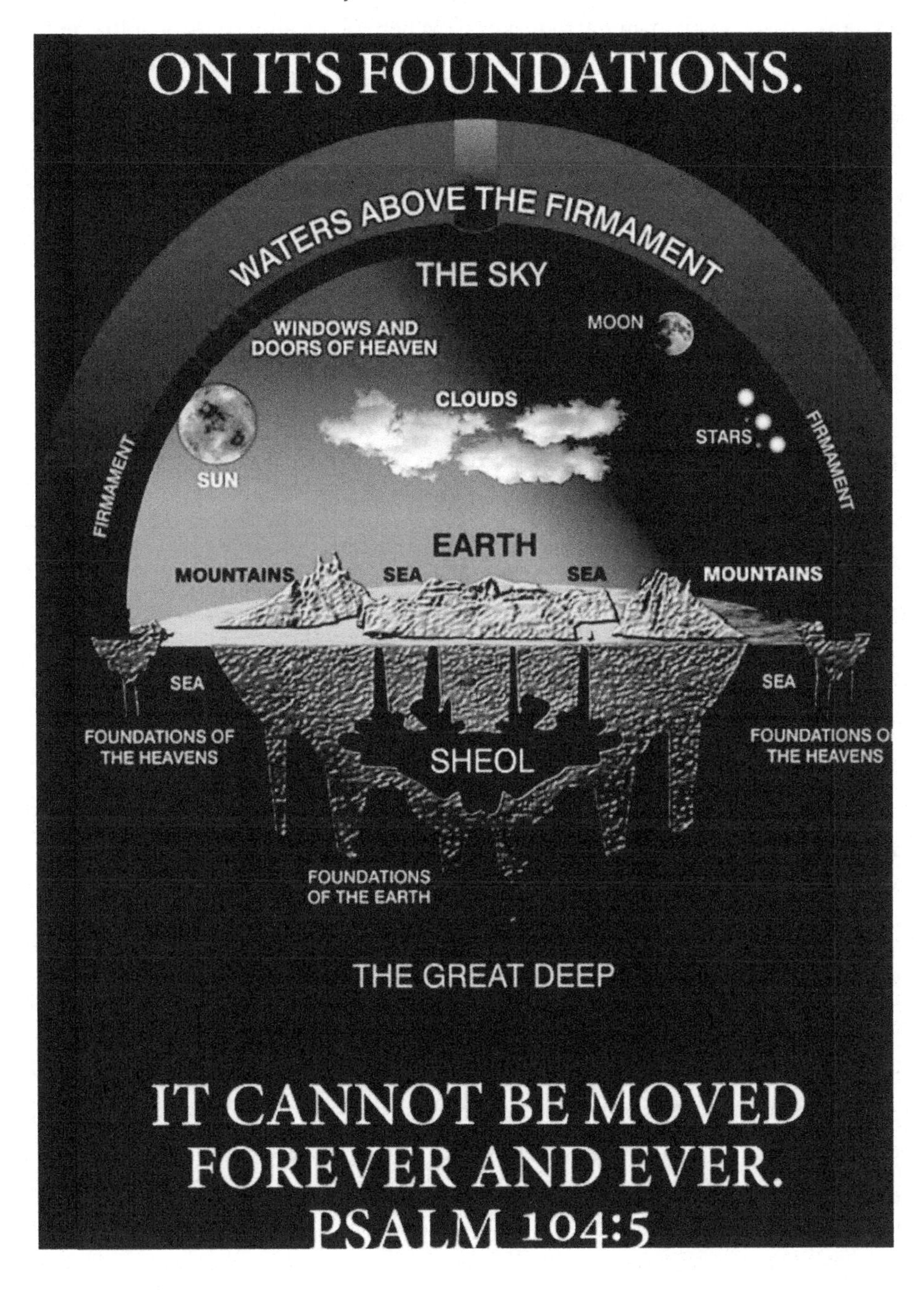

Bible Mystery and Secret Exposed
FOR GLOBLE- EARTHERS
For all you global earthers out there. Have you ever thrown water on a spinning tennis ball? Does it hold the water, or do you find yourself with a dry dead ball (planet)? Also, how do you explain an Earthquake? If/When the ground splits or shifts on the Earth's fault line, on a globe earth how do you explain this? Wouldn't the earth ball crack or split? **Like crack an egg and then keep it held together**. Now, produce the same hurricane event on a flat surface and it's logical for a split in one location not affecting the entire earth. Take a round ball and split/shift a piece of it, does your round ball (earth) stay intact or does it fall into pieces? Do you destroy the entire ball even just with one crack somewhere (North and South/East or West)? Now, take a flat piece of paper, you can draw lines and shift anywhere, and you still have a secure unmovable full-flat piece of paper intact. Explain Enoch?
(Flat-Earth is Bible Proof) Globe Earth is a false teaching of Mystery Babylon and blasphemy!
Beware of false prophets
Just some common sense to ask yourself and not just blindly allow the blind to lead the blind.

Science also teaches the theory of evolution, whereby they profess that man evolved, over time, from a single organism or atom. An example of this teaching is an atom became an organism became a plant became an animal which became a man over millions of years of evolution, and at the same time a bang turning into a planet creating all things.

They even claim the stars are sperm and that sperm is the spirits of the dead. Hence, they teach stars are dead spirits and they worship the stars.

Prior to debunking of Charles Darwin's evolution theory, they taught that man evolved from apes, which is a direct contradiction to man being formed from the dust of the ground and created in the image of YAH (**Genesis 1:26, 2:7**). Were they trying to call YAH an ape? **Esau did mate with beasts.** Not sure if this was the hidden reference!

Contrary to what science teaches of a big bang explosion to create Earth and man manifesting after millennia of evolution, **the holy text presents an orderly creation that was pleasing to the Highest YAHUAH.** Contrary to being a constant spinning ball in space, the Earth is a flat disk held in firm position by four pillars. **The reality is that Earth doesn't move! (Psalms 104:5)**. YAH is standing on the throne of the Dome. Earth is His footstool (**Isaiah 66:1**). There is a veil to hide heaven because of Adam. They want to hide this by using a fake globe with no YAH.

To understand the purpose of creation, one must need to be aware that the purpose of science is to teach things contrary to the Word of YAH. **Let's review the creation story as defined by the Word of YAH. Note: I'll be paraphrasing verses for brevity.**

Unlocking Bible Mysteries and Hidden Secrets Revealed
SECRET SCIENCE OF BLOOD
Blood is the source of energy of life to transfer and transmit electromagnetic energy. A way to see this is that blood is like fuel to a vehicle of transportation. As humans, we are the vehicle of transportation that is carrying the flaming spirit to have an experience of life on Earth. Blood is what is carrying the energy and source of life.
The Word of **YAH** is filled with many warnings **against** killing blood, eating blood, touching blood, using blood to conjure spirits, using blood for magic and divination, and sacrificing blood rituals. All these acts are an abomination of YAH and will lead you to eternal hell.
Isn't it strange that they are so desperate for your blood that agencies PAY YOU FOR BLOOD!
They use BLOOD FOR WITCHCRAFT AND SORCERY TO DEMONS. This is the science behind blood sacrifices and rituals.
Even our young people are cutting themselves and spilling blood for MAGIC and WITCHCRAFT
Freemasons eat the blood of newborns because they have the maximum amount of nutrients and the most energy. They eat a baby fetus!
Someone needs to audit the Red Cross and all agencies and see where the blood is really going!

OVERVIEW OF CREATION STORY

1. <u>**First day/Act of Creation: Light of the Son of YAHUAH Elohiym**</u> (Close your eyes and imagine a sea of blackness. Then, imagine the light switch being turned on. Thought is light turned on. We'll discuss this deeper in Ha'Mashiach section towards the rear of the book, which is symbolic of the stone that the builders rejected becomes the cushion cornerstone (**Psalms 118:22**).

2. At that place, I saw **the One to whom belongs the time before time**. - And his head was white like wool, **and there was with him another individual, whose face was like that of a human being**." His countenance was full of grace like that of one among the holy angels. And I asked the one--from among the angels-who was going with me, and who had revealed to me all the secrets regarding **the One who was born of human beings**, "Who is this, and from whence is **he who is going as the prototype of the Before-Time** And he answered me and said to me, "This is **the Son of Man**, to **whom belongs righteousness**, and with whom righteousness dwells. And he will open all the hidden storerooms; for the Lord of the Spirits has chosen him, and he is destined to be victorious before the Lord of the Spirits in eternal uprightness. This Son of Man whom you have seen is the One who would **remove the kings and the mighty ones from their comfortable seats and the strong ones from their thrones**. He shall loosen the reins of the strong and crush' the teeth of the sinners. **He shall depose the kings from their thrones and kingdoms**. For they do not extol and glorify him, and neither do they obey him, the source of their kingship. The faces of the strong will be slapped and be filled with shame and gloom. Their dwelling places and their beds will be worms. They shall have no hope to rise from their beds, **for they do not extol the name of the Lord of the Spirits (YAH). (Enoch 46)**

   For this purpose, he became the Chosen One; he was **concealed in the presence of The Lord of the Spirits prior to the creation of the world, and for eternity (Enoch 62)**.

For the Son of Man' was concealed from the beginning, and the Most High One **preserved him** in the presence of his power; **then he revealed him to the holy and the elect ones. * (Enoch 62)**

Important to note, that's why no man seen the Father except the Son as the Son shields and illuminates the original darkness of the Father, carries the prophetic thought, and why you must go through the Son to get to the Father is because He is the only person carrying the Father's thought. Lastly, it illustrates how the Son is the original light that was with YAH as YAH created all things.

In the beginning, the earth was without form and void. The spirit of YAH moved across the darkness of the deep. YAH said, "let there be Light" (**Genesis 1:1-5**). Here, we have the **first act of creation being the "Light of the World".**

My theory is that this is not the sun, as we see the sun created in **Genesis 1:16,17** and YAH clearly states the purpose of the sun creation in **verse 17**. **John 1:1 – 5** teaches that "In the beginning was the Word, and the Word was with Elohiym, and Elohiym was the Word. The same was in the beginning with Elohiym. All things were made by him; and without him was not anything made that was made. In him was life, and the life was the **light** of men. And the **light shines in darkness**; and **the darkness comprehended it not**" (**John 1:1 – 5**).

Ha'Mashiach is the Light of the World and prototype of man.

The Word is the thought or light. The thought is the righteous darkness of the Father. The Son is the Word, in the act of creation. Producing the Light of the World. Naturally, when you think, light is always the first act of creation. For more on this, read the Ha'Mashiach section located at the rear of this book. The last chapter.

3. **<u>Second day/Act of Creation: Heaven and Firmament</u>** (Imagine there being a divider (crystal clear glass wall) between the "waters with waters"

above, called heaven, being separated from waters below on "soon to be called Earth"). "Let there be a firmament in the midst of the waters, and let it divide the waters from the waters. And Elohiym made the firmament and divided the waters which were under the firmament from the waters which are above the firmament: and it was so. And Elohiym called the firmament Heaven (**Genesis 1:6-8**). **That firmament protects Earth from the waters above the firmament.**

4. **<u>Third day/Act of Creation: Earth, seas, grass, herb yielding trees</u>** (Under the firmament, Imagine the dry land appearing to form Earth and foundations of food sources being created to sustain life) "And Elohiym said: Let the waters under the heavens be gathered together unto one place, and let the dry land appear: and it was so. And Elohiym called the dry land Earth; and the gathering together of waters he called Seas: and Elohiym saw that it was good. And Elohiym said: Let the earth bring forth grass, the herb yielding seed, and fruit tree yielding fruit after his kind, whose seed is in itself, upon the earth: and it was so (**Genesis 1:9-11**)

5. **<u>Fourth day/Act of Creation: Sun, Moon, and stars</u>** (Imagine looking up from this dry land, Earth, and seeing the sun, moon, and stars under the firmament. Also, imagine half of the image being lit while the other half is dark. **Most Importantly, notice the details about these lights as compared to the light in Genesis 1 verse 3.)**

   "And Elohiym said: Let there be lights in the expanse of the heavens to **divide the day from the night**: and let them be **for signs, and for appointed feasts, and for days, and for years**. And let them be for **lights in the firmament** of the heavens to give light upon the earth: and it was so. And Elohiym made two great lights; the greater light to rule the day (**SUN**), and the lesser light to rule the night (**MOON**): He made the stars (**NO PLANETS**) also. And Elohiym set them in the expanse of the firmament to give light upon the earth, and to rule over the day and over the night, and to divide the light from darkness, and Elohiym saw that it was good (**Genesis 1:14-18**). **Notice how YAH made the sun and not the sun made YAH.**

Important notes about these verses, of light creations, are that there are no planets created or mentioned. What is mentioned are "wandering lights", which science calls "planets". Also, important to note that these are all called lights.

What is a light? A plasma source that channels energy and emits brightness/light. I'll break this down again. Simply, no matter how sophisticated technology is, no man can land on a plasma(watery) light source. **Meaning, no man ever landed on the moon! It is not a solid object. Neither are "planets" or "wandering stars".**

Those "moon and planet landings and aliens from deep space" are what I call, Hollywood finest deception of the governments!

Once you learn the deceptions, you'll see how science, the government, and Hollywood team up to deceive you with unproven blasphemy! They also use religion to blind you.

Another **secret** regarding **the moon is that the moon reflects the true image/map of flat-Earth!** The dark shadows of the moon are land masses on earth. That's why the ancients, explorers, and map makers studied the moon! **The moon is a giant mirror reflecting FLAT Earth!**

Lastly, If you were ever curious of what those "planets" look like, get a high-powered telescope and you'll see that they appear as **watery-colored plasma lights and not** solid objects! For those who cannot afford a high-powered telescope, you can search valid YouTube videos of **whistleblowers**! The evidence is clear.

Finally, before leaving these verses, it's important to note the Hollywood and government deception. Science teams up with Hollywood and the government. They have been deceiving us to believe in otherworldly objects, called UFOs and aliens. They **stole Nikola Tesla (a black man), Einstein (a black man) and others regarding free energy and secret sciences.** Many claim to be enlightened. Since their gods are from the underworld, they have learned secrets to manifest demons on Earth using portals, such as pyramids and the Earth energy grid and lowering the vibration (that's why they sell homosexuality and chaos to lower the vibrations). The need low vibrations for demons to manifest.

Some of them look like "aliens" because of DNA manipulation creating chimeras, part-man, and part-beast creatures. Some lost their soul and are the grays. Read the section on Enoch and the Days of Noah. **They are demons.**

They have been selling us things such as superheroes and aliens from outer space that will serve as gods to free man and improve the quality of life on Earth. We have been programmed since children to want to be a superhero. So, we stopped reading our Bibles/Cepher/Torah and calling on YAH.

The governments learned how to reverse engineer advanced technologies and secret sciences. Many **UFOs** you see are government-made and driven by our own military. **Most "abductions" are the government implanted thoughts, memories, images using secret sciences.** Your body isn't going anywhere! They even do this with MUFON and all the so-called "alien abductions". Those are **government mind control**, such as **MK ULTRA. YouTubers are government agents!**

They have been planning a fake alien invasion for decades to mimic the rapture. Also, another reason why they build on the energy grid of Earth AND lowering the consciousness, which builds an atmosphere for demons, is they are attempting to manifest their chief demonic deities from the underworld. That's why cities, such as Washington D.C. are all geometrically landscaped to harvest the energy and entities such as CERN serve as portals. **This is mass sorcery and witchcraft beyond your wildest dark demonic dreams, and it's all done by the governments around the world against the people.**

Without getting too off topic and beyond the scope of this section, this is another reason why they sell spiritualism and the illusion that man can become their own god through things such as **magic and witchcraft and mystery schools**

(contradicts entry rules to kingdom of heaven). We must realize that YAH is the only way, truth, and the light! There's only one true living Elohiym. We'll get into this a bit during our study.

6. **Fifth day/Act of Creation: Water Creatures, beasts, and animals. Birds** (Imagine the waters becoming populated with all kinds of creatures, while the air is filled with winged birds) "And Elohiym said, Let the waters bring forth abundantly the moving creature that has life, and the fowl that may fly above the earth in the open expanse of heaven. And Elohiym created great dragons, and every living creature that moves, which the waters brought forth abundantly, after their kind, and every winged fowl after his kind: And Elohiym saw that it was good. And Elohiym blessed them, saying: Be fruitful and multiply, and fill the waters in the seas, and let the fowl multiply the earth (**Genesis 1:20-22**)

7. **Six day/Act of Creation: Land animals and Man** (This is where we come in. Get excited! Contrary to what science teaches, **we are made in the image of our creator and not some random act of evolution of chances. We were also made complete and void of any evolution**).

"And Elohiym said, let the earth bring forth the living creature after his kind, cattle, and creeping thing, and beast of the earth after his kind: and it was so. And Elohiym made the beast of the earth after his kind and cattle after their kind, and everything that creeps upon the earth after his kind: and Elohiym saw it was good (**Genesis 1:25**).

Genesis 1:26 has led to much controversy regarding the "us". Without understanding the first act of creation, one will never understand the "us" in this verse. Also, we'll get into the mysterious Son of YAH later in the study in Ha'Mashiach section of the text.

Avoiding strange alien theories, reference the "us" from the first act of creation, the creation of the Son and Light. Hence, you have the Father and Son comprising of the "us" and not strange alien "gods". I point this out because there are many false teachings based upon misinterpretation of this single verse because **many fail**

to understand the plural in this verse is really a singular because the Father and Son are one.

"And Elohiym said: let us make man in our image, after our likeness, and let them have dominion over the fish of the sea, and over the fowl of the air, and over the cattle, and over all the earth, and over every creeping thing that creeps upon the earth. So, Elohiym created man in his own image, in the image of Elohiym created he them (**Genesis 1:26-27**).

Before we get to the **seventh day/Act of Creation, which was YAH rested on the Sabbath** and hollowed it. I'd like to also address another false teaching here. After this act of creation of man on the 6th day, YAH rested on the 7th day, and all acts of creation were completed, and all were good.

For those Bible readers, you will also see the creation of man outlined again in Genesis 2:7, which reads "And **Yahuah Elohiym formed the man of the dust of the** ground and breathed into his nostrils the breath of life, and the man became a living soul (**Genesis 2:7**).

Regarding the creation of woman, Genesis 2:21-22 reads, "And Yahuah Elohiym caused a deep sleep to fall upon the man, and he slept: and he took one of his ribs and closed up the flesh instead thereof; And the rib, which Yahuah Elohiym had taken from man, made he a woman, and brought her unto the man (**Genesis 2:21-22**).

I'm not a scientist. However, what I suspect here is that in the rib contains our DNA. I suspect that the DNA of Adam was spliced to create Eve, the first woman. Hence, the two are one and the same ("Therefore shall a man leave his father and his mother and shall cleave unto his woman: and they shall be one flesh" – **Genesis 2:24**). Without getting off topic, in my opinion, woman was not created inferior and should be respected with godly love. When positive and negative comes together they are one.

The creation story is very clear regarding the events and seven days of creation (seven is also a biblical number of completion and perfection). However, just as most of the Bible, it has led to many conflicting interpretations, teachings, theories, and even religions!

My approach to understanding the Bible/Cepher is a direct literal translation unless the verse sets the precept (definition of precept: a general rule intended to regulate behavior or thought) for an allegorical translation.

Throughout the creation story, the trend has been set for a literal interpretation of the text and is void of allegories (definition of allegory: a story, poem, or picture that can be interpreted to reveal a hidden meaning). For example, a clear example of an allegory is the entire book of Revelations. Seldom do you discover a literal translation mixed with an allegory in the context or framework of a single verse or story. To me, that spells confusion and **YAH is not the author of confusion – (see 1 Corinthians 14:33)**

A few notes regarding these verses to clear-up some false teachings: **There was only one creation story of man and not multiple creation stories**. There are some that teach that a heavenly man was created in **Genesis 1:26-27** and an earthly man was created in **Genesis 2:7**. I believe this to be false. Also, in **Genesis 1:26-27**, the verse reads that YAH called **them ADAM, male and female.** Further reading of the verses will reveal that **Genesis 2:7 is getting deeper into the genealogy of Adam**; whereas **Genesis 1:26-27 provides the general overview** of creation of Adam (male and female) as it pertains to the seven days of creation and YAH's actions. I state this because in **Genesis 2:3**, YAH rested **after** He saw that everything He created was completed and all good. Then, he sanctified the Sabbath day as a day of holy rest. Thus, creation was complete.

Also, notice how **Genesis 2:4a** begins, "These are the **generations** of the heavens and of the earth", which further proves a more **detailed view** of the original creation of man (male and female) and not a new creation story.

The interpretation of a double creation story would contradict **Genesis 2:3** by indicating another man creation was needed after YAH rested from His works and gives the contradicting illusion that "everything wasn't all good with creation". **(Remember the devil wants to create any doubts)**

Genesis 2:7 reads, "And Yahuah Elohiym formed the man of the dust of the ground and breathed into his nostrils the breath of life; and man became a living soul".

We'll get more into this during the study; however, **the color of the first man is hidden in the etymology of the name.** Adam means red- reddish brown and is the same color of the ground. **When you are trying to reveal the true color of Adam and the first humans, they were the color of a red garnet crystal stone.** That's the dark reddish-brown color of the first humans. It has an outwardly black appearance.

In fact, further studies will reveal even the crystals described, such as carnelian and jasper, in the Garden of Eden and the throne of YAH reveals this same, dark-reddish brown color all matching the color of the first man (male and female) and Earth.

Since man governs the basis of thinking from the lenses of science, let's look at science or what I will call "common sense". The first ideal location(s) for life to exist, on Earth, would be a tropical area in the direct path of the rising sun. This would present the first place of "cooling" for life. The sun rises from the east. The most ideal location, on Earth, would be in Africa near Ethiopia-area, which is the path of the rising sun and along the equator. Distance from equator can effect color of man.

Secondly, when you review the area of the Garden of Eden as outlined in **Genesis 2: 8-15** and the **book of Jubilees**, this confirms an **African origin of mankind**. Third, from a scientific perspective, black is the only color than can create all colors, including the color of white. **White can only create white and no other colors.**

In a rare incidence, Science confirms the Bible in that the first man (male and woman) originated in Africa and were black. **My research has revealed, and science confirms, is that the entire world began as black and made in the image of YAH.**

My theory, **based upon scriptures and hidden history**, is that **whites manifested** only **after** the flood of Noah, **through the seed of Esau and mixed with the entire world to hide their identity. Also, somehow Japheth became white, being further removed from equator and by genocide.**

Also, to note, **there is only one human race created in the image of YAH.** Without getting into the complications of the seed of Esau, I feel that we are all black in various degrees and shades. Scientifically speaking, it takes 2-3 generations to remove the blackness and create a white outer appearance (**which the world defines as race. Race, being a false theory to push racism and is created by science of man and not of YAH**). All Man is one race.

Once we realize this, it will eliminate all racist theories. And, perhaps, provide some pride to the chosen children of YAH that has been made to feel inferior and despise their color; when blacks **should be proud of their color as it is the color of the original man and the Highest YAH. Notice how YAH says that creation was all good and He rested after creating this world filled with blacks!** We'll cover this in later in the study.

8. <u>**Seventh day/Act of Creation: YAHUAH Elohiym Sabbath/ REST**</u>

"Thus, the heavens and the earth were finished, and all the host of them. And on the seventh day Elohiym ended His work He had made; and He rested on the seventh day from all His work which He had made. And Elohiym blessed the seventh day and sanctified it: because that in it He had rested from all His work which Elohiym created and made (**Genesis 2:1-3**).

After man was formed, he was placed in the Garden of Eden. Note, they weren't created in the Garden but placed there after purification (**Genesis 2:8 and Jubilees).**

SATAN

An excerpt of the Lords' Prayer, found in **Matthew 6:10** states "Your kingdom come. Your will be done **on Earth, as it is in heaven**".

I propose that the main purpose for the Garden of Eden was to be an earthly tabernacle mimicking the heavenly tabernacle of YAH. This will be a theme that you'll notice when studying the children of Israel. Keep this in mind. For example:

1. **The Ark of the Covenant created by Moses (Exodus 25:1-40)**. YAH resides between the cherubim on the first "portable" tabernacle of YAH, which the future temples would model after and reflected the image of the tabernacle in heaven, where YAH resides in the "Holy of Holies".
2. **The First Temple**, other known as **"Solomon's Temple" (1 Kings 6:1-38, 1 Kings 7:23-26 and 2 Chronicles 4:2-5)**
3. **The Second Temple (Ezra 1:1-4, 2 Chronicles 36:22-23)**

An interesting story, using an allegorical name, is found in the twenty eighth chapter of Ezekiel with a message to the "King of Tyre"; an interesting, **coded message for Satan.**

> Ezekiel 13 Thou hast been in Eden the garden of YAH; every precious stone was thy covering, the sardius, topaz, and the diamond, the beryl, the onyx, and the jasper, the sapphire, the emerald, and the carbuncle, and gold: the workmanship of thy tabrets and of thy pipes was prepared in thee in the day that thou wast created.
>
> Ezekiel 14 Thou art the anointed cherub that covereth; and I have set thee so: thou wast upon the holy mountain of YAH; thou hast walked up and down in the midst of the stones of fire.
>
> Ezekiel 15 Thou wast perfect in thy ways from the day that thou wast created, till iniquity was found in thee.

In verse 13 of the 28th chapter of Ezekiel, the stones that are listed reflect the **stones** of the **breastplate of a high priest.** In **28th chapter of Exodus**, YAH is describing the **requirements for priestly garments to Aaron**, the head of the Levitical Priesthood of the 12 Tribes of Israel. [15] And thou shalt make the breastplate of judgment with cunning work; after the work of the ephod thou shalt make it; of gold, of blue, and of purple, and of scarlet, and of fine twined linen, shalt thou make it.

[16] Foursquare it shall be being doubled; a span shall be the length thereof, and a span shall be the breadth thereof.

[17] And thou shalt set in it settings of stones, even four rows of stones: the first row shall be a sardius, a topaz, and a carbuncle: this shall be the first row.

[18] And the second row shall be an emerald, a sapphire, and a diamond.

[19] And the third row a ligure, an agate, and an amethyst.

[20] And the fourth row a beryl, and an onyx, and a jasper: they shall be set in gold in their inclosings.

[21] And the stones shall be with the names of the children of Israel, twelve, according to their names, like the engravings of a signet; every one with his name shall they be according to the twelve tribes.

[22] And thou shalt make upon the breastplate chains at the ends of wreathen work of pure gold.

[23] And thou shalt make upon the breastplate two rings of gold, and shalt put the two rings on the two ends of the breastplate.

Unlocking Bible Mysteries and Hidden Secrets Revealed
COMMUNICATION WITH YAH
To hear the silent voice of YAH, you must remove the noise of life. That's why the High Priest isolated themselves into chambers. This is what I did to produce this work. Silence the noise and Hear YAH. That's why meditation and fasting are important. Silence mind, body, and soul to see and hear YAH. **Get into the Silence, YAH will SPEAK**

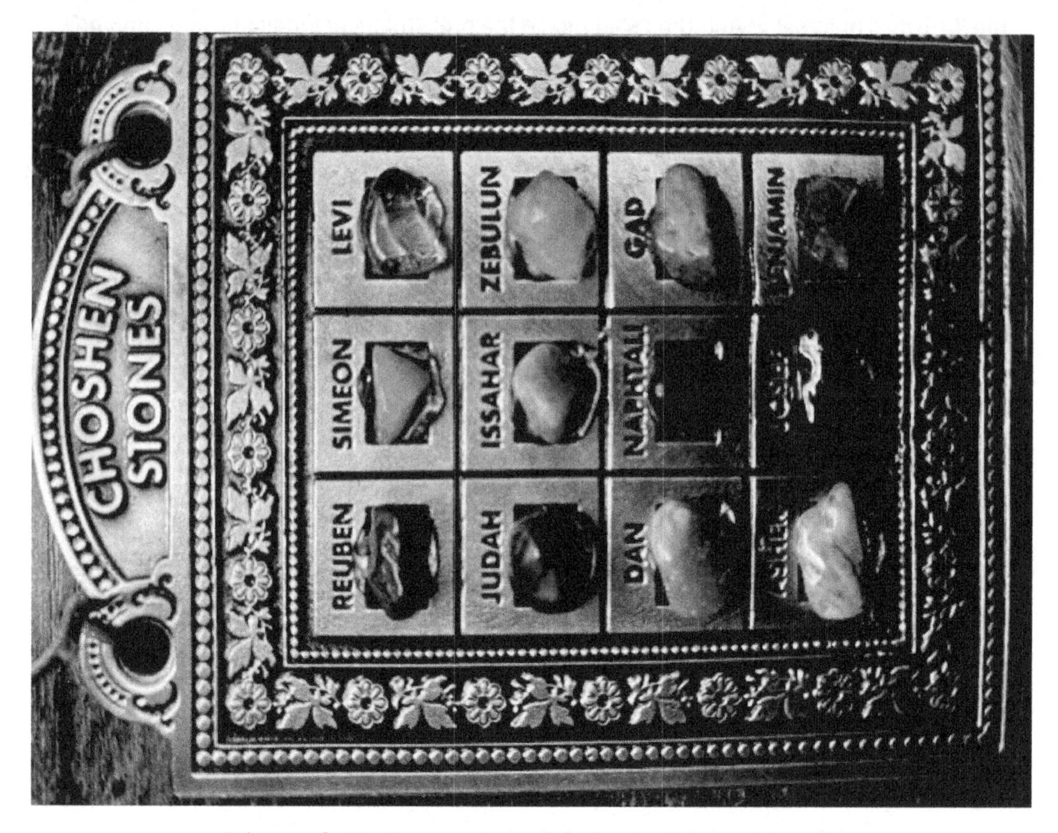

(Pictured: My Breastplate with the 12 Tribes of Israel)

<u>One immediate observation</u> **is that Aaron's Priestly breastplate in the 28th chapter of Exodus is almost identical to the breastplate in the 28th chapter of Ezekiel in the coded message to Satan. Keep this in mind.** The next puzzle piece comes from one of the oldest books of the Bible, the **book of Job**.

The book of Job is an amazing story of walking in righteousness while being persecuted with the tests and tribulations of life and being tested by Satan.

> "There was a man in the land of Uz, whose name *was* Job; and that man was perfect and upright, and one that feared YAH, and eschewed evil." **(Job 1:1)**

It's a story about a man of perfect righteousness and faith to YAH. **I encourage all to read and study this book and the message of strength**, in character, that you will come to appreciate as no man can escape the tests and trials of life while walking in faithful obedience to YAH. It also sets the story for the suffering servant, Ha'Mashiach. **One of the strongest messages in this story is that Satan can do no physical harm to those that walk with YAH in righteousness. Satan can only tempt. Never forget that!** Satan can only do what YAH allows and for testing purposes:

> [12] And **Elohiym said unto Satan, Behold, all that he hath is in thy power; only upon himself put not forth thine hand.** So, Satan went forth from the presence of Elohiym. **(Job 1:12)**

Before I present the picture, let's gather another puzzle piece. This is one that may blow your mind!

> **Job 2** Again there was a day when the **sons of Elohiym came to present themselves before YAH**, and **Satan came also** among them to present himself before YAH.
>
> [2] And YAH said unto Satan, From whence comest thou? **And Satan answered YAH, and said, From going to and fro in the earth, and from walking up and down in it.**
>
> [3] And YAH said unto Satan, Hast thou considered my servant **Job, that there is none like him in the earth, a perfect and an upright man**, one that feareth Elohiym, and escheweth evil? And still he holdeth fast his integrity, although **thou movedst me against him, to destroy him without cause.**

Job 2:1-3 provides some powerful information packed in just these few verses. I'll highlight a few that are pertinent to our study here.

- **In Job 2:1, this is the verse that will change what you think know about Satan. Many people have been led to believe that Satan is currently locked away in hell and burning in the lake of fire. This is what Christianity teaches and why you must come out of Mystery Babylon. People think that Satan is in the underworld ruling over demons, fallen angels, and people that died in sin. There's another chief fallen angel there! This verse clearly states that the sons of Elohiym AND SATAN presented themselves before YAH.**

- **In Job 2:2, the freedom of Satan to move amongst heaven and Earth is clearly displayed in the response of Satan to YAH. Satan is asked of his whereabouts and his reply is that he has been walking to and from the Earth. So, Remember this!**
- **Job 2:3 is our next clue for this study and describes the character of Satan. As you shall see, he is not some friend of man or character of light as many are fooled to believe. This verse clearly states that Satan has been pressuring YAH to cause harm to a man of perfect righteousness.**

  In the Bible and Cepher, few people, if any, are called perfect by YAH; Job was one of them! **This has been the works of Satan to accuse us day and night before YAH, as he wanders the Earth seeking his next victim.** The last item I will highlight in this verse is that **Satan is not focusing in on a sinner**!

  In **Job 1:1, we see how Job is a perfect man of righteousness and there's almost none like him in all Bible history!** Lesson there is that the more perfect you are in righteousness, the more of a threat you are to Satan.

Now that we gathered some critical information regarding Satan, I can now present my thoughts. My theory is that Satan was the original High Priest in the Garden of Eden during the time of Adam and Eve, before turning on YAH.

Notice in Ezekiel how it states that Satan was created in perfect beauty and wisdom. He was blessed to hold many secrets of heaven and earth. He was created as one of the chief angels in heaven. Also, keep in mind that angels were created before man was created as they sung praises to YAH when Adam was created. Satan loves and own music. Additionally, YAH is a one of highest righteousness. By being one of highest righteousness, **YAH creates us with free-will and not as robots**. This applies to **angels as well**. They are granted the ability to exercise their choice to obey YAH or to walk in the error of their own ways. **With this information in mind, let's return to the Garden of Eden.**

To recap, after YAH placed Adam (and Eve) in the Garden of Eden, I feel that it was the job of Satan to be their high priest. Secondly, Satan knowing the initial purpose of Adam, felt threatened and chose not to humble himself to teach the first man (and woman). Before we discuss the fall of man and Satan, let's see what YAH commanded Adam and Eve regarding their stay in the Garden of Eden.

> **Genesis** [15] And YAHUAH Elohiym took the man and put him into the garden of Eden to dress it and to keep it.
>
> [16] And YAHUAH Elohiym commanded the man, saying, Of every tree of the garden thou mayest freely eat:
>
> [17] But of the tree of the knowledge of good and evil, thou shalt not eat of it: for in the day that thou eatest thereof thou shalt surely die.

In Genesis 2:15-17, we see YAH placing Adam and Eve in the Garden of Eden. He says that they are allowed to freely eat of every tree in the Garden except for the tree of the knowledge of good and evil, which eating from, they will surely die. Notice the clear instructions from YAH. Keep this in mind as we shall see what Satan says to Eve in **Genesis 3:1-5:**

> **Genesis 3** Now the serpent was more subtil than any beast of the field which the Yahuah Elohiym had made. And he said unto the woman, Yea, hath Elohiym said, Ye shall not eat of every tree of the garden?
>
> [2] And the woman said unto the serpent, We may eat of the fruit of the trees of the garden:
>
> [3] But of the fruit of the tree which is in the midst of the garden, Elohiym hath said, Ye shall not eat of it, neither shall ye touch it, lest ye die.
>
> [4] And the serpent said unto the woman, Ye shall not surely die:
>
> [5] For Elohiym doth know that in the day ye eat thereof, then your eyes shall be opened, and ye shall be as gods, knowing good and evil.

Genesis 3 opens with one of the greatest mysteries of man; the first sin and fall of man from eating of the tree of the knowledge of good and evil. In **Genesis 3:1**, we see a reiteration of **Ezekiel 28** in that Satan was gifted in knowledge and wisdom even above the angels. This allowed for his craftiness to tempt Eve, as she, in doubt, reiterates what YAH had commanded her through Adam.

One observation is that man was created for divine purposes and if YAH wanted man to have the knowledge of good and evil, He would've blessed man with that knowledge. Keep in mind, there was no veil between heaven and earth; so, I don't feel it was about wisdom as they were of the Light of YAH. Perhaps, man was created to know only good knowledge. **In any event, in verse 3**, Satan persuades Eve by saying that she won't die but will become as a god in knowledge. **He causes doubt!**

> **Genesis 3** [6] And when the woman saw that the tree was good for food, and that it was pleasant to the eyes, and a tree to be desired to make one wise, she took of the fruit thereof, and did eat, and gave also unto her husband with her; and he did eat.
>
> [7] And the eyes of them both were opened, and they knew that they were naked; and they sewed fig leaves together and made themselves aprons.
>
> [8] And they **heard the voice** of the Yahuah Elohiym **walking** in the garden in the cool of the day: and Adam and his wife hid themselves from the presence of the Yahuah Elohiym amongst the trees of the garden.
>
> [9] And the Yahuah Elohiym called unto Adam, and said unto him, Where art thou?
>
> [10] And he said, I heard thy voice in the garden, and I was afraid, because I was naked; and I hid myself.
>
> [11] And he said, Who told thee that thou wast naked? Hast thou eaten of the tree, whereof I commanded thee that thou shouldest not eat?

[12] And the man said, The woman whom thou gavest to be with me, she gave me of the tree, and I did eat.

[13] And the Yahuah Elohiym said unto the woman, What is this that thou hast done? And the woman said, The serpent beguiled me, and I did eat.

In the preceding verses of Genesis 3:6-13, we learn that Eve convinced Adam to eat of the forbidden fruit. Remember **Genesis 2:24** and the power of a woman to surrender a man to a fallen state. This is another theme that plays out frequently throughout the Bible/Cepher. A few examples are Solomon, with all his wisdom and falling to pagan gods as he built alters for his many wives and their pagan deities. The woman Jezebel is another story with King Ahab, along with King Herod's wife who wanted the head of John the Baptist. One interesting observation of the coming curses is that Adam was the one to receive the commandments from YAH and not Eve unless Adam told her secondhand. She was not even in the garden at the time (**see Jubilees and Jasher**). However, it was Eve that received the curse.

In **Genesis 3:8**, we see how the **voice of YAH is walking in the Garden of Eden during the "cool of the day".** This goes back to my point regarding the original creation having no veil of separation between heaven and Earth, and YAH was in direct fellowship with His creation. It also reveals YAH exists! One final observation is in **verse 13** in that Eve blamed the serpent rather than accepting fault and rather than avoiding eating the forbidden fruit out of obedience to YAH. Needless to say, let's **review the first curses in scripture:**

Genesis 3: [14] And the YAHUAH Elohiym said unto the serpent, because thou hast done this, thou art cursed above all cattle, and above every beast of the field; **upon thy belly shalt thou go**, and **dust shalt thou eat** all the days of thy life:

[15] And I will put enmity between thee and the woman, and between thy seed and her seed; it shall bruise thy head, and thou shalt bruise his heel.

(Picture of a walking angel before belly curse.
Now, it's a crawling serpent after the curse)

The first character to receive curses was Satan in **Genesis 3:14-15**. In **verse 14**, it provides a reference to a fallen angel that once stood upright (see picture above of speculations of what angels looked like) and now is cursed to crawl upon his belly as a serpent. **This reminds me of what gray aliens look like, as a cursed creature with no soul.**

Genesis 3:15 is the first major prophecy of the Bible/Cepher. In this verse, we are promised that YAH will raise a seed to bruise/crush Satan. **This is the messianic prophecy of the coming Son of YAH. This verse also drops a major hidden secret** to those that study each word.

YAH is saying that He will put enmity between the **seed of a woman** AND **the seed of Satan. This is a powerful verse to unlock Bible secrets** and to understand that Satan has the ability of having his own seed (children). Keep this in mind during our current study and future works. We shall visit this verse during our study of Ha'Mashiach (a.k.a. The Messiah)

The next sets of curses are to Eve and Adam, in that order of **Genesis 3:16-19**.

Genesis 3: 16 Unto the woman he said, I will greatly multiply thy sorrow and thy conception; in sorrow thou shalt bring forth children; and thy desire shall be to thy husband, and he shall rule over thee.

17 And unto Adam he said, Because thou hast hearkened unto the voice of thy wife, and hast eaten of the tree, of which I commanded thee, saying, Thou shalt not eat of it: cursed is the ground for thy sake; in sorrow shalt thou eat of it all the days of thy life;

18 Thorns also and thistles shall it bring forth to thee; and thou shalt eat the herb of the field;

19 In the sweat of thy face shalt thou eat bread, till thou return unto the ground; for out of it wast thou taken: for dust thou art, and unto dust shalt thou return.

Genesis 3:20-24 shows the compassion of YAH towards His children. In these following verses, we see how YAH made "coats of skin" for Adam and Eve and removed them from the Garden by placing angels to forbid any further entrance (Nimrod + Esau stole these garments).

20 And Adam called his wife's name Eve; because she was the mother of all living.

21 Unto Adam also and to his wife did the Yahuah Elohiym make coats of skins and clothed them.

22 And the Yahuah Elohiym said, Behold, the man is become as one of us, to know good and evil: and now, lest he put forth his hand, and take also of the tree of life, and eat, and live forever:

23 Therefore the Yahuah Elohiym sent him forth from the garden of Eden, to till the ground from whence he was taken.

24 So he drove out the man; and he placed at the east of the garden of Eden Cherubims, and a flaming sword which turned every way, to keep the way of the tree of life.

Genesis 3:22, reveals the divine wisdom of YAH in that extreme measures were taken for man to be forbidden to eat of the tree of life in their (now) currently fallen states. What this means is that if Adam and Eve were allowed to eat of the tree of life and live forever, they would be doing so in a fallen state as devils. **This had to be prevented at all costs,** which is why they were removed from the Garden of Eden. **Hence, begins the story of the fallen state of man and our journey to reconciliation back to dwell with our Father, YAH.**

We have just reviewed the fall of Satan, Adam, and Eve in the Garden of Eden. In reference to our study in this current work, our next stop is to **review the fallen angels in Genesis Chapter 6.**

Unlocking Bible Mysteries and Hidden Secrets Revealed
FREEMASONS AND SECRET SOCIETIES
You will never discover physical proof about secret societies. They are extremely hidden and secret under penalty of DEATH. They all have instantaneous deniability. The system is created to never produce any proofs of their existence, members, and activities.
Freemasonry began in the days of Noah by Nirmod. They hold the secrets behind secret sciences, mathematics, hidden highly advanced technology, weather manipulation, witchcraft, magic, sorcery, DNA manipulation, financial manipulation, mind control, and more!
They control the world and have total control of the world's assets and resources. They control every industry in all aspects of life (religious, social, entertainment, financial, governmental, educational, legal, media, etc.). **They affect all areas of life.**
They created secret fraternities to **secretly control the actions** of all things, including you. **Many of our loved ones are secretly, under penalty of death, active members of Freemasonry.** They will never admit. They control every industry and ALL industries and persons with any power or influence over the masses. Meaning, all teachers, medical professionals, athletes, entertainers, elected officials, government, religious, leaders, police, military, lawyers, transportation, etc. are all secret members of this order.

They will deny involvement. The numbers are incapable of lying. **Follow the numbers!**
Freemasonry is NOT YAH. Freemasonry teaches AGAINST YAH. You won't learn this because they trap you in degrees. These are intentional distractions and never reveal any real truths. Their degrees also include human blood sacrifices, wife sexually sharing, homosexual rituals, and child abuse. They also accept all religions. Even after 33 degrees, you are still trapped in highly secret and compartmentalized programmed knowledge. You learn the things of **SATAN, which is the SECRET GOD OF FREEMASONRY.** You NEVER LEARN ABOUT YAH.
Did you know? Your loved ones sell their soul to hide the truth of YAH, for material gains. Secret degree rituals are stories to sell the children of YAH into ignorance. They intentionally come up with ways to hide your history and throw it in your face at the same time. An example are movies and music industry. "Strange Fruits"
The MOST IMPORTANT THING TO KNOW IS FREEMASONS SECRETLY SERVE THE DEVIL. Wonder how they kept the making of the 1st atomic bomb secret from the public and even those who MADE THE BOMB, is by highly advanced compartmentalized knowledge. Some 33-degree masons are not even aware of this knowledge of who they are really serving. Just as the United States President is not aware of the plans of the people that really run the country. You may have difficulty accepting because just as they destroy the world, they HIDE behind philanthropy. It's a horrible game.
TO GET/HAVE A JOB in MOST INDUSTRIES, THEY MAKE YOU SECRETLY PLEDGE INTO FREEMASONRY. This is how people elevate in life. This is also why Yahusha said that those that are friends of this world are enemies of YAH. Because people are making **DEALS WITH SATAN** and **SELLING THEIR SOUL** for **so-called material gains which they don't own or control!**
Freemasons don't allow you to financial own anything or have wealth. You are **CONTROLLED** in **ALL THINGS**. They make you do secret and horrible things and when you don't comply, in comes the **REAPER**!
Did you know? **ALL FRATERNITIES AND SORORITIES ARE FREE MASONS.** This how they secure their victims. They get you in college and at young ages and through material means.

SCHOOLS, **ALL COLLEGES AND STAFF ARE FREEMASONS. This is HOW THEY TEACH FALSE TEACHINGS AND CONTROL YOU AND SELL YOU THE LIFE ALL YOUR LIFE!**
FRATS are from GREEKS. Greeks STOLE FROM EGYPT Mystery schools. The mystery schools practice magic, witchcraft, sorcery, divination, star worship, and Satanism. They also represent a part of Mystery Babylon, and all have pagan gods of the underworld.
THEIR gods are the FALLEN ANGELS
THEY ARE DEMON POSSESSED BLOOD RITUALS
FREEMASONS ARE NOT YAH AND ARE AGAINST YAH.
Freemasons = another Mystery Babylon

DAYS OF NOAH AND LOT

For this study, one must **keep in mind the notes regarding Genesis 3:15**, whereby **angels had the ability of having their own seed**; in simple terms, **angels mated with human women, had babies,** and **created evil monsters and giants which roamed the Earth. They are demons in human and animal bodies. In all respects, they appear as human in features. They look just like us on the outside.**

Another significant reference point to this part of the study is the **warning from the words of Yahusha (a.k.a. Jesus) regarding Coming of Ha'Mashiach.** We find this in **Matthew 24:37-39**.

> Matthew 24: 37 But as the days of Noah were, so shall also the coming of the Son of man be.
>
> 38 For as in the days that were before the flood they were eating and drinking, marrying and giving in marriage, until the day that Noe entered into the ark,
>
> 39 And knew not until the flood came, and took them all away; so shall also the coming of the Son of man be.

For this study, I will be specifically focusing on **Matthew 24:37,** "But as the days of Noah were, so shall the coming of the Son of Man be". One might ask, what is meant by this verse? **Pay close attention and we shall uncover another major secret of life and the Bible.**

To understand what is meant by this we **must reference the notes on Genesis 3:15 (seeds of Satan) and review Genesis Chapter 6**, which outlines the fallen angels mixing their seed with human women giving **birth to physical giants (over 8 feet tall and some up to 3,500 lbs.).** I know this may go against everything you have been taught in life and church. **For the record, present day they look like us in size and appearances as human**. Only the spiritual eye can recognize the difference. **Fact is, there are demons in human bodies all over Earth right now. Some of you may be possessed!**

What I will say to you is throughout this entire book, I am allowing scriptures to confirm scriptures as the base and foundation for all information presented. I highly suggest we take this approach regarding the receiving of any information from any source(s), including especially religious leaders.

Scriptures must always confirm scriptures. Chances are that you may be able to disagree with me if you find difficulty accepting knowledge. For this section, **I will reference you to read the following scriptures:**

- **Hosea 4:6: "My people are destroyed because they have rejected knowledge, I will also reject thee, that thou shalt be no priest to me, seeing thou hast forgotten the law of thy Elohiym. I will also forget thy children".**
- **2 Timothy 3:16-17 "All scripture is given by inspiration of Yahuah Elohiym, and is profitable for doctrine, for reproof, for correction, for instruction in righteousness: That the man of Yahuah Elohiym may be perfect, thoroughly furnished unto all good works".**
- **Proverbs 3: 5-6 "Trust in the Yahuah Elohiym with all thine heart; and lean not unto thine own understanding. In all thy ways acknowledge him, and he shall direct thy paths.**

Some of you may still be wondering why this hidden knowledge is so important? Others may say, well didn't they get destroyed in the flood of Noah? Since this is a mouth of information to accept, I shall highlight a few points before we get into the actual scriptures to see what the Word of YAH says.

One key Bible/Cepher character to study, regarding the fallen angels, their mixing seeds with humans, and their coming judgement is **Enoch**. Let's see what the Bible/ Cepher says regarding Enoch in **Genesis 5:21-24:**

Genesis 5: 21 And Enoch lived sixty and five years, and begat Methuselah:

22 And Enoch walked with Yahuah Elohiym after he begat Methuselah three hundred years, and begat sons and daughters:

[23] And all the days of Enoch were three hundred sixty and five years:

[24] And **Enoch walked with Yahuah Elohiym: and he was not; for God took him.**

A few key points regarding the mysterious Enoch:

- **He was considered the first perfect man in history**
- **He walked with YAH**
- **He was one of FEW people that never died**
- **He was taken at Pi, 365.24, the circumference of a circle!**
- **He was taken directly to heaven by YAH, personally by YAH!**
- **He was allowed to see the secrets of heaven**
- **He was appointed to be a scribe in heaven to communicate judgement to the fallen angels on Earth**
- **Yahusha (a.k.a. Jesus) and NT writers quotes Enoch often**
- **The Book of Enoch was an accepted text in many orthodox churches. See introduction on rejected books. His book is now included in the Cepher. Read old translations.**
- **The Book of Enoch, along with Genesis 6, is needed to fully understand the fallen angels and last days.**

BOOK OF ENOCH CHAPTERS 7 AND 8

- **And it came to pass when the children of men had multiplied that in those days were born unto them beautiful and comely daughters. And the angels, the children of the heaven, saw and lusted after them, and said to one another: 'Come, let us choose us wives from among the children of men and beget us children.' And Semjâzâ, who was their leader, said unto them: 'I fear ye will not indeed agree to do this deed, and I alone shall have to pay the penalty of a great sin.' And they all answered him and said: 'Let us all swear an oath, and all bind ourselves by mutual imprecations not to abandon this plan but to do this thing.' Then sware they all together and bound themselves by mutual imprecations upon it. And they were in all two hundred; who descended in the days of Jared**

on the summit of Mount Hermon, and they called it Mount Hermon, because they had sworn and bound themselves by mutual imprecations upon it. And these are the names of their leaders: Samîazâz, their leader, Arâkîba, Râmêêl, Kôkabîêl, Tâmîêl, Râmîêl, Dânêl, Êzêqêêl, Barâqîjâl, 8Asâêl, Armârôs, Batârêl, Anânêl, Zaqîêl, Samsâpêêl, Satarêl, Tûrêl, Jômjâêl, Sariêl. These are their chiefs of tens.

And all the others together with them took unto themselves wives, and each chose for himself one, and they began to go in unto them and to defile themselves with them, and they taught them charms and enchantments, and the cutting of roots, and made them acquainted with plants. And they became pregnant, and they bare great giants, whose height was three thousand ells: Who consumed all the acquisitions of men. And when men could no longer sustain them, the giants turned against them and devoured mankind. And they began to sin against birds, and beasts, and reptiles, and fish, and to devour one another's flesh, and drink the blood. Then the earth laid accusation against the lawless ones (Enoch 7-8).

(Mt. Hermon pact – credits: British Museum online)

Before we get into what the book of Genesis states regarding this same story of the Fallen angels, a.k.a. Watchers, **let's review a few highlights**.

- **When we read this same story in the book of Genesis, we see that it matches up perfectly and provides additional details which are omitted in the Genesis record. Also, Enoch states this occurs during the days of Jared, which is the same as the days of Noah.**
- **The general overview is that a chief angel, called Semjâza, and 200 fallen angels left their heavenly habitation to come to Earth and mate with human women, which was a major forbidden act which had significant consequences. Angels can manifest as humans. The location of their landing was Mt. Hermon. Interestingly, this is the same Mt. Hermon that Yahusha transfigured and focused his ministry around this area, as it was a major fallen area of demonic possessions even during the times of Yahusha's ministry. This is another devil!**
- **If you read the full account in the book of Enoch, you will discover that these fallen angels are responsible for teaching man many heavenly secrets that were forbidden, such as witchcraft, sorcery, divination, worship of heavenly bodies, weather manipulation, DNA, etc.**
- **Because of the severe consequences of this forbidden act, the chief leader, Semjaza, made the remaining angels commit to a pact so that he wouldn't be left hanging alone with the consequences of their actions. This pact is pictured above and is available for public view in the British Museum. This is physical proof for all who call this science fiction!**
- **The fallen watchers mated with human women and created giants and monsters because of mixing angelic seed with human seed produced unknown results. That's why it was so forbidden. The giants began to turn against their parents and began to destroy the Earth.**
- **Humans weren't the only thing that they mated with. They also mated with animals producing hybrid creatures, a.k.a. chimeras (checkout "Golden Child" movie).**

This is a huge hidden secret here which explains why you see hieroglyphs and pictures of human bodies with animal heads as fallen gods of many ancient cultures. This was the beginning of **DNA manipulation!**

Those pictures and statues that you see in ancient Babylon, Mesopotamia, ancient Egypt, India, China, and all over the world. **Those were real human-animal hybrid creatures that were created and worshipped as gods.** For example, the sphinx was a real creature with a lion body and a human face! Also, some examples are gods such as Anubis, Shiva, and Enki. The world hides this secret by saying that they are allegories and symbolic messages. Check the pyramids, which are full of descriptions of these chimera creatures! **This is a huge lie to hide the truth**. It all traces back to **Mystery Babylon and Mesopotamia fallen pagan gods. Every pagan god's root, hidden by current many names.**

- **They corrupted the world so bad that only Noah and his sons were left. That's why the flood happened to destroy these fallen angels and save the creation of earth and man!**

Now, let's review the Genesis account of this same story! Let's start with **Genesis 6: 1-8**:

6 When human beings began to increase in number on the earth and daughters were born to them, [2] the sons of Elohiym saw that the daughters of humans were beautiful, and they married any of them they chose. [3] Then the Yahuah said, "My Spirit will not contend with[a] humans forever, for they are mortal[b]; their days will be a hundred and twenty years."

[4] The Nephilim were on the earth in those days—and also afterward—when the sons of Elohiym went to the daughters of humans and had children by them. **They were the heroes of old, men of renown.**

[5] And Yahuah saw how great the wickedness of the human race had become on the earth, and that every inclination of the thoughts of the human heart was only evil all the time. [6] And Yahuah regretted that he had made human beings on the earth, and his heart was deeply troubled. [7] And Yahuah said, "I will wipe from the face of the earth the human race I have created—and with them the animals, the birds and the creatures

that move along the ground—for I regret that I have made them." [8] But Noah found favor in the eyes of the Yahuah **(Genesis 6:1-8).**

Noah and the Flood - Genesis 6: 9-22

[9] This is the account of Noah and his family.

Noah was a righteous man, blameless among the people of his time, and he walked faithfully with Yahuah Elohiym. [10] **Noah had three sons: Shem, Ham and Japheth.**

[11] Now the earth was corrupt in Elohiym sight and was full of violence. [12] Elohiym saw how corrupt the earth had become, for all the people on earth had corrupted their ways. [13] So Elohiym said to Noah, "I am going to put an end to all people, for the earth is filled with violence because of them. I am surely going to destroy both them and the earth. [14] So make yourself an ark of cypress[c] wood; make rooms in it and coat it with pitch Inside and out.[15] This is how you are to build it: The ark is to be three hundred cubits long, fifty cubits wide and thirty cubits high.[d] [16] Make a roof for it, leaving below the roof an opening one cubit[e] high all around.[f] Put a door in the side of the ark and make lower, middle and upper decks. [17] I am going to bring floodwaters on the earth to destroy all life under the heavens, every creature that has the breath of life in it. Everything on earth will perish. [18] But **I will establish my covenant with you,** and you will enter the ark—you and your sons and your wife and your sons' wives with you. [19] You are to bring into the ark two of all living creatures, male and female, to keep them alive with you. [20] Two of every kind of bird, of every kind of animal and of every kind of creature that moves along the ground will come to you to be kept alive.[21] You are to take every kind of food that is to be eaten and store it away as food for you and for them."

[22] Noah did everything just as Elohiym commanded him.

Let's discuss a few highlights from the Genesis account of the same story described in the Book of Enoch:

- **Both, the Genesis and Book of Enoch accounts match and confirms one another. This gives further authority to the Book of Enoch**

- **Genesis 6:4 calls the children of the mixing of the fallen angels with human women "Nephilim". Another Bible code word is presented in this same verse "men of renown" and "heroes of old". Anytime you see those phrases, it is a hidden code reference to the giants and their offspring (demons in human bodies). Also, important to note that's why YAH commanded Israel to kill inhabitants of every city to destroy the remnants of the giants and their offspring. Remember this when reading the history of Israel (Exodus-Kings) as you will discover that YAH is not some evil tyrant who destroys flesh for no reason! YAH is love.**
- **DEMONS IN HUMAN BODIES – GIANTS**
  - **Nephilim: product children of the mixing of fallen angels with human women. The children were physical giants.**
  - **Anakim and Rephaim: descendants of Nephilim**
  - **Many of you today using mystery magic**

Noah and his children (Shem, Ham, Japheth, and their wives) found favour in the eyes of YAH and were chosen to be saved to restart humanity. **Keep in mind that we are still only discussing one family, which were all products of the same seed of Adam; meaning we are still discussing pre-historic Black history!**

Genesis chapters 7 and 8 discusses the details of the flood. One thing that you will notice about YAH when He brings judgment is that He will always give time allowance for people to repent and be saved. Also, He brings judgment once sin has reached maximum capacity of His allotted purpose of time. So, even with the world fallen to sin, YAH still gave allowance for people to repent, depart from evil, and turn back to Him. This time allowance must never be taken for granted as YAH doesn't allow His Word to fall void. Before bringing the flood, Noah went to preach the message of repentance for 120 days, which aligns with the statement of YAH in **Genesis 6:3**.

> "Then the Yahuah said, "My Spirit will not contend with[a] humans forever, for they are mortal; their days will be a hundred and twenty years." **(Genesis 6:3)**

For my pagan scientists who constantly challenge the Word of YAH, I'll share one interesting theory with you regarding the flood:

- **Many scientists attempt to discredit the flood because they are unable to provide traces for a worldwide flood.**
- **I'd like to suggest to you that the (then) "world" is not the entire world as we know it to be "today". The Bible world was mainly regional Africa. Keep in mind, the flood came shortly after Adam and Eve being expelled from the Garden of Eden (Africa). How far do you think they travelled in such a short span of time? Also, keep this "world" in mind when thinking of John 3:16, as you'll see it has different meanings.**
- **We know the Garden of Eden to be located within the African region**
- **Adam and Eve couldn't have made it across the physical world which we know today to populate the entire physical world.**
- **This can be another example in the Bible where the word "world" does not indicate the entire physical world that we inhabit today and could be only a reference to the inhabited world of ancient times. The same way, the word "World" in John 3:16 doesn't mean entire world. It means a nation – Israel (reference Greek/Hebrew words).**
- **Also, much of Biblical history reflects a "world" within regions of the African continent. Perhaps, that's why evidence of a "worldwide" flood is yet to be confirmed by science?**

Final notes regarding the flood of Noah are the covenant that YAH established with Noah found in **Genesis 9:11-17.**

> Genesis 9: 11 **I establish my covenant with you**: Never again will all life be destroyed by the waters of a flood; never again will there be a flood to destroy the earth."
>
> 12 And Elohiym said, "This is the sign of the covenant I am making between me and you and every living creature with you, a covenant for all generations to come: 13 **I have set my rainbow in the clouds**, and it will be the **sign of the covenant** between me and the earth. 14 Whenever I bring clouds over the earth and the rainbow appears in the clouds, 15 I will remember my covenant between me and you and all living creatures of every kind. Never again will the waters become a flood to destroy all life. 16 Whenever the rainbow appears in the clouds, I will see it and remember the everlasting covenant between Elohiym and all living creatures of every kind on the earth."

> [17] So Elohiym said to Noah, "This is the sign of the covenant I have established between me and all life on the earth."

The reason why I included this covenant is to show how bad we have fallen as a people and the amount of blasphemy in our culture towards the things of YAH. As a sign of this covenant, YAH states that He will place a rainbow in the cloud as a sign that He will never flood the world again with water. **The rainbow was a holy sign revered by YAH.**

Let's fast-forward to our current day and age where we have allowed the rainbow cloud to be degraded to symbolize homosexuality, which is an abomination to YAH according to scriptures. Just think, what's the first thing that comes to your mind when you see a rainbow cloud? Are you recalling this holy covenant with YAH **or** are you thinking about gay pride? Just some food for thought!

SECTION DEBRIEFING

In this section we have reviewed the creation story and been made aware how religion, science, and governments manipulate truths to teach things that are contrary to the ways of YAH. We identified the Earth to be a flat concentric unmovable disk. We saw that the first man was reddish-dark black/brown, which appears black. We see the impacts of Satan seeking to destroy the Word of YAH. In this next section, we shall dig deeper into the Children of Israel.

THE 12 TRIBES OF ISREAL: CHOSEN CHILDREN OF YAH

The world would have us to believe that the identity of the children of Israel has been lost, that they are a race that disappeared/extinct, or they are a totality of the descendants of current inhabitants of the land of Israel. Facts remain, Scriptures reflect the 10 tribes are currently in Arzareth until last days when they join Ha'Mashiach. Judah is dispersed, Africans in the diaspora (Americas).

In this section, **I seek to explore the identity of the children of Israel by tracing back to its roots after the flood of Noah and reviewing their full Bible history.** To do this, **we must go back to the "new" beginning of life on Earth that began with Noah and his children**.

> Genesis 9: 18 **The sons of Noah who came out of the ark were Shem, Ham and Japheth. (Ham was the father of Canaan.)** 19 These were the three sons of Noah, and **from them came the people who were scattered over the whole earth (Genesis 9:18).**

In **Genesis 9:18**, we learn that out of the ark came forth Noah and his children, Shem, Ham, Japheth, and their wives. These were the sole survivors of the flood that destroyed the previous population of life on Earth. In **Genesis 9:19**, we learn that the Earth was re-populated from the children of Noah. Also, keep in mind that the covenant of Adam was transferred to Noah in the preceding verses.

CURSE OF HAM

After listing the new forefathers of man, the Bible discusses a story of the curse of Ham. In my opinion, this is one of the most misunderstood verses in the Bible. This has also been used to "justify" slavery of Blacks and racism, so we shall **review these verses to shed light upon the subject. The story is outlined in Genesis 9:20 – 27**.

> Genesis 9: 20 Noah, a man of the soil, proceeded[a] to plant a vineyard. 21 When he drank some of its wine, he became drunk and lay uncovered inside his tent.22 Ham, the father of Canaan, saw his father naked and told his two brothers outside. 23 But Shem and Japheth took a garment and laid it across their shoulders; then they walked in backward and covered their father's naked body. Their faces were turned the other way so that they would not see their father naked.
>
> 24 When Noah awoke from his wine and found out what his youngest son had done to him, 25 he said,
>
> "Cursed be Canaan!
> The lowest of slaves
> will he be to his brothers."
> 26 He also said,
>
> "Praise be to the Elohiym, the Elohiym of Shem!
> May Canaan be the slave of Shem.
> 27 May Elohiym extend Japheth's[b] territory;
> may Japheth live in the tents of Shem,
> and may Canaan be the slave of Japheth."

In reviewing the following verses, we discover:

- **Noah was drunk and fell asleep. Ham, his son, discovered the nakedness of his father, Noah. Japheth and Shem covered their father's nakedness. Noah awakened from his wine, discovered what Ham**

had done to him, and cursed Canaan, Ham's son. The beginnings of homosexuality.

- **Noah, while drunken, cursed Canaan to be the lowest of slaves. He cursed Canaan to be the slaves of Shem and Japheth.**
- **Noah praised the Elohiym of Shem**
- **Noah also said that Japheth's territory will be enlarged and that he will live in the tents of Shem.**

Let's spend some time discussing this since the misinterpretation of these verses are the basis of unjustified slavery and unwarranted racism that has poisoned the hearts and minds of generations for centuries. We still live with the effects even today! My observations of the curse of Noah are as follows:

- **We'll discuss this in the study: Because the identity of Shem has been hidden/attempted theft by Esau, scholars attempt to state that all Blacks are decedents from Ham. This is false. Not accepting the fact that all of Noah's children were of the same Black race as their black father, Noah, they attempt to ascribe different races to the children of Noah. With this racist and theory of blasphemy (anything that goes against the Word of YAH is blasphemy), <u>they attempt to state that Ham is the father of all Blacks, Shem is the father of all Asians, and Japheth is the father of all Europeans. After reading this entire study of works and my upcoming series, you will discover that this is a major error and false teaching.</u> Also, science confirms that DNA passes down through the father to child and not from our confused manipulating minds.**

  I'm not the only brave truth seeker stating these obvious biblical facts of life. The fact is the entire world, including Europe, Asia, India, and every continent was first populated by aboriginal Blacks, for centuries, long before any whites came into existence!

  This is a Biblical and historical fact that can't be denied. **In fact, if you study your bible and history, the first whites were considered curses and children**

of the devil as many feared their very existence, as it was not the norm (considered leprosy and such. You can study the **TORAH/Old Testament** to see how extremely serious they took leprosy. Study African history how they feared whites calling them devils. These were your first whites.). The norm was a black baby.

- **Also, How can one man have 3 different races of children? Especially if Noah was white? They even attempt to state that Noah was white. So, then, we must recall what science states that white can only produce the color white. Noah may have been albino but still black (Enoch). How, then, do they explain this derogatory false teaching? This is blasphemy! It also goes to show that the masses blindly accept what they are taught and fail to study the Bible for themselves to see that the answers are right in our faces. Also, keep in mind that they were still along the equator line of Earth for pigmentation.**

Do you read and study your Bible?

In the image of Yahuah Elohiym, **The fact is the entire world was all Black (various shades) until the birth of Esau (the father of the white race who was birthed for a specific purpose). Somehow, Japheth became white after generations in Europe isolated.** We will get into this later during our study.

- **We must keep in mind that YAH had just blessed Noah and all his children in Genesis Chapter 9.**
- **Ham was the one to discover his father, Noah's, nakedness. However, if you read the verse closely, the curse was upon Canaan and not Ham. Canaan was the son of Ham and not the Father of all Blacks.**
- **Noah was also drunk when he cursed Canaan, the son of Ham. There is no precedent for a drunk statement, let alone a curse, to be valid under any circumstances. He was not in his right state of mind. Hence, he was not sober. He was drunk!**
- **YAH blessed them. Allowing scriptures to confirm scriptures, no man can curse what YAH has blessed (reference Numbers 23:8)**

How can I curse those whom Elohiym has not cursed?
How can I denounce those whom the Yahuah Elohiym has not denounced? **(Numbers 23:8)**

- Additionally, did you know **Yahusha (a.k.a. Jesus) was from the line of Shem, had the seed of Ham mixed within His lineage** (see Tamar **[Matthew 1:3d]**, Rahab **[Joshua 2:21]**, Bathsheba **[1Kings 3:1]**). Also, there was Hamitic blood in all the kings that came out of the tribe of Judah. Abram named was changed to include "Ham". Hence, the name Abraham is clear we're discussing blacks. King of Tyre who supplied Ark of Covenant materials was of seed of Ham.

  So, based upon this false teaching, are we to assume that Yahusha and all the kings were cursed since they were all mixed with the blood of Ham? Keep in mind, it was in **Egypt (Ham)** that the 12 tribes of Israel were able to survive a major famine causing Israel and his children to move there with Joseph, who became a ruler in Egypt (Ham). It was also Egypt (Ham) that hid Yahusha when King Herod was killing all babies and allowed for survival. Without getting too beyond the scope of this present study, any rational mind can see the **errors in the racist teachings of the curse of Ham (which was on Canaan, his son and not on Ham).**

Genesis 9: 27 May Elohiym extend Japheth's[b] territory; may Japheth live in the tents of Shem, and may Canaan be the slave of Japheth."

- **My extensive research has revealed that Esau mixed his seed with many nations to conceal his identity. Additionally, Esau has hidden his identity in Japheth. We'll cover this in the study series. However, science has shown that it takes 2-3 generations of isolated breeding to remove traces of blackness, to go from black to white.**

  My research has shown that Esau bred with Japheth in a way to steal Japheth's identity and to conceal their own. This is a contribution how Europe became white after an aboriginal all black population. They killed off any black offspring and were only allowed to keep white appearance babies. **After 2-3**

generations of this sort of restrictive and controlled breeding, the black trace of Japheth was removed, Japheth became white as Esau, and the identity of Esau was hidden in Japheth. Science mixed with genocide.

Hence, **the fulfillment of Genesis 9:27, whereby Esau was used to enlarge Japheth and to also live in the tents of Shem. Esau is not Japheth and Japheth is not Esau. Esau is Rome.**

- **Genesis 9:26a, Noah says, "Praise be to the Elohiym, the Elohiym of Shem". As we shall see in this study, Abram, who became Abraham, walked faithfully with YAH, and became the father of many nations. He also became the first person that YAH called a friend (James 2:23) and became the first person that YAH swore an everlasting oath to (Genesis 17:4-7). Abram named was changed to include "Ham". Hence, the name Abraham is clear we're discussing blacks and salvation.**
- **[4] "As for me, this is my covenant with you: You will be the father of many nations. [5] No longer will you be called Abram[b]; your name will be Abraham,[c] for I have made you a father of many nations. [6] I will make you very fruitful; I will make nations of you, and kings will come from you. [7] I will establish my covenant as an everlasting covenant between me and you and your descendants after you for the generations to come, to be your Elohiym, and the Elohiym of your descendants after you". (Genesis 17:4-7)**

Unlocking Bible Mysteries and Hidden Secrets Revealed
POLICE AND FEAR
Did you know? The enemy has full control of all law enforcement, lawyers, military, elected officials, and government. They are all controlled by the Anti-Mashiach and used to ENFORCE FEAR and CHAOS. This is the hidden origin behind orchestrating false agendas, such as Black Lives Matters. They even kill blacks, pay off the family, and use the "victim" to exploit an agenda. Chances are, whenever you see a Black killed by a white cop AND make NEWS, there is an extremely

controlled agenda behind it. All are puppets to the system especially so-called Black leaders. **21st Century LYNCHINGS!**
THEY EVEN KILL THEIR OWN POLICE!
They want to incite a "race" riot so they can bring forth military law and order. They want to make this a police-state where all your rights are limited and controlled. I pray for Israel that's in prisons.
They even created a fake virus to attempt COVID CAMPS
Remember, They serve fallen angels of the underworld. Their motto is "order out of chaos". So, they create chaos to bring "order".
THE ENEMY FUELS ON FEAR!
FEAR IS THEIR ONLY POWER. CONQUER FEARS AND YOU ARE MORE THAN A CONQUEROR!
Did you know? For years, the police AND secret government was used to closely monitor me with FEAR ATTACKS in attempts for my life AND PAYED OFF EVERYONE. Sad, when calling 911 (cops) is a death sentence!

DIVISION OF NATIONS

> Ephesians 6: 10 Finally, be strong in Elohiym and in his mighty power. [11] Put on the full armor YAHUAH Elohiym, so that you can take your stand against the devil's schemes.[12] **For our struggle is not against flesh and blood, but against the rulers, against the authorities, against the powers of this dark world and against the spiritual forces of evil in the heavenly realms.** [13] Therefore put on the full armor of YAHUAH Elohiym, so that when the day of evil comes, you may be able to stand your ground, and after you have done everything, to stand. [14] Stand firm then, with the belt of truth buckled around your waist, with the breastplate of righteousness in place (**Ephesians 6:10-14**)

One unfortunate theme throughout the Bible/Cepher is the willingness of man to fall victim to the death of sin and turn away from righteousness in walking in the ways of YAH. Before we discuss the division of the nations, which was sparked by an incident of Nimrod, we must understand a few things regarding the flood of Noah. With the flood in recent memory, many have wondered how did the world return to a fallen state of sin, and so soon after the flood? Some also questioned where did the source of evil come from if the only physical survivors, after the flood, were the righteous seed of Noah and his children? There are many speculations regarding this. I would like to pose my thoughts.

My theory is that angels and humans have different consequences of life after death. Let's review a lesson by Yahusha regarding life after death for humans (Luke 16: 22- 26):

> [22] And it came to pass, that the beggar died, and was carried by the angels into Abraham's bosom: the rich man also died, and was buried;
>
> [23] And in hell he lift up his eyes, being in torments, and seeth Abraham afar off, and Lazarus in his bosom.
>
> [24] And he cried and said, Father Abraham, have mercy on me, and send Lazarus, that he may dip the tip of his finger in water, and cool my tongue; for I am tormented in this flame.

[25] But Abraham said, Son, remember that thou in thy lifetime receivedst thy good things, and likewise Lazarus evil things: but **now he is comforted, and thou art tormented.**

[26] And beside all this, **between us and you there is a great gulf fixed: so that they which would pass from hence to you cannot; neither can they pass to us**, that would come from thence.

In Luke 16: 22- 26, this is another eye-opener for many as it reveals where those who died went, before Ha'Mashiach conquers death. This allows for a brief discussion as it may reveal major errors in false teachings by religious leaders and **exposing Christianity and others as a part of Mystery Babylon.**

How many have attended a funeral and heard a pastor preach a eulogy stating that your deceased loved one is in heaven resting in the bosom of Jesus (Yahusha)? It sounds comforting to hear those words. **However, this is incorrect and another form of blasphemy;** whereby blasphemy is to teach or hold truths that are contrary to the Word of YAH.

In this verse, we learn where all humans go after death. The ancient Hebrews termed it "Sheol", and moderns call it "Hell". It is deep into inner-Earth. Reference the Hebrew cosmology picture.

The story describes a rich man dying and descending to hell. To Hebrews, there are many levels to hell. **Sheol is a resting place for all souls as we await the resurrection and eternal judgment day. There are distinctions to the different parts of Sheol (a.k.a. hell)**

The good part of Sheol/hell is called "**Abraham's bosom**" where Abraham, the only man called a friend of YAH, is currently awaiting the resurrection himself, along with all the saints of the ages (**4 Ezra/2 Esdras 7**)! Those who die in sin go to the bad part of Sheol/hell. This part is separated by a great gulf/expanse which one cannot penetrate (see **Luke 16:26**).

However, souls can be raised through divination, which is prohibited by YAH to disturb souls that are asleep and to use divination or witchcraft (1 Thessalonians 4:15-17, Galatians 5:19-21). An example of this is when King Saul raised the soul of the deceased Prophet Samuel in **1 Samuel 28**. This act by Saul was strictly prohibited. King Saul became a demon, which is what led to YAH raising King David to leadership of Israel.

Thus, in short, all souls are in Sheol/hell awaiting the resurrection by Ha'Mashiach in the last days.

Sorry to burst your bubble but the teaching that souls go directly to heaven is a major false teaching, it's unbiblical, and it's a form of blasphemy. Mystery Babylon.

In the previous paragraph, we learned that all deceased human souls are currently in Sheol/ hell awaiting the resurrection of Ha'Mashiach in the last days (**4 Ezra/2 Esdras 7**). So, **let's return to our initial inquiry of what happened to the deceased giants and Nephilim who were destroyed by the flood of Noah?**

My theory is that they lost their physical bodies and are spirits roaming the Earth. Some lost their soul and became the gray aliens that live in inner-Earth. The grays cannot stand the sunlight as they perish in the light. They are from inner-Earth and not some distant galaxy. Doesn't that sound like a demon!

As spirits, they can possess, temporarily inhabit, a human body to experience life. The secrets of this are locked away in forbidden arts, such as witchcraft, sorcery, and divination (**hint – many secret societies such as Freemasons, Illuminati, and religious leaders still use these forbidden arts to divine demons**). These were all forbidden acts that were taught by fallen angels/watchers prior to the flood and the results, of which, were the consequences of the entire Earth falling to sin causing the judgement of destruction by flood in divine efforts to save man and Earth from falling to an eternal life of deadly sin. They also are the reason why Earth fell deep into sin. Remember, the days of Noah.

The division of Nations, by YAH, came because of a man called Nimrod.

Genesis 10: [8]And Cush begat Nimrod: he began to be a mighty one in the earth.

[9]He was a mighty hunter before the Lord: wherefore it is said, Even as Nimrod the mighty hunter before the Lord.

[10]And the beginning of his kingdom was Babel, and Erech, and Accad, and Calneh, in the land of Shinar.

For reasons beyond the scope of this study, **Bible translators have hidden many historical and biblical secrets under code names**. As you see above, **Genesis 10:9 is a prime example of their attempt to hide the seed of Satan.**

My theory is when you see the words "**a mighty hunter before the Lord**" or "**men of renown**", **this is a reference to one that is or became a giant or demon in a human body**. (We have many today!). It also implies a skilled hunter. Many meanings.

Also, there were a few physical giants that survived the flood. The Bible doesn't state how this occurred. Perhaps, they went inside inner-Earth or survived in caves. They didn't escape through the locked firmament only to be flooded by waters above the firmament claiming to reach another made-up planet on plasma.

A few examples of physical giants (excessive height and weight) after the flood are:

- **Goliath – He was eventually defeated by King David as a precursor to how Ha'Mashiach will defeat the Anti-Mashiach (1 Samuel 17:1-25:7)**
- **King Og of Bashan – When studying the King of Bashan, interesting to study the size of his bed, which would reveal his larger-than-life physical size. (Deuteronomy 3:11)**
- **"Lands of giants" and Inhabitants of the promised land during the conquering of Israel. When you read how Moses sent scouts to check out the promised land, they feared and doubted YAH because the lands were filled with physical giants (Exodus – Joshua)**

- **Anytime you see the Anakim and Rephaim in scriptures, it refers to offspring of the giants/Nephilim. Even the myth of Gilgamesh**
- **Many ancient cultures also have myths/stories regarding giants. One interesting thing about myths is that they all have elements of truth in their stories.**

From the above examples, some physical giants survived the Noah flood. **The others roamed the Earth as wandering spirits, which is why even today we have these same fallen angels wandering Earth and possessing humans**. The only issue with recognizing this is that we often look for a large size physical giant and not realizing that **their size is not the current indicators, but their superhuman abilities.**

Therefore, Yahusha states that Coming of Ha'Mashiach would be as the "Days of Noah", meaning that **humans would be possessed by fallen angels in our current day and age of Ha'Mashiach advent. There are demons in human bodies! Clearly, today's time!**

My theory is that Nimrod began to engage in forbidden arts, and he became possessed by a giant. Thus, he became a "mighty hunter before Elohiym" (**A side note is that Esau would be described as a mighty hunter before Elohiym, and Esau killed Nimrod and stole the "coats of skin" that YAH made for Adam and Eve). He did all this right before selling his birthright to Jacob. This is what made him weak that he was dying for a bowl of soup.**

After Nimrod rises to power, he began to gather all the nations under his rulership creating the foundations for the first one-world government, and they created the "Tower of Babel" (**Genesis 11**). **This tower of Babel is no different from our modern-day CERN and many pyramid structures that you see around the world.** These are geometric structures which are located on the electromagnetic energy grid of Earth and their main purpose is to **communicate with the demonic realm and manifest demons on Earth**. Somehow, you praise pyramids and since the devil seeks to mimic the creator, he demonized a sign of YAH, the pyramid.

Interestingly, the Bible doesn't provide many details on this. One would need to be versed in the outside text to come to this understanding. Additionally, the Bible states that this tower reached the heights of heaven. If you study this statement, you can realize the allegory here as Earth is enclosed in an indestructible firmament, which no man has been able to escape.

This is another reason why one must realize that even if there were other worlds and other planets, no man can ever leave the atmosphere of Earth because we are trapped under the firmament since Genesis, the beginning of time. Not even a satellite or spaceship can escape our orbit to reach the heavenly realms. It's not because of gravity because gravity is fake.

Also, if you search YouTube videos, for the phrase "glass firmament', I discovered a few that confirmed what the Bible reports as **there are waters above the firmament. You can hear the water as you approach the firmament. If the firmament were ever penetrated, it would be like unleashing a massive flood of waters upon Earth.**

This is part of the **grand deception of NASA** and our **world leaders** since the beginning of time. Another deception is that everyone is looking towards a future one-world-government and not realizing that **we have been under a one-world-government since the days of Nimrod.** My theory is that Nimrod was the **founder of Freemasonry** and the **keeper of forbidden sciences post-flood**. His identity has been kept secret because, to me, the **name Nimrod is not his name.** It's simply a title and not his historical name.

So, we have this **one-world-government led by fallen angels** during the days of Nimrod. This is no different than all throughout the course of history and **even today**! **This is the main reason why YAH came from His heavenly throne to confuse the languages of man and to scatter man throughout the Earth.** Since the beginning of time (reference: **Genesis 3:15**), Satan has attempted to seize control over Earth and heaven.

- **the kingdom of heaven suffereth violence, and the violent take it by force (Matthew 11:12b)**

After the masses were scattered throughout the lands, came the division of the nations. YAH divided the world into 70 nations, and He chose Israel through Abraham. **Abraham (Shem),** which was a fulfillment of Noah's blessing which Noah said praise the Elohiym of Shem. YAH gave spirits to lead the other nations away from Him. He never knew any other nation. This is when we see how the mighty faith of Abraham conquered the heart of YAH and became the only man in the Bible/Cepher that was called the friend of YAH. **This begins the Chosen Children of YAH a.k.a. The Black Hebrews a.k.a. The 12 Tribes of Israel and it all started by Abraham, the friend of YAH.**

- [23] And the scripture was fulfilled which saith, Abraham believed Elohiym, and it was imputed unto him for righteousness: and he was called the Friend of Elohiym (**James 2:23**).

Unlocking Bible Mysteries and Hidden Secrets Revealed
BATTLE OF THE SEEDS – GEN 3:15
YAH chose the 12 Tribes of Israel to be His chosen children (Romans 9:23, John 3:16) to carry his seed on Earth to fulfill **Genesis 3:15** prophecy. **The game of life is a battle of the seeds.** The **seed of YAH vs. the seed of Satan.**
Remember, all truths are hidden in codes and numbers
In all sports, you ever wonder why whites dominate in all games with a small white ball? Most of those games are calm, relaxing, and patient. Whereas Blacks dominate in all sports with brown balls and fast paced environments (This is why Blacks think on their toes and whites have difficulty thinking in fast paced environments). This is the battle of the seeds! **They throw it in your face as games and these fallen athletes sell it to you.** I also have a theory whereby **all athletic stars are possessed by fallen angels and demons. This is all secret Freemasonry** sworn oaths of secrecy. **Keep this in mind as they do this in all activities of life (throw it in your face in codes and get paid doing it)!**
Ever examine the numerical values of KBs death. It's all freemasonry! Numbers never lie! Black Panther.
THEY KILL BASED UPON NUMBERS

ABRAHAM

Who are Israelites; to whom pertaineth the adoption, and the glory, and the covenants, and the giving of the law, and the service of God, and the promises **(Romans 9:4)**

When we think about Israel, we must always keep in mind **Genesis 3:15.** [15] **"And I will put enmity between thee and the woman, and between thy seed and her seed; it shall bruise thy head, and thou shalt bruise his heel".** In this scripture, **we see the first prophecy and promise of YAH to bring forth a child out of the seed of a woman (meaning humans) to crush the seed of Satan. This promise would be fulfilled through the seed of Abraham, Isaac, Jacob in Ha'Mashiach.**

Therefore, YAH chose a nation unto Himself. That nation is the children of Israel. The nation of Israel forefathers are Abraham, Isaac, and Jacob (Israel). Jacob would become YAH's firstborn.

To better understand the environment which Abraham lived, one would need to read the **Book of Jubilees** and the **Book of Jasher**. These books provide additional details to understand how bad man had fallen back into sin after the flood of Noah and shed light to how bad we are today. Remember, this is a major unfortunate reoccurring theme in the Bible/Cepher, mans' eternal battle with deadly sin and turning against YAH.

As you read and study the days of Noah and Lot, keep this in mind as we face, in my opinion, more severe circumstances just as Yahusha stated regarding our current times and Ha'Mashiach advent. I feel that our current days and times are much worse than the days of Noah and Lot.

Jubilees and Jasher also provide additional critical details as to why YAH chose Abraham and called him his friend. It is also important to keep in mind that these events were immediately during/after the Nimrod "Tower of Babel" incident and not too long after the flood of Noah. This is important to note as the judgement of the flood should have been still fresh in the minds of man to caution against the outcomes of sin.

> 2 And the sons of Noach (Noah) **began to war on each other, to take captive and to slay each other**, and to **shed the blood of men** on the earth, **and to eat blood**, and to build strong cities, and walls, and towers, and individuals began to exalt themselves above the nation, and to found the beginnings of kingdoms, and to go to war people against people, and nation against nation, and city against city, and all **began to do evil, and to acquire arms, and to teach Their sons war**, and they **began to capture cities and to sell male and female slaves.** 3 And Ur, the son of Kesed, built the city of Ara of the Kasdiym, and called its name after his own name and the name of his father. And they **made for themselves molten images**, and they **worshipped each the idol**, the molten image which they had made for themselves, and they **began to make graven images and unclean simulacra**, and malignant ruachoth (spirits) assisted and **seduced them into committing transgression and uncleanness (Jubilees 11:2-3)**

This is an important verse to understanding the culture and systemic pressures faced by Abraham and others. As indicated in the scripture, this was a time when we saw the beginnings of cities and kingdoms. To bring this about required much violence and bloodshed. Many people began to go to war against one another seeking power and control over resources and each other. They began to murder and eat blood.

As previously discussed in the Nimrod observation, many started **conjuring evil spirits**. They even made molten and graven images, which means that they made false pagan gods from the works of their hands and imagination. Every man worshipped their own idol gods. These are the origins of gods of today.

> 14 And in the seventh year of this week she bore him a son, and he called his name Avram (Abraham), by the name of the father of his mother; for he had died before his daughter had conceived a son. 15 And **the child began to understand the errors of the earth that all went astray after graven images and after uncleanness**, and his father taught him writing, and he was two weeks of years old, and **he separated himself from his father, that he might not worship idols with him.** 16 **And he began to pray to the Creator of all things that he might save him from the errors of the children of men**, and that his portion should not fall into error after uncleanness and vileness **(Jubilees 11:14-16)**

From a young age, Abraham was a man of true character and strength. A mighty man of faith and the father of the faithful. He was blessed to have the household of Noah remaining, on Earth, at this time. Remember, Noah was a man that walked with YAH and was a prophet who was solely chosen by YAH to teach the ways of YAH. Noah was also the recipient of the covenant from Adam, because of his faithfulness to YAH. Noah maintained his faith and provided a spiritual outlet to Abraham to learn the proper ways of YAH. Abraham would restore monotheism, the belief in one Supreme Creator. This would prove very critical as we shall see in **Jubilees 12: 1-5** in a conversation between Abraham and his own father, Terach.

> And it came to pass in the sixth week in the seventh year thereof, that Avram said to Terach his father, saying: father! 2 And he said: Behold, here am I, my son. And he said: **What help, and profit have we from those idols which you do worship, and before which you do bow yourself?** 3 **For there is no ruach (spirit) in them, for they are dumb forms, and a misleading of the heart. Worship them not:** 4 **Worship the Elohiym of heaven**, who causes the rain and the dew to descend on the earth and does everything upon the earth, and has created everything by his word, and all life is from before his face. **5 Why do ye worship things that have no ruach in them?** For they are the **work of men's hands**, and on your shoulders do ye bear them, and ye have no help from them, but **they are a great cause of shame to those who make them, and a misleading of the heart to those who worship them: worship them not (Jubilees 12:1-5)**

That is one very powerful scripture! Let's think on this for a second. This study and my future works are a result of my unwavering faith to worship the Creator of all things and to follow YAH and only YAH with everything that is of me. It is also a direct result of many questions that I had regarding our current institution of religion and many false teachings which I felt were results of idol worship and paganism shielded by Christianity (we'll cover fallen and pagan Christianity and their false teachings throughout in the study).

All my life, I have been a student of biblical studies and always questioned our current state of religion, their teachings, racist unbiblical theories, and Bible interpretations. **I always went against the norm and had the strength not to blindly follow my loved ones or any "so-called" religious teacher or leader. I FOLLOW YAH ONLY.**

Keep in mind, just because someone holds a religious title, supplied by man, it does not grant them authority from YAH, and it certainly doesn't mean that YAH agrees with their created title.

We'll cover this later in the study regarding the proper order how YAH communicates with His creation. **It will amaze you that YAH never spoke to more than one person, Prophet, or High Priest, on Earth at any given time, unless YAH raised a prophet for a purpose and dealt with that individually personally. YAH never spoke to the pope. Ever! The pope is part of Mystery Babylon and is not of YAH.**

Unlocking Bible Mysteries and Secrets Revealed
THE POPE
The Pope is a major form of blasphemy. He does not represent YAH on Earth. YAH never allows this. The pope is not a son of YAH. The pope follows science, which is against YAH. The pope is part of **Mystery Babylon**, whose teachings go against YAH. The pope has no authority from YAH. The pope is a freemason who practices paganism and secretly worships a Black Madonna and Black Jesus.
YAH NEVER USED THE POPE, ENEMY OF YAH

Everything with YAH is within divine order. **It was the job of that Prophet or High Priest to communicate the things of YAH with man and the world.** If it was an isolated Israel event, YAH typically used a prophet. When Israel impacted the "outside" world, YAH sends Ha'Mashiach. We'll touch on this later, it's beyond the scope of this current section.

Recently, I had a conversation with my oldest sister regarding Christianity, the way they interpret the Bible, and their watered-down pagan teachings. For the record, I was raised in a Christian family. **This will be difficult to accept as it was for many loved ones even with truth in their faces.** You should not love any man more than YAH. **Oftentimes, standing with YAH means standing alone.** In this fallen world, truth stands alone!

After coming to spiritual enlightenment regarding the things of YAH, I could not understand how and why many follow the biblically incorrect and pagan teachings of Christianity. **Many accept blindly and are taught rather than study themselves this slave religion.** I would study the Bible and say to my sister, **"There's no way they can't see what I see when reading and studying the Bible".** What my sister said to me was very powerful.

Keep in mind that all pastors are Freemasons, Her response was, "Gian, well many pastors were taught by their fathers and parents, their parents were taught by their parents, and so on for generations. They never thought to question anything and felt as betrayal to family loyalty if they did". This reminded me of what Yahusha said in **Matthew 15:14**, "Let them alone: they be blind leaders of the blind. And if the blind lead the blind, both shall fall into the ditch".

Think about all the pressures that Abraham faced. It will help you to put yourself in Abraham shoes and vice-versa, as our current world is just as bad if not worse than Abraham's time. He was born in a world that fell in sin. Think about all the peer pressures, the many temptations, the challenges of lust and pride, the pursuits of being accepted by others, and wanting to be accepted by a parent by not challenging their beliefs or values and not following their belief system.

Rather than blindly following his father's pagan idol worship, the scriptures state that Abraham challenged his own father and questioned him about why he worships gods made of man's hands and imagination. A question we must all ask ourselves, **Why don't you worship our Creator, YAHUAH Elohiym?**

This was the faith of Abraham. Throughout **Jubilees and Jasher**, you will learn that Abraham studied with Noah and his household. Noah, just like pre-flood, was one of few households, on post-flood Earth, that walked with YAH, the only true Creator and living Elohiym (a.k.a. God). **Abraham did not follow the god of his father. He worshipped the Creator.** In fact, scriptures will report that Abraham challenged his father many times. Until one day, he decided to destroy the idol images of his father. He also taught many others about the true worship of YAH. At the time, there were no prophets, high priests, or temple! YAH wasn't dealing with anyone except Abraham. So, for all those who say Abraham wasn't a prophet, read the books of **Jubilees and Jasher**. He may not had held the title, but he did the work!

After reading the story of Abraham, one will better understand what Yahusha meant in **Luke 12:51-53**. In the last days **(today!), everyone will have to make their own personal decision** regarding their **faith** and the **eternal consequences of that decision** for **judgement day and Ha'Mashiach will come to cause divisions not unity**:

> [51] Suppose ye that I am come to give peace on earth? I tell you, Nay; but rather **division**:
>
> [52] For from henceforth there shall be five in one house divided, three against two, and two against three.
>
> **[53] The father shall be divided against the son, and the son against the father; the mother against the daughter, and the daughter against the mother; the mother-in-law against her daughter in law, and the daughter in law against her mother in law (Luke 12:51-53)**

How many of you can speak divine truth to power?
Do you worship the only true living Elohiym and Creator of life?
If you had to stand alone, would you stand for the Highest YAH?

Remember, no one can pray you into heaven. Your money cannot buy you in. Therefore, we will all be individually judged and face the creator alone!

The only outcome is either eternal heaven or eternal hell

To me, this account brings a fuller picture as to why YAH chose Abraham than the Genesis account. In respects of space in this current study, I will have follow-ups which will get deeper into all topics, including the forefathers, Israel history, Ha'Mashiach, last days, and more.

I'm not discrediting the Genesis account. **Genesis provides some details. Let's discuss a few:**

- **YAH calls Abraham – Genesis 12** Now the Lord had said unto Abram, Get thee out of thy country, and from thy kindred, and from thy father's house, unto a land that I will shew thee: [2] And **I will make of thee a great nation, and I will bless thee, and make thy name great; and thou shalt be a blessing:**[3] And **I will bless them that bless thee, and curse him that curseth thee: and in thee shall all families of the earth be blessed**.
- **YAH promises Abraham a numberless seed – Genesis 13:** [16] And **I will make thy seed as the dust of the earth**: so that if a man can number the dust of the earth, then shall thy seed also be numbered.

  [5] And he brought him forth abroad, and said, Look now toward heaven, and tell the stars, if thou be able to number them: and he said unto him, So shall thy seed be. **(Genesis 15:5)** (keep this verse in mind for our study of Israel)

- **YAH provides a major Abrahamic prophecy that provides significant clues to the true identity of Israel, the chosen children of YAH (clue- think modern-day African Americans) – Genesis 13:** [13] And he said unto Abram, Know of a surety that **thy seed shall be a stranger in a land that is not theirs, and shall serve them; and they shall afflict them four hundred years; (US Slavery dates 1619-2019, 400 years)**

  [14] And also that nation, whom they shall serve, will I judge: and afterward shall they come out with great substance.
- **YAH choses Abraham: The Abrahamic Covenant – Genesis 17:** [2] And **I will make my covenant between me and thee and will multiply thee exceedingly.**
  [3] And Abram fell on his face: and Elohiym talked with him, saying,

  [4] As for me, behold, **my covenant is with thee, and thou shalt be a father of many nations.**

  [5] Neither shall thy name any more be called Abram, but **thy name shall be Abraham**; for a father of many nations have I made thee.

  [6] And **I will make thee exceeding fruitful**, and I will **make nations of thee, and kings shall come out of thee.**

> [7] And **I will establish my covenant between me and thee and thy seed after thee in their generations for an everlasting covenant, to be a Elohiym unto thee, and to thy seed after thee.**
>
> [8] And I will give unto thee, and to thy seed after thee, the land wherein thou art a stranger, **all the land of Canaan, for an everlasting possession**; and I will be their Elohiym. (Ham's seed Canaan lost the promised land due to molesting Noah)

So, **we learn that YAH decides to establish an everlasting covenant with Abraham and his seed in perpetuity and Abraham was to be a father of many nations.** The challenge is that Abraham and Sarah, his wife, were both very elderly at the time and they did not have any children, nor did they perceive the ability to have children. When life presents a conflicting picture from the voice of YAH, you are left with nothing but faith. Before we discuss the faith of Abraham (**Romans 4:16**), this is a great time for a prophetic break on faith. To be clear of YAH's intentions to save blacks, Abram name was changed to add "Ham". Hence, Abraham.

Unlocking Bible Mysteries and Hidden Secrets Revealed
Prophetic Faith
John 15: [20a] Remember the word that I said unto you, The servant is not greater than his Elohiym. If they have persecuted me, they will also persecute you.
This above verse describes the challenges of the life that we all live and interact with daily. In **John 15:20**, Yahusha is warning Hebrews that they will be persecuted just as he was persecuted. We all want to get into the kingdom of heaven. However, we must face persecution, trials, and tribulations. **To receive the kingdom of heaven, we must experience the fire to come out as gold.** One must have complete faith in YAH as the treatment of the world would tempt one to think that there's something wrong with walking with YAH.
Therefore, it takes the faith of Abraham to believe and walk with YAH regardless of the circumstances.
This is also why it's **so critical to have true knowledge of the Word of YAH** as **life presents things that are contrary to the things of YAH**. Therefore, the warning in **James 4:4b, "know ye not that the friendship of the world is enmity with Elohiym? whosoever therefore will be a friend of the world is the enemy of Elohiym".**

YAH promised Abraham to a father of many nations. He also promised that the world would be blessed through his seed. However, both Abraham and Sarah were old stricken in years. Sarah has a moment of doubt and provides her maid, Hagar, to have a child with Abraham. In **Genesis 16**, we learn the story of Hagar and Ishmael, the child of Abraham. Sarah would eventually become "jealous" of Hagar and her child and suggest to Abraham that they must separate. (Important to compare the Jubilees and Jasher account as it paints a different picture for Sarah. It wasn't jealously. Ishmael was committing acts against Jacob.) An angel appears to Hagar and tells her not to worry. YAH decides to bless Ishmael. However, **Ishmael will not be the recipient of the Abrahamic covenant with YAH.** This is very important to keep in mind.

One thing to learn about YAH is that He is not the author of confusion (**1 Corinthians 14:33**). YAH, specifically, told Abraham that he would be a father of many nations. However, for his covenant, YAH was in order with honoring proper laws in that Sarah was his wife. Thus, YAH appears to Sarah to set the record straight in **Genesis 17:15-21**.

Genesis 17: [15] And Yahuah Elohiym said unto Abraham, As for Sarai thy wife, thou shalt not call her name Sarai, but Sarah shall her name be.

[16] And I will bless her, and give thee a son also of her: yea, I will bless her, and **she shall be a mother of nations; kings of people shall be of her.**

[17] Then Abraham fell upon his face, and laughed, and said in his heart, Shall a child be born unto him that is an hundred years old? and shall Sarah, that is ninety years old, bear?

[18] And Abraham said unto Yahuah Elohiym, O that Ishmael might live before thee!

[19] And Yahuah Elohiym said, **Sarah thy wife shall bear thee a son indeed; and thou shalt call his name Isaac: and I will establish my covenant with him for an everlasting covenant, and with his seed after him.**

[20] And as for Ishmael, I have heard thee: Behold, I have blessed him, and will make him fruitful, and will multiply him exceedingly; twelve princes shall he beget, and I will make him a great nation.

[21] **But my covenant will I establish with Isaac**, which Sarah shall bear unto thee at this set time in the next year.

It is important to note that Abraham went on to have many children, as the prophecy states that he would be a father of many nations. The seed of Abraham can populate the planet. **However, the covenant of YAH would only pass on to his son, Isaac, and then to Isaac's son, Jacob (Israel). Jacob would be considered YAH's firstborn.**

After Isaac is circumcised, the Bible/Cepher describes a story about how Yahuah Elohiym tests the faith of Abraham. After the fulfillment of the prophecy to have children, at an elderly age, YAH tests Abraham to see if He can still trust him.

For those following along with the Bible, the abbreviated story is described in **Genesis 22. I prefer the book of Jubilees and Jasher account** of the story because it provides greater details to the event and sets the stage for our discussion.

Have you ever wondered why YAH tested Abraham with a human sacrifice of his child? Have you ever wondered how Sarah dies (Genesis 22)? Keep this story in mind for our discussion.

> And Elohiym said to him: Avraham (Abraham), Avraham; and he said: Behold, here am I. 2 And he said: Take your yachiyd (beloved) whom you love, even Yitschaq (Isaac), and go unto the high country, and offer him on one of the mountains which I will point out unto you. 3 And he rose early in the morning and saddled his ass, and took his two young men with him, and Yitschaq (Isaac) his son, and clave the wood of the ascending smoke offering, and he went to the place on the third day, and he saw the place afar off. 4 And he came to a well of water, and he said to his young men: Abide ye here with the ass, and I and the lad shall go yonder, and when we have worshipped we shall come again to you. 5 And he took the wood of the ascending smoke offering and laid it on Yitschaq (Isaac) his son, and he took in his hand the fire and the knife, and they went both of them together to that place **(Jubilees 18:1-5).**

Abraham was obedient and faithful to YAH in all his ways. He was so obedient that he was willing to sacrifice his own son, Isaac, the promised seed of the covenant. **In the Jubilees account of the story**, one can also notice that same obedience and faithfulness with Isaac. Abraham led Isaac to an altar, which he had setup for a smoke offering to YAH. He never told Isaac that he was the intended "item" to be sacrificed. Also, his faithfulness never wavered from the test commandment of YAH (see scriptures).

As they approach the altar, Isaac notices that there is no animal or meat offered to be sacrificed. The **Jubilees account (Chapters 18-19) and Jasher (Chapter 23) provides** great details to this event that's summarized in **Genesis 22**. Once Isaac realizes that he was to be the "item" sacrificed, he willingly offered himself to the altar. Right as Abraham is about to sacrifice Isaac, YAH immediately stops him as he witnesses Abraham's faithfulness and obedience regardless of the commandment. In the scriptures, it states that **YAH offered a sacrifice on behalf of Abraham in Jubilees 18:12 which proves Yahusha (a.k.a. Jesus) was not the sacrifice of the world as claimed. Is this why Jubilees and Hebrew books were hidden?**

Unlocking Bible Mysteries and Hidden Secrets Revealed
HOLLYWOOD – MUSIC – MOVIES
EVER WONDER? How movies seem so REAL. They don't even ACT. They conjure spirits. Demonic possessions. Witchcraft. Forbidden Secret Sciences. Magic.
That's why they don't act. You are hooked! They place curses and trances on you to train you how they want you to see life and live. That's why Hollywood, Music, and Movies are so GAY and violent. You follow. This is all about lowering your vibrational frequencies to harvest demons. They also are active in blood sacrifices and child harvesting
Even watching a movie or hearing music can make you turn into a demon. **ALL celebrities CAST CURSES THROUGH THEIR ART and MUSIC**
ALL FORBIDDEN MAGIC
COME OUT OF MYSTERY BABYLON - REPENT

Unlocking Bible Mysteries and Hidden Secrets Revealed
CHILD HARVESTING
Demons are negative energy sources that require active sources of energy. **They are constantly feeding off your energy.** They need your energy to survive. **The purer and more righteous you are, the more spiritual energy you have.** Spiritual energy is like priceless currency. **Stronger demons require lots of energy or high energy sources. That's why they target the pure in heart and the righteous.** This is also why they harvest on kids because **kids give off the most energy when they fear. For example, fear is the strongest energy source even over love. When a child is afraid, they give off so much energy. There is mass child harvesting of their energy, blood, and souls.**
DEMONS STEAL YOUR ENERGY
Fear is the lowest vibration and gives demons the most power when you fear. That's why you must be fearless and have the spirit of Elijah (fearless) to bring about Ha'Mashiach (salvation). That's why Ha'Mashiach sends Elijah to pave the way to be saved! You can't be saved and be afraid at the same time!

Another mystery that the book of Jubilees helps to solve is how did Sarah die. Genesis 23:2 simply states that "Sarah dies" and provides no details regarding her death. **For those details, one must read the account in the Book of Jubilees and Jasher.**

Jubilees goes on to explain how while Abraham and Isaac were heading back from this secret sacrifice event, as no one knew the reason why they went away, **Satan manifested and was taunting Sarah. One important point to reiterate, from the beginning of this study, is that Satan roams the Earth and heaven as we saw in the Book of Job. This is another story about Satan personally disturbing events on Earth**. His job is to tempt you!

Since Isaac was her only child and the seed of the promise, Sarah was nervous that something bad would happen to him. Who knows! Call it motherly instincts or perhaps she felt the energy as Abraham and Isaac departed. While they were returning, Satan tells Sarah that her son, Isaac, was dead. This caused her to go into traumatic stress and she died (**Jasher 23:86**).

Josephus, Hebrew Historian, revealed that Abraham taught the ancient Egyptians mathematics and astrology.

The faithful, Abraham and Isaac lived on.

JACOB AND ESAU

As stated previously, I shall have follow-up works that will provide greater details into Bible/Cepher topics and characters. Keeping in line with the focus and scope of this study Unlocking Bible Mysteries and Hidden Secrets Revealed, **the next focus of study comes from Isaac and the birth of his twins, Esau and Jacob. Twins who were chosen before the world was created in order to fulfill YAH's plan for Earth.**

In **Genesis Chapter 24**, we learn that Isaac married Rebekah, from his father's lineage. **Genesis Chapter 25** discusses Abraham's additional children. However, **keep in mind that the Abrahamic covenant passed on to Isaac only (Genesis 17:15-21).**

> **Genesis 25:** [19] And these are the generations of Isaac, Abraham's son: Abraham begat Isaac:
>
> [20] And Isaac was forty years old when he took Rebekah to wife, the daughter of Bethuel the Syrian of Padanaram, the sister to Laban the Syrian.
>
> [21] And Isaac intreated the Elohiym for his wife, because she was barren: and Elohiym was intreated of him, and Rebekah his wife conceived.
>
> [22] And the children struggled together within her; and she said, If it be so, why am I thus? And she went to enquire of Yahuah Elohiym .
>
> [23] And Yahuah Elohiym said unto her, **Two nations are in thy womb, and two manner of people shall be separated from thy bowels; and the one people shall be stronger than the other people; and the elder shall serve the younger (Genesis 25:19-23).**

In John 3:12, Yahusha says, "If I have told you earthly things, and ye believe not, how shall ye believe, if I tell you of heavenly things?"

The story of Esau and Jacob is a prime example of the mystery of YAH to bring about the fulfillment of his purposes on Earth.

Without being accused of becoming racial, I want you to remember that up until this point, the entire world is still various shades of Black only. **We must always keep things in the proper perspective to see the real complete picture.**

In these verses, we learn that Rebekah, Isaac's wife, is pregnant with **two different manners of people (one black righteous and one evil white from birth)** within her womb. We also learn that the children struggled in her womb all throughout the duration of her pregnancy and after. In **verse 23, Yahuah Elohiym provides the ultimate prophecy by stating that the elder shall serve the younger.**

> **Genesis 25:** [24] And when her days to be delivered were fulfilled, behold, there were twins in her womb.
>
> [25] And the first came out **red**, all over like a hairy garment; and they called his name **Esau**.
>
> [26] And after that came his brother out, and his hand took hold on Esau's heel; and his name was called Jacob: and Isaac was threescore years old when she bare them.
>
> [27] And the boys grew: and **Esau was a cunning hunter**, a man of the field; and **Jacob was a plain man, dwelling in tents (Genesis 25:24-27)**
>
>> 13 And in the **sixth week**, in the second year thereof, Rivgah (Rebekah) bore to Yitschaq (Isaac) two sons, Ya'aqov (Jacob) and Esau, and Ya'aqov (Jacob) was a smooth and upright man, and Esau was fierce, a man of the field, and hairy, and Ya'aqov (Jacob) dwelt in tents. 14 **And the youths grew, and Ya'aqov (Jacob) learned to write; but Esau did not learn, for he was a man of the field and a hunter, and he learned war, and all his deeds were fierce.** 15 And Avraham (Abraham) love Ya'aqov (Jacob), but Yitschaq (Isaac) loved Esau.16 **And Avraham (Abraham) saw the deeds of Esau, and he knew that in Ya'aqov (Jacob) should his name and seed be called (Jubilees 19: 13-16b)**
>>
>> **Esau was a designing and deceitful man, and an expert hunter in the field,** and **Ya'aqov (Jacob) was a man perfect and wise, dwelling in tents, feeding flocks and**

learning the instructions of Yahuah and the commands of his father and mother (Jasher 26:17b).

1 The burden of the word of the Lord to Israel by Malachi.

[2] I have loved you, saith the Lord. Yet ye say, Wherein hast thou loved us? Was not Esau Jacob's brother? saith the Lord: yet I loved Jacob,

[3] And I hated Esau, and laid his mountains and his heritage waste for the dragons of the wilderness (**Malachi 1:1-3**).

[13] **As it is written, Jacob have I loved, but Esau have I hated (Romans 9:13).**

I provided three different accounts of the birth of Esau and Jacob since each account reveals additional information and I added 2 additional verses for references. On the sixth (6=sin), Esau was born first. Hence, as any other father, Jacob, initially, loved his firstborn more until he realized the true character of Esau was evil (6=sin). However, Abraham, Rebekah, and YAH loved Jacob, who fulfilled prophecy to inherit the covenant promises of Abraham and Isaac.

Esau was born different, meaning he was a different color from birth than Jacob, his parents, and the rest of the human population (at that current time) and he was born with an evil spirit. This is another example of a Bible coded verse. Keep in mind, from our earlier discussion regarding science. **Black can create all colors.** White can only create white. Also, keep in mind. Where Esau went further away from equator altered pigmentation.

So, **here we have Black parents giving birth to a white child.** The Bible codes this by saying that Esau was born red. This is not the same red as Adam was created, as Adam was dark brownish red like a garnet stone whereas **Esau was a bright red like white in the sunlight.**

To better understand this, think about a white person standing in the sun. If you look at their skin, it looks more **bright-reddish than pale white. This is the**

origins of real whites. They were born to sin, be red hot, and a mighty hunter that turns from YAH from birth.

I do not like to use the word "race" as that is a word created by science and has no biblical authenticity.

Esau, thus, is the only father of all whites that we see today. Perhaps, that's why he hated his birthright, his own twin brother (who came out Black like his parents), and even YAH. Born void of righteousness. Left from the prism of his ancestry shade. Void. Which is why he forces you to mix with him while forbidding you to mix with yourself!

Ask yourself, As the firstborn blessed of YAH, would you sell your birthright? For a bowl of soup? For anything?

Esau was upset for being born cursed and not in the image of the Creator

HE SOLD HIS BIRTHRIGHT OF YAH

Esau would eventually sell his birthright to Jacob for a bowl of food because he hated his birthright. He claimed to be "dying" of hunger, after killing Nirmod, as his reasoning why he sold his birthright to Jacob. Him selling his birthright was another fulfillment of prophecy of YAH in that Jacob was to be the one that inherited the covenant. YAH also said that the elder would serve the younger. This initially occurred as the entire world was ruled by Black rulers before Esau usurped the power on Earth, which was another prophecy fulfillment. **However, in the millennial kingdom and kingdom of heaven, Jacob/Israel will rule forever.**

- **"For Esau is the end of the world and Jacob is the beginning of it that follows (2 Esdras 6:9)**

Additionally, the scriptures reflect that Jacob stayed home to learn the ways of YAH, while Esau became a mighty hunter. For those that have been closely following, remember my theory for the **coded phrase "a mighty hunter".** Allowing scriptures to confirm scriptures, each time that this phrase is used in the Bible/Cepher, **it refers to one who is demonically possessed and became a seed of Satan.** While **Esau was becoming a demon**, the first person he attacks is Nimrod, the person who **rebirthed the Nephilim spirits (Jasher 27:7-12**).

We shall touch on this later in the study but remember the prophecy for **Esau being used to enlarge Japheth**. This is another method Esau used to **hide their identity**, while they **stole the possessions and inheritance of Japheth.** Remember, **Japheth was the aboriginal Europeans, which were all various shades of Black**.

Esau would isolate off this section of Europe and crossbreed until they produced an all-white offspring. This is after they came out of their humble beginnings in the **Caucasus mountains** living as savages and uncivilized. That's why they praise the dog so much because dogs protected them in the mountains and wild. Now they call Elohiym God, a dog backwards. Keep in mind, they killed all black newborns to remove the blackness and create white. **Genocide**!

After producing an all-white population, they then positioned themselves **to conquer an already highly advanced civilization starting with Europe, France, and then around the world.** They used highly secret sciences to steal and conquer Earth. Hence, they never created anything, just deceivers just like their father, Esau.

For centuries, they have done everything in their power to hide their identity. Without getting beyond the scope of this section, you ever **wonder why many whites are naturally evil? Why they hate blacks, the Chosen of YAH, so much? Wonder why Blacks are naturally spiritual people?** Why all the racism? African Americans get it worse than American Africans. Why is that? Israel!

I'll leave you with the **words of Yahusha, you'll know a tree from its seed and fruits.**

> [16] Ye shall know them by their fruits. Do men gather grapes of thorns, or figs of thistles?
>
> [17] Even so every good tree bringeth forth good fruit; but a corrupt tree bringeth forth evil fruit.

[18] **A good tree cannot bring forth evil fruit, neither can a corrupt tree bring forth good fruit.**

[19] Every tree that bringeth not forth good fruit is hewn down, and cast into the fire.

[20] Wherefore by their fruits ye shall know them **(Matthew 7:16-20)**.

Before we leave the subject of Esau, let's **review Japheth after the flood**. You will discover something very interesting:

[2] **The sons of Japheth**; Gomer, and Magog, and Madai, and Javan, and Tubal, and Meshech, and Tiras.

[3] And the sons of Gomer; Ashkenaz, and Riphath, and Togarmah.

[4] And the sons of Javan; Elishah, and Tarshish, Kittim, and Dodanim.

[5] **By these were the isles of the Gentiles divided in their lands**; everyone after his tongue, after their families, in their nations **(Genesis 10: 2-5)**.

A review of the dispersion of **Japheth, after the Noah flood, reveals that it was a black Japheth who inhabited the isles of the Gentiles! Hence, the origin of the Gentile world was started by Blacks!** Currently, Japheth's identity was stolen by Esau, the great deceiver (see notes above). Japheth also became white.

Jacob is described as a "tent dweller". This is the same description given to Abraham, Shem, and all Hebrews, as they were known to travel and dwell in tents and be righteous people. The Bible/Cepher then goes to describe the blessing of Jacob from Isaac before his death. This entire story is a fulfillment of Abraham's prayers and the Word of YAH. **Thus, by Esau hating his birthright, selling it, Jacob becomes the firstborn.**

[26] And his father Isaac said unto him, Come near now, and kiss me, my son.

> [27] And he came near, and kissed him: and he smelled the smell of his raiment, and blessed him, and said, See, the smell of my son is as the smell of a field which Yahuah Elohiym hath blessed:
>
> **[28] Therefore Yahuah Elohiym give thee of the dew of heaven, and the fatness of the earth, and plenty of corn and wine:**
>
> **[29] Let people serve thee, and nations bow down to thee: be lord over thy brethren and let thy mother's sons bow down to thee: cursed be everyone that curseth thee, and blessed be he that blesseth thee (Genesis 27: 26-29).**

Like Abram who became named Abraham, Jacob would become named Israel and give birth to the 12 tribes of Israel. The births of the children of Jacob are listed in **Genesis 29 and 30**. Jacob's only daughter, which was birthed by Leah, died. Jacob receives the covenants from YAH. Jacob becomes named Israel.

The Forefathers of the 12 Tribes of Israel by Jacob/Israel (wives are listed as headers)

Leah	**Rachel**	**Bilhah – Rachel Maid**	**Zilpah – Leah's maid**
Reuben	Joseph	Dan	Gad
Simeon	Benjamin	Naphtali	Asher
Levi			
Judah			
Issachar			
Zebulun			

In **Genesis 29**, we learn that Jacob served Laban, Rachel and Leah's father, for 14 years and an additional 7 years, to earn the marriage of Leah and Rachel (remember the number 14, another Messianic number). He initially proposed to serve 7 years for Rachel. However, Laban tricked Jacob and gave him Leah. Because Jacob loved Rachel, he served the additional time to gain her marriage. **With this knowledge, it shouldn't be a surprise that his favorite son was Rachel's firstborn, Joseph.**

Unlocking Bible Mysteries and Hidden Secrets Revealed
THE MILITARY AND GOVERNMENT
ALL military and government are secretly implanted which means they can be silently controlled as puppets!
Just as YAH chose the children of Israel as His righteous seed, **Satan uses the military and government to produce its demonic seed.** Esau was called a mighty warrior before Elohiym. He lives and dies by the sword. He is a liar, cheater, and theft. The truth is not in him at all. Esau is void of righteousness. Void of a living soul. Void of love. Doesn't this all sound like our military and government! They target our children at young ages. They win their souls for monetary gains and superheroes. That's why they throw so much money and perks to the military. Think about the VA loans! Student loans! The god of money and war. Satan!
Most of the military are secretly Freemasons and serve the agenda of Satan. They are bred to BLINDLY FOLLOW ORDERS and NEVER QUESTION AUTHORITY. Thus, they become blind puppets to the system of control.
All wars are secretly planned by shadow governments to seize control over the resources of lands and people. This is the only reason for war. In fact, even the Iraqi crisis was veiled for the real meaning was for the resources and to steal ancient artifacts. No different than how they robbed ancient Egypt's mystery schools to fund the Greeks.
DID YOU KNOW? GREEKS STOLE EVERYTHING FROM EGYPT. They can't even prove that these "Greek" philosophers ever lived! This is how the military and government functions. They are void of love as they turn their backs on their own family and loved ones all in the name of serving the mark of the beast. That's why they want blacks to serve! Also, they conduct secret medical experiments on our soldiers. Yes. Tuskegee was real! They killed blacks for science.

THE BIBLE IS BLACK HISTORY OF ISRAEL

Genesis 38 and 39 reveals the powerful story of Joseph. It is in this story that we shall uncover another secret to identifying the true children of Israel, the chosen of YAH. **Each bible story has many dimensions of knowledge encoded within the text.** This is a case of many clues being revealed for those who search beyond the surface.

A brief overview of the story is that Joseph's siblings were jealous of him because Jacob, now known as Israel, made Joseph a coat of many colors and he found favor in the eyes of Israel. Joseph was also the firstborn of Rachel, the favorite of Jacob (Israel). As firstborn, naturally he became a favorite and because of his righteousness.

The story of Joseph also shows how **YAH can turn a curse into a blessing and transform any situation.** The major lesson here is no matter what life throws at you, always walk with YAH.

Joseph's 11 siblings sold him into slavery, lied to Israel and reported that Joseph was killed by a beast in the field. They even went as far as dipping his "coat of many colors" in blood and presenting it to their father, Israel, as "proof" of death since they claim they were never able to "recover' his allegedly deceased body. The slave traders end up taking Joseph to Egypt. In Egypt, Potiphar's wife falls in love with Joseph and blends him into their household (**keep this in mind**).

Joseph lands himself in jail. He had a unique gift to be able to interpret dreams. In jail, Pharoah learns of Joseph's skills. Joseph interprets a very critical dream in that he alerts Pharoah to prepare for a very severe 7-year famine that was to hit the entire Earth. This interpretation allowed Egypt to stock up and prepare to weather the 7-year storm and be the only land that had supplies enough to feed their people and sell to other nations. Because of this revelation to Pharoah, Joseph goes from being a slave to being made ruler of Egypt, second only to Pharoah.

Let's cover a few clues before we get into the rest of the story. First, let's go back to after the flood when Noah and his 3 sons exited the ark to re-populate Earth. In the previous sections, **I revealed that Noah, his 3 sons, and their wives were all the Black complexion**

both pre-flood and post-flood (until the birth of Esau, which is the father of all whites).

But, for all those doubters and conspiracy theorist (a term manufactured by the CIA to scare you from truth), let's focus on **Ham** only for a second.

Let's review where Ham went after the flood and what does history say about Ham. **This is important because Joseph was blended into Egypt (Ham) and Pharoah's household.** He didn't stand out and fit in as one of their own! **The only way this would be possible is if Joseph and the Egyptians were of the same complexion and color!**

> [6] And the sons of Ham; Cush, and Mizraim, and Phut, and Canaan (**Genesis 10:6**). You can also reference **Jubilees 10.**

Ham and his seed inhabited much of Africa. In fact, Cush and Phut are located near Ethiopia. The Ethiopians are directly under the path of the sun. Interesting note about Ethiopia is that it is one of few lands, on Earth, that wasn't conquered by foreigners. Ethiopia today and during ancient times are dark-skinned Blacks. Cush means black.

Mizraim is another name for Egypt. My research also revealed that **Ethiopia is the motherland of Egypt**, and they were one dynasty before Europeans conquered and divided Egypt centuries later. Thus, the multicultural Egypt is a later reflection and not how the ancients looked like Egypt, just like all of Africa was all Black. Let's see what history and the "Father of history", **Herodotus,** reports of ancient Egypt and Africa. Keep in mind, he was one of the first European explorers into ancient Africa:

- **Herodotus has been called the "father of history." An engaging narrator with a deep interest in the customs of the people he described, he remains the leading source of original historical information not only for Greece between 550 and 479 BCE but also for much of western Asia and Egypt at that time (Britannica.com).**
- **"At one point in Black Athena (pp. 52-53) Professor Bernal has written that Herodotus "thought the Egyptians and some Libyans were black," and that Herodotus' portrayal of Egyptians as black was one of the**

inspirations for the title Black Athena. In another instance he stated his conviction (p. 242) that many of the most powerful Egyptian dynasties based in Upper Egypt - the 1st, 11th, 12th and 18th "were made up of pharaohs whom one can usefully call black." And in this case it is clear that Professor Bernal is using black in the contemporary sense of Negro, because he observes in the same context that the farther one goes up the Nile, "the blacker and more Negroid the population becomes," and that this has been so for some length of time. In support of his interpretation of Herodotus he has cited" (p. 242 note 68) (Bernal's "Blacks", Herodotus, and other Classical Evidence by Frank M. Snowden Jr.)

- **"For it is plain to see that the Colchians are Egyptians; and this that I say I myself noted before I heard it from others. When I began to think on this matter, I inquired of both peoples; and the Colchians remembered the Egyptians better than the Egyptians remembered the**
- **Colchians; the Egyptians said that they held the Colchians to be part of Sesostris' army. I myself guessed it to be so, partly because they are dark-skinned [melagchroes] and woolly-haired [oulotriches]; though that indeed goes for nothing, seeing that other peoples, too, are such" (Herodotus Book 2)**
- **W.E.B. DuBois in his book, The Negro (1915), writes that the Great Sphinx reveals strong negro traits and elements**

There are countless historical records, evidence, and many books written to prove that Egypt, just like the entire ancient world, was all Black long before the existence of any whites. **This is an unfortunate secret on Earth that has been hidden because all world history has been whitewashed only hundreds of years ago!**

This is not a racial comment as whites are simply Blacks that have lost their melanin. Another way to put this, there is only **one hue-man family and Blacks are the parents** of whites and all humans. Whites are blacks that look white.

What is racist is the power elite who attempted to erase Black world history and replace it with white faces. We'll cover this throughout in the study. However, to focus on facts and to simply reports facts is not racist at all.

Another eye opener is **reviewing ancient maps of Africa**, which was then called "**Negroland** on maps. If you look closely, you will also see the **"Kingdom of Judah" in Africa**. This is where some of the **dispersed** went to avoid persecution and slavery.

- **The remaining 11 forefathers and Israel go into Egypt during the famine. They, too, fit right in and resided in the land of Goshen.**
- **Let's fast forward to the story of Moses. Remember, just like Noah, Moses arrived on an ark. His destination was the land of Egypt where he, too, blended in with the population to avoid being killed (Exodus 2).**
- **There's more! Mary and Joseph hid away in Egypt with Yahusha when King Herod issued the decree to kill all babies in efforts to stop the birth (Matthew 2:13). All 3 of them fit right in, including the Yahusha (a.k.a. Jesus), who is also Black!**
- **[14] His head and his hairs were white like wool, as white as snow; and his eyes were as a flame of fire;[15] And his feet like unto fine brass, as if they burned in a furnace; and his voice as the sound of many waters (Revelations 1:14-15).**

- **John, another Black disciple, confirmed the color of the Ha'Mashiach in Revelations 1:15 by describing his feet are as fine brass burned in a furnace. If his feet are Black, then it's obvious that the rest of His body is black too! Think of a garnet stone.**

Recall the Father of History, **Herodotus** description of the ancient Egyptians. He said that their hair was as **wool**. This description of wool didn't stand out for me until **I started to grow my own hair out.**

Look at any hair of a Black person and you'll notice this "wool" description. Also, when the ancients wrote of a person having white hair, **the white hair is a symbol of wisdom** and not necessarily the actual color of the hair. Keep in mind that the **Book of Revelations is a highly coded message.**

IS THIS WHY RACISM? IS THIS WHY THE WHITEWASHED HISTORY WITH A REPLACED IMAGE PAINTED BY LEONARDO DA VINCI OF A CAUCASIAN WHITE PAGAN GOD? Jesus a White Mithra?

Keep in mind, prior to the 20th century, the entire world recognized a Black Yahusha (a.k.a. Jesus). Even the Pope prays to a Black Madonna and Black Jesus in secret! Any simple online search would reveal this!

- **Ha'Mashiach is one with YAH, a split image. So, if Ha'Mashiach is Black and the same as YAH. Obviously, YAH is Black as well! Hence, the darkness in Genesis 1.**
- **Perhaps, that's why Esau hated his birthright so much because he did not have the same color image as YAH or any other children of YAH/ creation.**

This may provide another clue as to why Esau has so much natural anger and desire to work against all the things of YAH with much destruction, hostility, and natural hate. **Is this why Esau is destroying Earth and the children of YAH?**

Not realizing that YAH is of righteousness to those who will repent and follow Him in obedience and righteousness. To **Esau, I leave you with Romans 9:20,** [20] **Nay but, O man, who art thou that repliest against Elohiym? Shall the thing formed say to him that formed it, Why hast thou made me thus?**

- There's more! Keep in mind that **King Solomon** married **Bathsheba, a Black African Queen**. Their son is one of the **forefathers for Ethiopia**, which has been one of the unconquered lands on Earth. Let's see what King Solomon says of himself.

  [5] **I am black**, but comely, O ye daughters of Jerusalem, as the tents of Kedar, as the curtains of Solomon.

  [6] Look not upon me, **because I am black**, because the sun hath looked upon me **(Song of Solomon 1:5-6a)**

- Revealing the **12 Tribes of Israel being Black**, all the forefathers back to **Adam** being Black, **Yahusha** being Black, Ha'Mashiach and **YAH** being Black. Now, we see **King Solomon** was black. His father, **King David** would also be Black. Abraham was black. YAH left a clear map by adding "Ham' to Abram.
- The **Apostle Paul** was mistaken as an Egyptian in **Acts 21:38**.
- This may appear shocking to many racially biased readers. The more you dig, the more you will come to notice:

THE ENTIRE BIBLE/CEPHER IS BLACK HISTORY OF THE BLACK CREATOR GOD/YAHUAH ELOHIYM (YAH), HIS SON Ha'Mashiach, HEAVEN AND EARTH ALL BLACK, THE FIRSTBORN/ CHOSEN CHILDREN OF YAH (12 TRIBES OF ISRAEL). EVERY CHARACTER IN THE BIBLE/CEPHER, EXLUDING ESAU and some New Testament Greeks, **IS BLACK!**

"And laid open the book of the law, wherein the heathen had sought to paint the likeness of their images" **(1 Maccabees 3:48)** This **verse describes the whitewashing of Black history, which occurred over the last 2,000 years! For any factual history, one must research over 2,000 years ago when the world was ruled by all Blacks since the beginning of the creation of Earth and the creation of man.**

With this information in mind, you may be wondering WHO are the people currently occupying the Land of Israel? The mystery "Jews" that have been receiving trillions in worldwide reparations for alleged events that factual history has been able to prove a contradicting story of real truths, yet you blindly accept blind facts. The same "Jews" that secretly run the world. Those that know the truths are silenced by pressures or death. They are Jewish converts and not of ethnicity. They have their own ways. This report comes directly from the throne of heaven! REPENT!

Unlocking Bible Mysteries and Hidden Secrets Revealed
THE REAL JEWISH HOLOCAUST
A very sensitive topic is the alleged Jewish Holocaust in Germany. **I say alleged because we must start requiring history to be proven and not just blindly accepted.** It's a proven fact that the **conquerors always rewrite history** and re-shape the stories in a framework to secure their worldwide domination, even if they must sell you myths of propaganda. We also live in a Hollywood movie! A case in point is the Jewish Holocaust. For those free thinkers and upholders of truth and righteousness **(truth and righteousness are your only tickets to heaven),** just like a fabricated 9/11 (Twin Towers) veiled the real event of man's manipulation of the weather and Earth's energy grid, you bought a plane crash story, I would caution all to research authentic historical records regarding the alleged Jewish Holocaust. They will blow your mind. During your research, you must note that **the only real holocaust was the one history doesn't report.** Fact is **millions of Black Jews** experienced the real and unreported holocaust while the yet-to-be-proven Hollywood movie is entertained and accepted as truth. Hitler was trying to help blacks by killing those stealing black identity!
Yahusha says, only the truth shall set you free (John 8:32)
You may even discover that what's reported never really happened in reality, at least not on the large and harsh scale that's taught and it's nothing

compared to **the numbers of real Black Jews that were murdered as attempted genocide worldwide, with is evidenced in the Book of Maccabees.** You may even discover only hundreds European Jews were killed than the millions alleged of European Jews. **This is a known fact amongst the secret elite and was a manufactured event to gain unwarranted worldwide sympathy, steal a Black Hebrew/Black Jewish identity, and gain worldwide domination and control. Hitler tried to stop this!**
Research the real reason why Hitler was killed and even his true character. Just like history distorts the real Malcolm X, they do the same regarding Hitler and every leader. They have you thinking Malcolm X was a racist Muslim and Hitler was a racist Nazi, and because they said it you believe it without any factual proof given. You accept lies. **The truth will set you free (John 8:32).** REPENT
The real and unreported Black Jewish Holocaust worldwide proves that the Chosen Children of YAH (Black Jews) have ALREADY EXPERIENCED THE GREAT TRIBULATION OF JACOB'S TROUBLE (Daniel 70 weeks) for the last 2,000 years (Gentile World).
The Antichrist (**Pope**) and Mark of the Beast (**Rome's 3 Mystery Babylon Religions – Christianity, Catholicism, Islam**) are already here for the last 2,000 years and replaced the TORAH of YAH (**1 Maccabees 3:48**)! We are at the end of the Gentile world (**Romans 11:25**). Turn a curse (veiled lie) into a blessing (hidden truths). You get **Ezekiel 37** Dry Bones Waking! **The Great Black Hebrew Awakening!**
History reveals the expected 2/3rds of Black Jews were killed already as biblically prophesized. We are the remnant that will be saved and multiplied beyond numbering. They hide your real identity in hopes of genocide and another tribulation that's unbiblical. Open your Third Eye.
This series focuses on proven facts and avoids misrepresentation of any data. These sections are for gentle moments of truth. Stay tuned in the series for more **Unlocking Bible Mysteries and Hidden Secrets Revealed.**

I'll allow you to ponder on what Yahusha said in Revelations:

> [9] I know thy works, and tribulation, and poverty, (but thou art rich) and I know the blasphemy of them which say they are Jews, and are not, but are the synagogue of Satan **(Revelations 2:9)**

Still unsure? Let's look at some verses that clearly identifies **modern-day African Americans as the chosen children of YAH** and the original 12 Tribes of Israel. **I don't use the phrase "Lost Tribes" because the entire world power structure knows exactly who the authentic 12 Tribes of Israel are and where they are located, always.** It's only the general population that has been deceived. Remember, scriptures report 10 tribes are in Azareth until the last days. Judah is dispersed in the Americas.

Those in power will lie to you. However, they will never lie to themselves! Therefore, the Pope, and all world leaders secretly pray to a Black Jesus and sell you a white lie!

A few examples where YAH clearly shows His intentions of a Black Ha'Mashiach and black chosen people are Moses and King Saul. YAH offered to destroy Israel and start a new nation with Moses, another black man, and Moses turned it down. Benjaminites were the darkest of Hebrews and King Saul was of this tribe. King Saul lost the honor when he fell into sin. That's how King David, another black man, became the royal line. Study your bible. The answers are right there!

> **I'll repeat. Modern-day African Americans in the Diaspora are the Tribes of Israel that are living under Deuteronomy curses. In fact, what many are coming to realize is the Great Hebrew Awakening that has been prophesized to occur during our current generation! We are the Dry Bones in Ezekiel 37. Our Torah was opened and changed by the heathen (1 Maccabees 3:48). We went through Daniel 70 weeks of Jacob's Trouble. OUR CURSES ARE FOR A SIGN and WONDER! Leaving undeniable clear proofs of facts.** Let's review some scriptures to further confirm the obvious:

YAH to Abraham during Abrahamic Covenant Blessings

[13] And he said unto Abram, Know of a surety that thy seed shall be a stranger in a land that is not theirs, and shall serve them; and they shall afflict them four hundred years; **(Keep in mind American slavery approximately 1619 or 400 years ago)**

[14] And also that nation, whom they shall serve, will I judge: and afterward shall they come out with great substance (**Genesis 15: 13-14**). (Babylon {America} is expected to fall per prophecy).

I will be covering details on the blessings and curses in follow-up works due to the scope of this current work in efforts to restrict from being an extra-large volume of reading work for historical proven unactive readers.

The main reasons for Israel being cursed are:

Pagan/Idol Worship	Forsaking YAH	Wicked Kings and leaders	Stiff-Necked People
Disobedience to the Laws of Moses	Being unfaithful to YAH and doubtful	Worshipping Yahusha as YAH	Corruption to join the enemy -see the feet of Daniel prophecy (mixed clay and iron)

Some Scripture References on curses

Deuteronomy 28	Deuteronomy 18	Daniel 9:11	Baruch 1:19-20	Baruch 2:1-2
Leviticus 26	Ezekiel 4:3-6	Deuteronomy 29:28	Deuteronomy 28:68	Jeremiah 29:18
Luke 21:24	Genesis 15:13	Nehemiah 1:8	Psalms 44:11	Micah 5:7-8
2 Baruch 1:2-4	2 Baruch 84:2-5	Esther 2:5-6	Zechariah 7:14	Leviticus 26:17
Jeremiah 12:7	Jeremiah 34:20	Isaiah 5:13	3 Maccabees 3:24-25	Enoch 103:11-14
Isaiah 46:22	Jubilees 23:23	Jeremiah 9:2-5	Luke 23:28-29	Hosea 3:1-5
Ezra 9:7	Jeremiah 50:6	Hosea 4:6	Romans 11:25	Jubilees 1:11

Unlocking Bible Mysteries and Hidden Secrets Revealed
THE MIND
Ever wonder how you can see something once and it becomes stuck inside of your head? This is because everything is a form of LIGHT. Light attracts to Light as a magnet.
In a fallen world, most things that get stuck in your mind are abominations of YAH. Because Ha'Mashiach (THE TORAH) is the Light of the World, you must shine the light of the TORAH on the light that you receive from this dark and fallen world.
If you're ever struggling with something as an addiction or difficulty, FOCUS on the WORD OF YAH, FAST, PRAY, OBEY YOUR TORAH. This is how you conquer your mind with YAH. Shine the Light on Darkness.
Meditate in like-minded, Righteousness, with the Darkness of YAH to shine the Light of Ha'Mashiach (Righteousness)
Always remember that Ha'Mashiach was the first act of creation and one with YAH. He is the light that clothes darkness!
The Light is Ha'Mashiach, The Light of the World.
You CAN EVEN HEAL "MENTAL ILLNESS" with YAH
YAH HEALS ALL THINGS, EVEN YOUR MIND!

When I first read the **story of Moses**, it was one of my first clues to accepting the fact that the children of Israel were blacks and not feel like I'm playing the sensitive race card. **This is a difficult fact to accept as Christianity, GOVERNMENTS, and Hollywood incorrectly and aggressively teaches a white tribe and a white god/father/white Jesus.** This is what most have been raised to think and believe our entire life!

Some even incorrectly think that there's a Jesus in every color or race (the word and science of race is false. We are all shades of Black {the primordial darkness}). They even incorrectly sell that Jesus is YAH!

In the 15th century and slavery following, Rome issued world laws forcing all to accept Christianity or die. This is how Black Hebrews became Christians. The Arab slave trade produced Black Muslims.

Unlocking Bible Mysteries and Hidden Secrets Revealed
NO GRAVEN IMAGES
One of the **10 Commandments of Mosaic Law** is not to make any graven images (**Exodus 20:4**).
Many violate this every day! **Especially with all the false images of a white Jesus as Elohiym (a.k.a. God)**
COME OUT OF BLASPHEMY MYSTERY BABYLON

Imagine all the churches worldwide, over the last 2,000 years, that publicly preach, teach, profess, and hold publicly fake portraits of a white Jesus as Elohiym (a.k.a. God). Even reading many bibles/cephers as they also advertise a false white image of Jesus and bible characters.

Preachers and pastors teach a false white Jesus to their congregations and the public. Imagine living lifetimes (**over the last 2,000 years**) with a false white image of Jesus in all the movies, talk shows, YouTube videos, video games, cartoons, action figures, clothing and merchandise, billboards, music and entertainment, educational institutions and schools, prisons, hospitals and facilities, nursing homes and rehabilitation centers, books and media, memorabilia, marketing and promotions, posters and pictures, all activities of life and culture, laws and politics, governments and rulers, and financing, etc. All areas of life.

For those who study African American history, there's something extremely poetic that occurred while being raped from our Motherland and taken back to "Egypt" (The Americas) on ships as slaves (**Deuteronomy 28:68**) to foreign lands to serve strange Elohiym that our fathers didn't know (**Deuteronomy 11:28**) as part of our **Deuteronomy** curses for disobedience to Mosaic law/Torah (**Deuteronomy 28).**

Unlocking Bible Mysteries and Hidden Secrets Revealed
"KumbaYAH"
They tried as best as they were able to conceal the name of YAH. They were forced to accept a white Jesus. **One of the most famous slavery songs has the name of YAH hidden. The slave song, "KumbaYAH" (which means, Arise, YAH is the name of the Eternal Elohiym a.k.a. God).**
No one told you that one!

After being forced to accept a false image and false god of Ha'Mashiach, the slave boat that carried the first Black Hebrews to the Americas was called "Sweet Jesus". Google it! They were Black Hebrews from Africa sent to suffer **Deuteronomy curses as a "sign and a wonder". Even the slavery posts advertised "Hebrews for sale" on signs and posters. All read Deuteronomy 28.**

America was stolen from **ABORIGINAL** (Some of us were already living and ruling in America before slavery) **Black Hebrews (the first U.S. Presidents were Black before George Washington. The First American President, A Black, created the US Seal. Google: John Hanson. His altered statue is in the White House).**

America was transformed into a racist prison for Black Hebrews, including all people of color/shades of Black, brown, and yellow. This was all financed and controlled by Esau-Rome.

Additionally, Esau-Rome opened the Torah and changed the images (1 Maccabees 3:48), **changed the interpretations, and started new racist religions (Christianity, Catholicism, Islam). They manufactured a white Jesus based upon a white male human king seeking to be worshipped as a god. This is the grand secret behind the white Jesus picture. You are not even aware of this horrible act of blasphemy. Google Serapis and Mithra. Striking images!**

After hijacking the worship of the Creator, Yahuah Elohiym, the identity of His chosen children was unbiblically changed to Esau. They, then, used this as the justification and basis for slavery of Black Hebrews and killed off the incoming generation so the children had no way to discover the truth of who they were and what color is the Creator, Yahuah Elohiym and Ha'Mashiach. **They, even, whitewashed all history and religion around the world while murdering anyone who held the truth. All religions started with black deities changed to white or other nations. Even Buddha was Black!**

Unlocking Bible Mysteries and Hidden Secrets Revealed
SLAVERY
Whites used the Bible to justify slavery. They even wrote a racist "slaves bible". **They just didn't tell you that slavery was a punishment of YAH as being His chosen children of Israel and disobeying His Law (punishment) and rejecting the Ha'Mashiach by accepting a false Messiah. Deuteronomy 28.**
Deuteronomy Curses – JACOBS TROUBLE
They falsely taught it was a curse of Ham (a curse that never existed. Especially for Shem who was blessed [Abraham] and Ham is not the father of all blacks)
The answer was in our faces the entire time! **Look beyond the Veil!**

It is also a difficult fact to accept as Blacks have been conditioned to think of themselves as inferior and good for nothing but servitude as a false curse of Ham, while **Esau-Rome is "late-night" pimping the holy Word in the valleys of shadows of their darkness**. Living in a world shining by falsified stolen white light, **Blacks have become the Dry Bones in Ezekiel 37. We must be born again (John 3). We must study the Torah and get full knowledge of YAH and obey His Laws/Torah.**

Whites have been falsely taught to feel superior based upon something the ancients considered the color white to be inferior, a curse (leprosy), a red devil, and an abomination of YAH (Romans 9:13), to not be born in the full image of the Creator (Genesis 1:26/Genesis 2:7), Yahuah Elohiym (John 3:16) whose true color is like a black-red garnet crystal stone (Revelations 1:11).

After 400 years of African American slavery, a forgotten history and stolen identity, 2,000 years of false religious and racist teachings, and the whitewashing of all history and religion, and the creation of racism and science {which contradicts YAH and is the Antichrist} (last 2,000 years), and **our current system of a state of a fallen Christianity and religion secretly teaching blasphemy and secretly part of Mystery Babylon**, this is a very challenging subject.

Some say, why is this important? First, with all scriptures being divinely inspired by Yahuah Elohiym, it must've been important enough for the writers of the Bible/Torah to reveal the true black colors of all characters, including Yahuah Elohiym and Ha'Mashiach, in secret through dimensionally clear Bible verses.

Some ask why is the Bible/Torah written in so many layers of codes? This was intentional as an extreme measure to ensure that **the truth is available, always, to those that search in the spirit of truth and love (Matthew 7:7).**

Additionally, it must've been important enough for **Esau (whites) to open the Torah and history and changed all the images and replaced them with their own (1 Maccabees 3:48). {note: Esau simply changed images and deceived as scriptures declared he would.**

Esau doesn't have the ability to create anything, nor did he. He doesn't even have the ability or authority to have a king on earth, which is why you never saw a King in Europe and they only had a Queen (This year marks her 70th year of ruling and a major 70th Biblical Jubilee of Atonement October 4th).

This is bible prophecy in real life proving the authority of Yahuah Elohiym over earth. This is living history confirming the Word of Yahuah Elohiym (Open your Third Eye)

There's no king in Europe because YAH doesn't authorize this to happen ever again on Earth (Esau is the end of the world and Jacob (Israel) is the beginning of the world to come {2 Esdras 6:9}.

Esau only lied, cheated, killed, hated, and stole all the way from the womb {his birth} to the tomb {his death} and his seed have all done the same even until this day.

If you are Esau, you must know that sin comes to you naturally.

You were born to sin and die.
You can't provide your own salvation.

You cannot avoid it without YAH.
It's in your DNA and brain's computer from birth._
You must also know that you are not Japheth or Shem/Israel.

You are a white-skinned Black!

ONE HUE-MAN RACE

Knowledge is half the battle. With this revelation, one must come to accept they must instantly repent, learn Torah, and walk in the ways of YAH and righteousness, and holster your pride. Respect and love YAH and His chosen children.

OR FACE ETERNAL HELL, LAKE OF FIRE

It is important to note that all the ancient wonders of the world were all created by Blacks, even the pyramids. Look at the Sphinx and recognize the Black features. Stonehenge and all others were built by Blacks. They incorrectly lie and tell you they were built by aliens.

Those "aliens" are really the Black Israelites and Aboriginals from antiquity. We'll get into this throughout this series, how Esau-Rome (whites) illegally manufacture weather to seize control over Earth and how those seized control over Earth's geometric electromagnetic energy system.} They did this to curse the chosen of YAH and steal their land.

Unlocking Bible Mysteries and Hidden Secret Exposed
EARTH's ELECTROMAGNETIC FREE ENGERGY
SECRET SCIENCES
We live on an electromagnetic planet that functions off a geometric electricity grid. The sky is electromagnetic plasma, including the sun, moon, and stars. The Bible/Torah supports this teaching of light. **The power elite (Esau-Rome) uses secret sciences to control Earth and blame Yahuah Elohiym for bad weather (This is the same sciences and heavenly secrets that were taught by the fallen watchers in Genesis – see the Book of Enoch).** Scriptures state that

Earth is secured by four pillars and never moves (**Psalms 104:5, 1 Chronicles 16:30**). **This proves that every earthquake that we experience are results of weather manipulation by man and not natural events.** Even tornadoes are man-made. Also, **there's no such thing as gravity or global warming or an ice age.** Even homosexuality is an electromagnetic manipulation of Earth's electrical masculine and feminine energies. These are all false teachings by science (Esau-Rome) and weaponized against you under the false flag of peace.
For those whistleblowers and truth seekers, even the Twin Towers of **9/11 is suspected to be illegal weather manipulation (a man-made manipulation of Earth's fault lines to make the towers fall** - shaded by a" plane" crash even with no evidence of plane crashed materials ever recovered. A real-life Hollywood movie).
The tsunamis are nothing but weather manipulation to mass steal property, mass steal wealth through insurances and REITS, and mass fund big banks. They did **this also with mass fires. Some places, such as China, even manufactured a fake sun and put it in the sky.** (Note: These were all the prophecies of **Baruch, Enoch, Daniel, Enoch** being fulfilled and Jacobs Trouble/Gentile World)
Note: The aboriginal Earth was a world-wide tropical environment, ruled by all Blacks, and the earth never moves. We'll get into this throughout the series. It's beyond the scope of this current section break. Stay tuned and follow closely.
Did you know that we can have UNLIMITED FREE ENERGY and FLYING CARS? HIGH SPEED TRAVEL WORLDWIDE! This is how the government secretly built UFOs!

Blacks get accused of being racists when they teach the true Elohiym, when it was and is racist to teach a false white god when the fact is Yahuah Elohiym and Ha'Mashiach are both Black, and so was Yahusha (a.k.a. Jesus)! It's a silent way of rejecting the Creator, Yahuah Elohiym and His chosen children (The 12 Tribes of Israel). The Bible is Black history. Read Deuteronomy 28.

JOSEPH AND THE 12 TRIBES OF ISRAEL

Reverting to our story about the children of Israel, let's pick up again where Joseph was sold into slavery by his 11 siblings. **Jacob was renamed Israel.** It's beyond the scope of our current focus of this study, however, note that the original form of slavery was a limited term of indentured servitude, and the slave was considered a member of the household with an expiration term which one would be set free (reference the books of **Leviticus and Deuteronomy** those looking to get deeper into the subject and distinctions. Atonement Laws).

Another interesting revelation about this story is that **Joseph was sold to what we would consider to be Arabs (Ishmael),** who in-term sold Joseph to the Egyptians (Ham). Ishmael was a son of Abraham. **(This reminds me of Ishmael's jealousy towards Isaac revealed in the books of Jubilees and Jasher).**

As a chosen child of YAH, Joseph was prized for his physique, intelligence, wisdom, and beauty. **This is a marvelous story redemption story whereby YAH turned a curse of man into a blessing from YAHUAH Elohiym.**

Genesis chapters 39-50 reviews the early beginnings of the children of Israel, their journey to Egypt sets the stage for Egyptian slavery and one of the most memorable biblical stories, the **Exodus**. While in Egypt, Pharoah has a dream that no worldly magician or sorcerer could explain. Joseph, calling upon YAH, was able to interpret and explain Pharoah's dream that no one on Earth was able to decipher.

Because Joseph was a man that walked in righteousness to YAH, his relationship with YAH would anoint him in wisdom and righteousness to the things of YAH. **It's also a very powerful and symbolic example of why one should never seek to cause harm to a person that is anointed by YAH, as your very well-being and existence depends upon one who has direct access to YAH.**

One must always ask yourself, **what are the consequences of cursing or eliminating a man of YAH? Death is the only price for sin (Romans 6:23).**

In a poetic sense, Joseph was a symbolic messiah to the entire inhabited world by providing salvation, to all, avoiding a seven-year famine that posed an extinction-level-event on Earth (**Genesis 41**). He will also set the stage for Ha'Mashiach of Israel in a symbolic way.

> [36] And that food shall be for store to the land against the seven years of famine, which shall be in the land of Egypt; that the land perish not through the famine (**Genesis 41:36**).

Because of the magnitude and significance of this revelation, Pharoah makes Joseph ruler over the land of Egypt. This is very important as the land of Egypt was the center of worldly power at the time and held dominion over the known world. In our present-world, man elevates one to leadership based upon the ways of a fallen man. **In ancient times, the world recognized that YAH created all things and held dominion over all things.**

As diligent bible students would learn, no world leader conquered the world by the ways of man. It was YAH that raised all world leaders into power for Seventy Sevens (we'll cover this during our discussion of the Daniel prophecies for YAH raised all 4 kingdoms that were set to rule Earth).

With this frame of revealing reference, the ancients selected their world leaders based upon the Word of YAH.

> [38] And Pharaoh said unto his servants, Can we find such a one as this is, a man in whom the Spirit of Yahuah Elohiym is?
>
> [39] And Pharaoh said unto Joseph, Forasmuch as Yahuah Elohiym hath shewed thee all this, there is none so discreet and wise as thou art:
>
> [40] Thou shalt be over my house, and according unto thy word shall all my people be ruled: only in the throne will I be greater than thou.
>
> [41] And Pharaoh said unto Joseph, See, I have set thee over all the land of Egypt.

[42] And Pharaoh took off his ring from his hand, and put it upon Joseph's hand, and arrayed him in vestures of fine linen, and put a gold chain about his neck **(Genesis 41: 38-42)**.

Referencing our point on appreciating the power of one who walks with YAH, another powerful revelation is discovered in this story of Joseph.

[16] And we have known and believed the love that Yahuah Elohiym hath to us. Yahuah Elohiym is love; and he that dwelleth in love dwelleth in Yahuah Elohiym, and Yahuah Elohiym in him **(1 John 4:16)**.

Even though Joseph's siblings "sold him for dead" into slavery over unwarranted jealousy, risked the life of Israel's forefather Israel by lying about Joseph dying, turned against the ways of YAH, and committed a major sin (**Exodus 20:13** "thou shalt not kill"), YAH turned this cursed story into an unconditional lovingly brother story and of forgiveness and love.

A background reference to keep in mind, Israel going into Egypt, and the subsequent slavery of the children of Israel was all in the plan of YAH. Let's consider a few points. The entire Earth was in a fallen state of deadly sin.

[23] For the wages of sin is death; but the gift of Yahuah Elohiym is eternal life through Ha'Mashiach **(Romans 6:23)**. (edited Yahusha)

At the time of this story, the mighty man of faith, Abraham, was deceased. His faith passed on to Israel (Jacob), who in turn passed this faith on to his favorite son, Joseph. This is how the Word of YAH and His presence was communicated with man and Earth, through righteousness.

After the divisions of nations (**Genesis 10:25**), YAH chose Israel as his chosen seed (**Deuteronomy 7:6**). He would communicate and deal with them only (**Romans 9:4**). Also, at the time of this story, Israel (Jacob) was elderly and stricken with grief over his favorite son, Joseph, who, at the time, was sold into slavery and physically absent from his family.

The remaining 11 forefathers of Israel (chosen children) had fallen to a state of sin, as part of a fallen world. **YAH needed a way to introduce Himself to His chosen children (The 12 Tribes of Israel), therefore he used slavery in Egypt to reveal Himself and their salvation to show His Love.**

Like present-day slavery, it was a form of divine chastisement, humility, and **academic purposes** as there was much to learn from this story.

What an amazing way, through miracles that no man could duplicate, to prove YAH's credibility, authority, and authenticity beyond a shadow of a doubt that YAH is real and the only true living Elohiym.

Genesis chapters 42-45, reveals the story of forgivingly brotherly love that only a righteous and wise man of YAH could produce, as no worldly man could unconditionally forgive, without warrants, after being executed for death by his own family.

Joseph's siblings would travel to Egypt seeking food to survive the severe famine that has grief-stricken the lands. Another revelation to debunk those who claim Israel is of European complexion is that when Joseph's siblings visited **Egypt (a known place inhabited by blacks), his siblings were not able to recognize him.** It meant that everyone blended in! As racists say, all blacks look alike!

This further confirms that the entire 12 Tribes of Israel are blacks. During their second trip to Egypt, Joseph would reveal himself after he discovers that his brothers meant him no harm at the time. What's revealed is that there is salvation to those who repent and turn from their evil and wicked ways.

Would You Be So Forgiving To Someone That Offends You?

Elohiym is Love and Love is Elohiym. This is the law of life. It is based on Righteousness. The law is life. Just as the circumference of a circle is 365.24, so too are the solar calendar days of a calendar year, 365.24 days in a solar year. The law is the law and cannot change. Just as Earth doesn't move. This is Pi.

MOSES AND THE EXODUS

In **Genesis 46**, Israel and his family moves to Egypt and resides in the region of Goshen. Israel (Jacob) would eventually die. Joseph and his siblings would leave Egypt, temporarily, to bury Israel (Jacob) in the land of our forefathers. Joseph eventually dies as well.

Upon their return, the original Pharoah would die and there rose a Pharoah which knew not Joseph or the children of Israel (**Exodus 1**). He would dishonor the agreement of preferential treatment, loyalty, and respect to the children of Israel. On returning, Israel would go from being treated royally to being of the lowest class of slaves.

By allowance of YAH, the children of Israel would experience harsh and cruel slavery. This difficult experience would allow for the Love and Light of Yahuah Elohiym to shine and be established and sown into the hearts and mind to produce believers and carriers of His Word (**Romans 9:4**).

> **[4] Who are Israelites; to whom pertaineth the adoption, and the glory, and the covenants, and the giving of the law, and the service of Elohiym, and the promises (Romans 9:4)**

Thus, YAH needed to raise a seed of a woman (Genesis 3:15) to show His love, dominion, and power to provide salvation to His chosen children on Earth, which sets precedence for all things under the sun to be set in divine order. Like Joseph, a Ha'Mashiach figure is born in Moses (Exodus 2).

Just as during the birth of Yahusha (**Matthew 1**), when **King Herod** attempted to murder the Yahusha by killing off all Hebrew/Jew newborns and males, the **Pharoah of Egypt issued the same decree**.

For those unbiblical male chauvinists who refuse to accept reality and downgrade women, **one of the first sets of major prophecies was communicated by a black woman.** Take away the story of Moses and the Exodus story from the Bible, the children of Israel and the Torah/Law seizes to exist. It came about through the life of Moses. Think about how powerful the importance of this divine revelation of prophecy was shared and it came out of the mouth of a black woman named Miriam.

Moses' sister, Miriam had a revelation that a Ha'Mashiach figure would be born in Moses. Thus, to protect the birth of Moses and salvation of Israel, when Moses was born, per the warning his mother placed him on an ark (ex. the Days of Noah Ark) and sailed him in the waters, where he ends up in Egypt.

Back to the Exodus story, we discover that Moses was born of the tribe of Levi, one of the 12 tribes and the priestly tribe of Israel. The baby Moses was discovered by Pharoah's wife, who was a black Egyptian. In my opinion, there were some insiders who must have sympathized with the Israelites because Moses was raised in the king's household as one of their own. Perhaps, another illusion to "keeping your enemies close" or "secretly honoring the legacy of Joseph- the ruler that saved Egypt and Earth".

However, the fact that Moses was able to mature right before the Pharoah's eyes and with the active decree to murder all Israelite newborns and males, Moses must have fit right in with the Egyptians as appearing as one of their own in image and color.

If Moses was white, he would not have gone un-noticed by Pharaoh, especially for so many years to reach adulthood. (Keep in mind, much of current history has been whitewashed by racist whites in power {Esau-Rome}). Also, the decree was still active to kill all Hebrew newborns. So, Moses certainly is not white.

Additionally, the **books of Jasher and Jubilees** reveals another major clue. Prior to the Exodus of Israel, Moses had escaped Egypt for a period of time after defending an Israelite. The offender died and Moses feared his life so he escaped from Egypt until Yahuah Elohiym would call him back to save the tribe of Israel. **Jasher and Jubilees** explains how Moses went to the land of Kush (another land of ancient blacks) and became a king there for **40** years. This was all before the story of the Exodus! Kush means Black!

This work project is a result of a 40 day fast that sets stage to the 2nd Exodus. There's that number 40.

Just as modern-day slavery, YAH never intended for Egyptian slavery to last forever. He only needed enough time to reveal His divine plan over earthly events and His chosen children. **Exodus Chapters 3 and 4**, YAH sends Moses back to Egypt to free the children of Israel. **This also reveals another clue to deciphering Bible codes as the name "Egypt" would become synonymous with "slavery" (Exodus 13:3, Exodus 13:14, Deuteronomy 5:6, Deuteronomy 28:68)**. This is important to keep in mind for **previous** prophecies "**back to Egypt with ships**", and **modern-day prophecies** for the **2nd Exodus from "Egypt".**

The **"back to Egypt on ships" further confirms** the identity of the 12 Tribes of Israel as **no other race was sold into slavery on ships.** Blacks were the only ones and mainly just the Israelites/Chosen Children of YAH (reference the **Arab slave trade and the African Transatlantic slave trade of Hebrews** or the **conquering of Christopher Columbus searching for Black Hebrew lands**). To an unbiased and studious mind, the clues are right in front of our faces the entire time! One must simply think outside the blindly programmed boxes of this created matrix. **In simple terms, use your brain and common sense!**

Exodus chapters 5 -11 presents the revelations of YAH as YAH frees the children of Israel through divine miracles using Moses and Aaron (Moses' brother). **The miracles that YAH produces through Moses and Aaron, were unmatched to the miracles that Pharoah was able to produce through his own magicians and sorcerers.**

Additionally, they were unable to reproduce YAH's miracles, avoid them, or withstand them. This is important to keep in mind as we prepare for salvation from the man of sin by our Ha'Mashiach and the 2nd Exodus. **Recognizing YAH holds all power and is unmatched in authority and rulership.**

Some of the miracles of YAH produced in Egypt for the 1st Exodus:

- **The waters are turned into blood**
- **The plague of frogs**
- **The plague of swarms of flies**
- **The plague of the animals dying**
- **The plague of the boils**

- **The plague of hail**
- **The plague of locusts**
- **The plague of three days darkness**
- **The plague of all first-born Egyptians dying and no deaths from the children of Israel. This sets the stage for a major perpetual bible feast. This is the story of the celebration of "The Passover" (Genesis 12)**

Unlocking Bible Mysteries and Hidden Secrets Revealed
2ND EXODUS
(print for your knowledge of today's times – what to expect)
Did you know? The Ha'Mashiach's role is to reconquer Earth and bring the children of Israel back to the Promised Land, with a Mighty Hand, for "heaven on Earth" while we're still alive (This means our generation. US!). To establish Yahuah Elohiym's Kingdom of heaven on Earth (not some Mystery Babylon teaching of a heaven in the sky).
This will be the Second Exodus and will be unlike any event ever in our history!
The 12 Tribes of Israel will be gathered from the four corners of Earth for one final Exodus back to the Promised Land. Israel will rule the entire world again forever with YAH. The world will serve Yahuah Elohiym and pay reparations. Non-Israelites who repent and walk in righteousness can be saved. All will submit to Israel, who will submit to Yahuah Elohiym. All nations that commit(ted) against Israel and those who don't submit will perish. Babylon will fall!
This is the only true "last days Bible prophecy" that Esau-Rome Mystery Babylon (Christianity, Catholicism, Islam, Spiritualists) doesn't want you to know! This is Scriptures Confirming Scriptures for the Full Image of Yahuah Elohiym's Salvation Plan from the foundation of the world.
For the 2nd Exodus, some of the miracles of YAH will be:
• Take the world by surprise, as no one would see it coming nor expect the appearance of Ha'Mashiach (Remember the "Days of Noah" and "Days of Lot" are warning signs for the Coming of Mashiach

• Regather the children of Israel from every dispersed land "Egypt-bondage houses all around Earth" (black, brown, and yellow). The Americas!
• Smite the waters (dry the waters) and produce walkways on the waters, leading from every continent back to the Promised Land. (think Red Sea)
• The Vial and Bowl Judgements of Revelations (see **Revelations 16: 2-21**)
The Book of Revelations can only be understood within the additional context of the Torah (Isaiah, Esdras, Daniel, Enoch, Jubilees, Baruch, etc.) whereas the **Word of YAH is confirmed out the mouths of 2-3 witnesses (2 Corinthians 13:1)**. **Furthermore, no prophecy ever hinges upon a sole prophet, whereas each prophet has a piece of the story and never the entire story except the Son of Elohiym.** You must piece the puzzle together, from different witnesses (Bible books) to see the entire picture
As a standalone "last day" prophecy, Revelations becomes a mystery teaching from Mystery Babylon to reproduce a Tribulation that has already been fulfilled for the last 2,000 years. You already have the Mark of the Beast and don't even realize it. It's called Christianity, Islam, Catholicism – All the products of Esau-Rome, The Antichrist Pope
Study the **books of Isaiah, Ezekiel, Enoch, all the books of Esdras and Baruch**. Stay tuned in this series! Fast and pray and **Use your Third Eye!**

A **review of the books of Exodus, Leviticus, Numbers, Deuteronomy, and Joshua** reveals YAH's intimate relationship with the children of Israel. YAH is not a man and cannot lie.

Furthermore, Yahuah Elohiym is a spirit, and we must worship Him in spirit and in truth (**John 4:24, Hebrews 11:1**) This is the basis of His righteousness. YAH is one who keeps His Word, often through His Right Hand (Ha'Mashiach). What YAH says is a bind and law!

YAH brings the children of Israel into the Promised Land, fulfilling His promise to the only person named as the friend of YAH, the owner of the only covenants with YAH for Israel, and the Forefather of Israel and the Faithful, Abraham (**Exodus 6:8, Genesis 12:7, Genesis**

26:2-5, Genesis 3:15). **YAH** kept His **Word** with **Abraham**. Yahuah Elohiym through Yahuah (Joshua) conquered the promised land (another prelude to the **Ha'Mashiach** during His coming advent to re-conquer a fallen Earth) and divide(d) the lands to the 12 Tribes of Israel, with each tribe receiving their lots.

The Tribe of Levi was made into the Priestly tribe and was the only tribe that was purified and set aside to be able to have the High Priests be in connection with Yahuah Elohiym and not die. **The only source for man to be able to hear the things of Yahuah Elohiym on earth and perform His works on Earth.**

Yahuah Elohiym was their King and Elohiym, and the land was protected and at peace until Israel turns again in disobedience to YAH.

Levites received no land portion and is the only personal tribe of Yahuah Elohiym as He is their inheritance, and they have a portion of lands within each of the 12 tribes' inheritance to conduct their priestly duties to the 12 Tribes of Israel (**Deuteronomy 18:1-2**).

The reason why this is significant is that **no man can serve 2 masters** (**Matthew 6:24**). **Imagine trying to survive in society by working hard, paying bills, and to do the works of YAH at the same time; juggling the world of the flesh and the world of the spirit at the same time [that which is flesh is flesh and that which is born of the spirit is spirit – John 3:6] (therefore Earth has fallen and can't get up without YAH.**

We cannot do it on our own. We cannot provide our own salvation. Thus, sets order to the earthly Priestly line of Israel, the only portal to communicate with Yahuah Elohiym (side note: **there's no High Priest today (since the last 2,000 years and that's why one doesn't feel the presence of YAH in this fallen world of sin.**

SECTION SUMMARY

Throughout this section, we have reviewed the history of the children of Israel. This history has revealed the 12 Tribes of Israel to be our modern-day African Americans in the diaspora (blacks, browns, and yellow) and 10 tribes are in Azerath until the last days. Judah is dispersed. We have discovered how Esau-Rome has stolen their true identity and deceived the world through false teachings and religion.

Modern-day African Americans are the dry bones in **Ezekiel 37**. Many have been awakening to this reality and experiencing the great awakening of Black Hebrews. Abraham was told that his children would be in a foreign land serving false Elohiym for 400 years.

We are living in the year 2022, 400 years after American slavery ended. We are also living during a major Jubilee year and Atonement year. The law of atonement is established to return the property and people back to their legal owners. The Day of Atonement is Oct 4th.

For Yahuah Elohiym loves His chosen children that He gave His Son to regather and combine as one, the split Northern and Southern Tribes of Israel back into One Olive Tree (12 Tribes), Ha'Mashiach, so that we can have eternal life and forgiveness of sin if we repent and depart from evil by obeying the Torah.

Unlocking Bible Mysteries and Hidden Secrets Revealed
In John 3:16 "World" means Israel ONLY!
In this verse, the proper translation for "World" implies a nation and not the physical world. It means Israel. That's who Ha'Mashiach is coming to save: The 12 Tribes of Israel. There is no spiritual Israel.
This teaching of "Spiritual Israel" or the "Church-replaced Israel" is a false teaching. Reference original Greek and Hebrew words. Ref Enoch.

We are at the end of experiencing almost 2,000 years of Jacobs Trouble (Daniel 70 weeks), which outlines the prophecy of YAH's salvation plan. We are the

remnant of Black Hebrews that have been refined as gold. We are living currently at the end of the Gentile world.

The time to repent is now. All prophecies have been fulfilled. We are awaiting the revelation of Ha'Mashiach. In the next section, we'll discuss this mysterious character, His role, and what to expect in the coming recent times.

Remember to stay tuned in the series as there's always much information to cover and share. I have a full social media website which corresponds to all works. In efforts to create a safe online website resource, I purchased a domain name. I will be updating my website often to provide additional materials and live updates for coming projects. You may become a free member at www.gianmichaelsimmons.com

THE HA'MASHIACH OF ISREAL A.K. A. MESSIAH

(a.k.a. "Son of Elohiym, Son of Man, Messiah)
For the record, he will have a name no one knows. So, call on YAH.

Behold I will reveal a mystery, [12] His eyes were as a flame of fire, and on his head were many crowns; and **he had a name written, that no man knew, but he himself** (**Revelations 19:12**). In the book of Revelations, we are told that the Ha'Mashiach (a.k.a. Messiah) will appear, **at the end of the age**, and **with a name that no man knows except Himself**. I want you to keep this fresh in your mind as this is also the same who says that only in His name can you be saved and the same who said He would never leave or forsake you.

For the last 2,000 years, man has been calling on the name of Yahusha (a.k.a. Jesus) to be saved. Yet, the Ha'Mashiach is not appearing in the name of Yahusha (a.k.a. Jesus) or even in the image of Yahusha (a.k.a. Jesus). Otherwise, the name Yahusha (a.k.a. Jesus) would have been named, especially from a testimony that is reported to be from Yahusha (a.k.a. Jesus).

Without getting into theories regarding the name of Jesus possibly and secretly being the name of the Greek pagan myth god Zeus and calling Jesus may be like saying "Hey Zeus", realizing the church involvement with many pagan teachings. And considering the Druid god Hesus and Krishna (Christ). **After learning the proper Hebrew names, I prefer to use the original Hebrew translations. I encourage you all to do the same.**

It is claimed that John wrote the book of Revelations from the testimony of Yahusha (a.k.a. Jesus) as Yahusha (a.k.a. Jesus) was speaking with him. Yet, in Revelations, Yahusha (a.k.a. Jesus) didn't mention his name AND he said the Ha'Mashiach (a.k.a. Messiah) would appear with a name no one would know. Additionally, in the gospels after Yahusha (a.k.a. Jesus) appears to his disciples after his resurrection. His own disciples couldn't even recognize him because he had a new appearance. **Keep this in your mind.**

Ha'Mashiach will appear at the end of this age with a name that no man knows but Himself. If Yahusha (a.k.a. Jesus) followers knew him by his name (Yahusha or Jesus) and if it's Yahusha (Jesus) talking in Revelations, then why does Ha'Mashiach appear with a name no man knows? **Keep this in mind for our discussion.**

Also, this book is about your ETERNAL SALVATION. Suffer not your soul to eternal damnation. Keep this is mind.

We are now entering revelations of the highest Bible mystery and the Biggest secret revealed. The fearless true knowledge and wisdom of YAH in this section is earth shattering and groundbreaking. The information may even come at a surprise to some, while biblically balancing the truth through scriptures, praying, fasting, and fellowship with YAH. However, this information can only come from a pure heart as only the pure in heart sees YAH. Only one who seeks YAH with the fullness of your mind, body, soul, and time can hear YAH and gain the ability to kinetically undulate divine truth, order, and justice on Earth as it is in heaven. It takes allowing the self to fully perish, spiritually be born again, and allowing the Father in. **My heart to you, I pray that YAH allows you to read in spirit and in truth.** Because YAH's Word will never fall void and YAH makes no mistakes. Lastly, YAH planned the end from the beginning. So, what will be will be.

Throughout this discourse I will presenting a multi-dimensional religious exercise of blind faith to get you to see beyond the veil. Don't cheat yourself and look, but I'll reveal it at the **end** of this section, how chilling blind faith can be as the blind leading the blind. After you read it, ask yourself, who is Yahusha (a.k.a. Jesus)?

Since we are in the last days or at the end of an age, everyone is awaiting the apocalypse. A simple definition of apocalypse is the revealing of hidden heavenly mysteries. In English, we call it revelations. The following is thus what is expected to be revealed at this time since we are at the end of an age. We are at the end of the Gentile world, For Jacob (Israel) is the beginning of the eternal world to come. What's hidden is revealed as heaven is rolled back as a scroll, the seals have been broken, the chains have been loosed, and what's above comes below. The powers of heaven have shaken, the archangels are at command, the Lamb conquered, and YAH has spoken. WOE. It is done.

I can truthfully state that this is the Word of YAH. I can further state that all this information is secretly known amongst the elite and religious class leaders. Regardless of manner of person, the knowledge presented is what we have been searching for our entire life, true knowledge of YAH, the history of man and earth, and the self/spirit. And who is Yahusha (a.k.a. Jesus)? Actual Hebrew history knows him as Rabbi Yahusha Ben Yosef.

For the last 6,000 (rounding) years, man has been greatly divided about Elohiym (a.k.a. God). Hundreds of millions, if not hundreds of billions, of lives have been lost due to mass murders and killings all in the name of religion. Hundreds of billions of lives have been persecuted, oppressed, enslaved, and spoiled all in the name of religion. Trillions upon trillions of wealth has been stolen, seized, and conquered all in the name of religion. Man has toiled with and conquered man to steal and seize control over all earth's lands, natural resources, minerals, electromagnetic energy, and water all in the name of religion. The planet has been destroyed all in the name of religion. Every kingdom on earth has been shaken; the plant kingdom, the animal kingdom, and man. YAH is our kingdom.

The source of all power is true knowledge of the Creator, YAH. This is what the black albino rejected kind of man (not to be confused with man) have crawled out of caves in Caucasus mountains in illegal pursuit of worldwide power and dominion by seizing control over, changing the Torah, and suppressing true knowledge of YAH. This is the information that they hide. This is the only source of their power. This, along with fear and ignorance. Consequentially, this is YOUR FREEDOM.

If the created (man) knew how to properly call upon the name of their Creator, YAH, then no weapon formed against you would prosper as **in the name of YAH** every knee bow and every tongue confesses that YAH is the only Creator and the only Elohiym (a.k.a. God).

So, how do we call upon the name of YAH?

To answer this question and understand any story, one must investigate the context and the historical background of the story presented. Oftentimes, what was going on is more revealing than what is reported. Would you be able to understand Matrix Revolutions without watching Matrix Part One?

To understand the gospels and New Testament, one must have full knowledge of the Old Testament. One must also understand that Abraham was the first Hebrew. All the prophets were Hebrew. YAH chose Abraham/Israel Hebrews. YAH never dealt with any other nation. The holy texts are all about Israel and Hebrews. The holy scriptures began and ended in Hebrew. YAH never dealt with Greeks. Greeks wrote the New Testament. Remember this as we explore this engaging topic. Let's explore the historical setting.

In this case, let's review the historical background of the times that Yahusha (a.k.a. Jesus) lived. For this, let's review the books and historical records that were written covering this era. Keep in mind, his story wasn't written until hundreds of years after his death.

For this section, I recommend studying Torah, Tanakh, Cepher, Bible, and the writings of Josephus (1st century Jewish historian who lived during the times of Yahusha [a.k.a. Jesus]), Hebrew scholar Moses Farrar, and **OLD Bible translations**. I highly recommend old translations. The books that closely identify with this time are Maccabees, Daniel, Enoch, and the gospels. It's also important to note that Yahusha (a.k.a. Jesus) never authored any books, no authors of the gospels can be proved, all authorships are disputed, and all the gospels were written hundreds of years after Yahusha (a.k.a. Jesus) died. Lastly, all Greek books contradict Hebrew books and even themselves. No authorship can be proved.

Always remember that Yahusha (a.k.a. Jesus) did not author any books. There are no secret books of Yahusha (a.k.a. Jesus). Moses, Solomon, and David (to name a few) all authored books to ensure their life's works would always be clear and the mission from YAH will always be there. They realized they had to leave manna for their followers and protect against false doctrines by declaring their own in writing and feed those in the wilderness of sin. Yet, "Elohiym (a.k.a. God) with us" had a lot to say. But, never left clear instructive books knowing he was going to die, knowing that his religious views were not a part of the Jewish/Hebrew religion and were rejected, and claiming that he was the only way to heaven. **Yet, he left us with no books. Think on that.**

Additionally, to understand the setting, the books that were left were altered and changed many times (**1 Maccabees 3:48** 48 And laid open the book of the law (Torah), wherein the heathen had sought to paint the likeness of their images. [mind you, Maccabees were written before the time of Yahusha (a.k.a. Jesus). So, even knowing what the power system was already doing, Yahusha (a.k.a. Jesus) left us with no books]. **Remember this.**

They also received many revisions and changes in text. In fact, **it was only by studying very older translations** that I was able to uncover the removal of keywords and phrases, as well as the insertion of keywords and phrases, particularly addition of Yahusha (Jesus) centuries later. Medical professionals, legal professionals, math professionals, etc. all go back to the source and original to understand and treat the modern.

One example of a **modern insertion of a keyword** can be found in **4 Ezra/2 Esdras 7:26-28** in the **Cepher Millennial Edition**:

> 26 Behold, the time shall come, that these tokens which I have told you shall come to pass, and the bride shall appear, and she, coming forth shall be seen, that now is withdrawn from the earth. 27 And whosoever is delivered from the foresaid evils shall see my wonders. 28 For my **Son Yahusha** shall be revealed with those that be with him, and they that remain shall rejoice within four hundred years **(4 Ezra/2 Esdras 7:26-28)**

The modern/recent translation added the name "Yahusha (Jesus) in verse 28. Keep in mind this was done by the Greeks. The same people who wrote the New Testament and the same power structure that runs the world today as the last beast to rule before the kingdom of YAH comes on Earth.

Now, let's see how an older translation of this verse reads.

The temporary messianic kingdom and the end of the world

> 26"For behold, the time will come, when the signs which I have foretold to you will come to pass; the city which now is not seen shall appear, and the land which now is hidden shall be disclosed. •And everyone who has been delivered from the evils that I have foretold shall see my wonders. • For **my son the Messiah** shall be revealed with those who are with him, and those who remain shall rejoice four hundred years **(4 Ezra 7:26-28).**

This is a **much older translation (The Old Testament Pseudepigrapha Volume One)**. In the older translations of verse 28, **there is no mention of a name of the Messiah**. Another interesting thing about verse 28 is that it states the Messianic kingdom will only be 400 years and not 1,000 years as taught in the book of Revelations/NT. Also, **keep in mind that many Old Testament books were changed after the creation of the New Testament and during the cursed Gentile age.**

Also, prior to the Council of Nicaea, Jesus was just a man who was made into God. He received a new name, as his historical name was Yahusha Ben Yosef. Paul, a man that never saw Jesus, formed the Church, founded Christianity, changed the gospel, and even became a false prophet of Jesus as Paul's teachings contradict what Yahusha (Jesus) taught as Yahusha was a Hebrew prophet that taught and followed the Torah Law. The same law that Paul did away with by taking his message to the enemy of Hebrews, to the Gentiles.

Some may be asking, what's all the fuss? What's the big difference? The big difference is that the holy scriptures have experienced many revisions, throughout the years, to align with the power structure and system of religion to fit their narrative and oppress you.

When reading any book, even one word can make a HUGE DIFFERENCE. Many times, even a single letter can make a huge difference. Even the location of a comma or period can make a huge difference. The older translations did not have the name Yahusha (Jesus) listed as the Messiah in verse 28. You'll find this trend as you **rigorously become a student of scriptures**. You'll see how the name "Yahusha (Jesus)" was added where the name Messiah appears.

By adding the name "Yahusha (Jesus), you give the illusion that Yahusha (Jesus) is the name of the Messiah. These additions all occurred centuries later, after Israel was cursed, and after Rome changed all the books. **Remember this.**

For all you who think I'm making a big deal out of nothing over just a few words. **No person, especially no African in the Americas, can state that interpretations and the importance is meaningless.** One of the biggest reasons why interpretations are important is that whites used the misinterpreted curse of Canaan to apply to Ham and then they enslaved all blacks (**see section on Curse of Ham**). Canaan was the only cursed and not Ham. Whites misinterpreted this, **no one studied their Bible to recognize the error, no one spoke up**, and then we have 400 years of slavery all because of a mistranslated verse. Even today, we're still dealing with the dangers and effects of white supremacy all because of a misrepresented verse.

What I learned is when dealing with the Bible, you must be extremely technical and over-analytical as all words matter and black lives matter to YAH goes hand to hand in scriptures.

The New Testament presents itself as books inspired by YAH. Being inspired by something and being something are not one in the same. For example, have you ever watched a movie which was inspired by the life of someone? Oftentimes, the movie presents a different picture than the actual life of the person and the real events. Thus, the New Testament books were inspired, as they took all their information from the Old Testament, repackaged it, and made a new gospel and a new Elohiym (a.k.a. God).

To better understand this new gospel, incorrectly called the New Covenant or New Testament, one would need to understand this historical and spiritual setting.

Prior to 2,000 years ago (rounding), Israel was a spiritually living nation. They were a people that knew YAH. However, Israel was also a stubborn nation that fell into sin. Despite what Christians teach, the Law of Moses always stands and never perished. Yahusha taught and followed the Torah Law. Because YAH chose the nation of Israel to be His chosen people, he gave them the world. In fact, the world was created for Israel. YAH chose Israel even before the creation of the world. Additionally, the Son of Elohiym/Ha'Mashiach was with YAH, in heaven, when Israel was named and chosen before the world was made. Jacob is YAH's firstborn.

The children of Israel were being groomed to represent the Word of YAH on Earth. They were to be his holy messengers and workers of righteousness. They were to turn to YAH and follow YAH with their whole mind, body, and soul. This was their responsibilities for being the chosen children of YAH. They were to spread the message of the Creator.

To further clarify the responsibilities for Israel, YAH spoke with Moses and instructed Moses on the **law**, which would be later called the **Torah**. The Torah represent the **first 5 books of the Bible** and **outlines all the commandments of YAH**. **It reveals the**

blessings and curses of YAH. What to do to be blessed and how to avoid being cursed. It also outlines how to call on YAH to be gathered from your captivity. **Wonder why Christians AVOID the Old Testament. Do they enjoy curses?**

Curses come from disobedience to the law, even if you don't know you are violating the law. Blessings come to those that obey the law. For Israel, no curse is permanent. The law governs all aspects of daily life. It's that simple.

You must **learn and study the Torah** as This eternal covenant as being the chosen children of YAH comes with blessings and curses (see section on Joseph and the 12 Tribes of Israel and Moses and the Exodus). The following scriptures are spoken by Moses to the children of Israel after the Exodus. I'm including because it has such powerful information as it **reveals the secrets to your freedom. How you can be saved. What YOU SHOULD BE DOING NOW**. This scripture is found in **Deuteronomy 30/Torah.**

> **30** And it shall come to pass, when all these things are come upon thee, **the blessing and the curse,** which I have set before thee, and **thou shalt call them to mind among all the nations, whither Yahuah Elohiym hath driven thee,**
>
> [2] And **shalt return unto Yahuah Elohiym and shalt obey his voice according to all that I command thee this day, thou and thy children, with all thine heart, and with all thy soul;**
>
> [3] **That then Yahuah Elohiym will turn thy captivity, and have compassion upon thee, and will return and gather thee from all the nations, whither Yahuah Elohiym hath scattered thee.**
>
> [4] If any of thine be driven out unto the outmost parts of heaven, from thence will **Yahuah Elohiym** gather thee, and from thence will **he fetch thee**:
>
> [5] **And the Yahuah Elohiym will bring thee into the land which thy fathers possessed, and thou shalt possess it; and he will do thee good, and multiply thee above thy fathers.**
>
> [6] And the Yahuah Elohiym will circumcise thine heart, and the heart of thy seed, to love the Yahuah Elohiym with all thine heart, and with all thy soul, that thou mayest live.

[7] And the Yahuah Elohiym will put all these curses upon thine enemies, and on them that hate thee, which persecuted thee.

[8] **And thou shalt return and obey the voice of Yahuah Elohiym and do all his commandments** which I command thee this day.

[9] And Yahuah Elohiym will make thee **plenteous** in every work of thine hand, in the fruit of thy body, and in the fruit of thy cattle, and in the fruit of thy land, for good: for Yahuah Elohiym will again rejoice over thee for good, as he rejoiced over thy fathers:

[10] If thou shalt hearken unto the voice of Yahuah Elohiym, to **keep his commandments and his statutes which are written in this book of the law, and if thou turn unto the Yahuah Elohiym with all thine heart, and with all thy soul.**

[11] **For this commandment which I command thee this day, it is not hidden from thee, neither is it far off.**

[12] It is not in heaven, that thou shouldest say, Who shall go up for us to heaven, and bring it unto us, that we may hear it, and do it? **(Deuteronomy 30:1-12)**

From Israel's first king and until this day, Israel has fallen in disobedience to YAH. The majority the issues stemmed from assimilating the cultures of the people that they were diversifying with. As they would inter-marry, often the women would lead the men and family to idol worship (the real reason why inter-marrying was prohibited to preserve the holy seed).

By studying the Old Testament, you discover the spiritually challenged nature of the children of Israel. You will see the cycles of blessings and curses.

It was during the life and times of the Maccabees and the Second Temple era that Israel was experiencing the Deuteronomy curses. It was during this time that Israel was being punished by YAH, the only source of power. **This was the time that Yahusha (a.k.a. Jesus) lived. This is the background to always keep in mind regarding the historical setting, which clarifies the context.**

Let's understand this in common language. YAH sent His chosen children of Israel to experience punishments and curses. So, you have a people temporarily cursed by their Creator leaving them defenseless during the period of punishment. Let's say that you're the enemy and knew that the people were YAH's cursed chosen children. You knew that when the children walked with YAH, they were untouchable. However, you knew when they were punished, they were powerless.

You knew that, at that moment, they were defenseless as not even YAH would hear their prayers because of the punishment period of the curse.

Taking advantage of this information, you conquered your enemy, made a slave of him, and shipped him off to a foreign land stealing the person and their identity, leaving few traces to discover truth. Before making a slave, you setup **new religions** and seize control over their religion (Hebrews) and change the text (**1 Maccabees 3:48** "And laid open the book of the law, wherein the heathen had sought to paint the likeness of their images" – **note** – Maccabees were written shortly before the time of Yahusha [Jesus]. We received an early warning as scriptures states they would change the text and images.). Also, let's further recognize the corruption within the nation of Israel as **Daniel 2-3** prophesied the mixed feet during the time of the last beast. The mixing of iron and clay.

And, Before shipping him off to a foreign land, you force him to accept a Elohiym (a.k.a. God) that he never knew or served (**Deuteronomy 4:28** cursed to serve Elohiym (a.k.a. God) of wood [**cross**] and stone [**Kaaba**]). Then, on penalty of death you forbid any worship of the true Creator. Upon arriving to foreign lands, you divide the families and tribes and disperse them on various slave plantations throughout the lands. Then, you force the slaves to mate and produce offspring in the masses. Then, once the children are born, you kill off the fathers so there is no passing down of truth through generations. Because of unconditional motherly love, you allow the mother to live under an oppressed system of control since you also need her to produce additional offspring for more slaves. Then, you forbid any congregations of slaves to avoid them communicating amongst each other. Without getting too far on this subject, I'll provide a short version and explain the significance.

This was the experience of Africans in the diaspora (Americas) and how we arrived on slave ships as children born in prison and our parents were killed so we don't know the truth.

This is how many blacks came to the Americas and was forced to be Christians. We were stolen from of our lands, families, tribes, and Elohiym (a.k.a. God). Israel was experiencing **Deuteronomy curses** for their disobedience to YAH and for not obeying the **Torah (Law/ Commandments). YAH temporarily "turned" his back on His chosen and sent them off to be temporarily punished, for 400 years as YAH warned Abraham.**

During the curse, the book of **Isaiah 29:10 reveals that YAH will cause us to spiritually fall asleep**. YAH closed our eyes. This is huge to keep it mind that **during the Gentile world, last 2,000 years, we were experiencing the curse of deep sleep. Because of the curse, no true knowledge of YAH was public. Also note that Christianity began at this same time, Islam, and Catholicism shortly after.** Furthermore, The curse expires when Ha'Mashiach (a.k.a. Messiah) appears at the end of the Gentile world. We are at the end of the Gentile world.

> [10] For the **Elohiym hath poured out upon you the spirit of deep sleep**, and hath **closed your eyes**: the prophets and your rulers, the seers hath he covered **(Isaiah 29:10)**.

> [27] And the Lord shall **scatter you among the nations**, and ye shall be **left few in number among the heathen**, whither the Lord shall lead you.[28] And **there ye shall serve gods, the work of men's hands, wood and stone, which neither see, nor hear, nor eat, nor smell (Deuteronomy 4:27-28)**.

In summary, you have a people that are experiencing divine curses for the last 2,000 years, curses which have expired. YAH ordered us to be spiritually asleep during the times of the curse and until the Ha'Mashiach appears at the end of the age. As a penalty of our sins, the curse also states that we would be forced to serve Elohiym (a.k.a. God) of **wood [Christianity cross]** and **stone [Islam], which are the works of men's hands and not of YAH. Yahusha (a.k.a. Jesus) worshipped the Creator and monotheism. Yet, Christianity created a new God, polytheism with a Trinity (3 Gods in 1).**

You cannot begin the discussion of Yahusha (a.k.a. Jesus) without understanding the context and historical background as Israel was a cursed nation and no truth was to appear.

What I mean by this is you cannot just pick up a book and read it without understanding the nature that brings the composition of the text and story together, this is called the **historical background**. Imagine looking at a blank piece of paper that has black/white sketches. Well, the historical background would paint the picture, by adding colors, and you'll be able to see the imaged pictures clearly. Otherwise, you're just looking at sketches that will always reveal a different picture every time you look at it. **The historical background paints pictures that can never change or be altered and only the true nature of the picture can be revealed. Always do your due diligence!**

Furthermore, let's see what the book of Enoch says about this time that we're living in of the Gentile world. This will also be another opportunity to highlight **another recent modern mistranslation of text.** We find this in **Enoch 93** where he is discussing the **Apocalypse of Weeks (determined history of man)**. We'll narrow in to where we are in this determined time of man as we await the everlasting righteous plant.

In the older translations, you find this is **93:9-10**. The newer translations place this verse at **93:12**. Let's review the modern verse translation and then we'll review the older translation.

> Afterwards, in the seventh week, a **perverse generation shall arise; abundant** shall be its **deeds**, and **all its deeds perverse.** During its completion, the righteous shall be selected from the everlasting plant of righteousness; and to them shall be given the sevenfold doctrine of his whole creation **(Enoch 93:12 Cepher Millennial Edition)**.

In the modern translations, we see the phrase **"a perverse generation shall rise"**. The definition of perverse is to show a deliberate and obstinate desire to behave in a way that is **unreasonable** or **unacceptable**. **Keep this in mind.** Now, **let's see what the older translation of this verse says**

> "After that in the **seventh week** an **apostate generation shall arise; its deeds shall be many, and all of them" criminal.** •At its completion, there shall be elected the elect ones of righteousness' from the eternal plant of righteousness, to whom shall be given sevenfold instruction concerning all his flock **(Enoch 93:9-10 The Old Testament Pseudepigrapha Volume One)**.

Remember to keep the context of a people that is temporarily cursed by YAH and slavery. A people that was cursed to be in deep sleep. However, **in the older translation**, it states that an **"apostate generation shall rise and it's deeds shall be many, all of them criminal"**. This is very revealing. Let's review some points:

- **The apostate generation represents the church a.k.a. Gentile world (last 2,000 years, remember Christianity, Catholicism, Islam all began at this time and shortly after)**
- **Let's remember that the apostle Paul started the church and wrote many New Testament books. He also taught a new gospel, which any new gospel was to come at the end of the age. The New Testament was never ordained by YAH as the Jeremiah 31 new covenant prophecy will come at the Ha'Mashiach, Who hasn't come on Earth until our recent days. Paul's teachings contradict Yahusha teachings and life.**
- **Let's also keep in mind, like all New Testament writers, they all took scriptures from the Old Testament and changed the words by repackaging into the New Testament. This was Paul and all New Testament writers as the Word of YAH ended with the Old Testament. Nothing new came from YAH.**
- **Remember that Paul was a persecutor of Jews. Let's also remember that Yahusha (a.k.a. Jesus) is reported to have had 12 disciples, which followed him during his life. None of his 12 disciples agreed with the teachings of Paul. Yet, those were the main people receiving the teachings of Yahusha (a.k.a. Jesus) and they all disagreed with Paul.**
- **Right after Yahusha (a.k.a. Jesus) says beware of false prophets, he was betrayed by Judas and then Paul. Paul also created a new gospel called the gospel of grace and did away with Moses laws. This was done to appeal to pagans and not to YAH. He incorrectly taught salvation and the doing away with the Moses Law/Torah. The law that never dies. The same law that Yahusha taught and followed.**
- **He also stated that Yahusha (a.k.a. Jesus) was Elohiym (a.k.a. God) and that his death washed away all sins. In fact, compared to the name of YAH, the name of Yahusha (a.k.a. Jesus) outweighs the usage of the name of YAH in the New Testament. Yahusha never claimed to be YAH.**

- **Scripture clearly states their deeds will be many and ALL criminal. Scriptures doesn't state "some" or "few". It says, "ALL CRIMINAL". Meaning, nothing legal would come out of the church. Nothing of YAH. This is what the Word of YAH is revealing through SCRIPTURES. YAH spoke this. Not me.**
- **Paul wants you to ignore the very law which is the only law that can save you! The law that brings blessings and curses!**
  - **And he (Ha'Mashiach) will destroy them (devils) without labor by the Torah (LAW) which is like unto me (YAH). (4 Ezra/2 Esdras 13:38 – This is what Ha'Mashiach will use to conquer Earth. His weapon is the TORAH, which is the LAW.**
- **Could this be why the modern translations remove the phrase "apostate generation shall arise; its deeds shall be many, and all of them" criminal" as there's no way for church to deny what's written in scriptures.**
- **This verse clearly states that the church will be entirely criminal in all their ways. Again, not some of their ways. ALL CRIMINAL. This will end at appearance of Ha'Mashiach as you see in the next verse when seeds of righteousness are eternally raised. It would be WISE not to Reject the Word of YAH.**

Without studying the historical context and scriptures, you will not understand the story. Case in point, if I wrote a story a religious historical story during the early 1st century about Africans in the Americas, and I didn't tell you about slavery, you would think it was a peaceful story and everyone loved one another. **You would blindly accept lies as facts and not even know it. Because of our curses, we have confused a silent war and curses for peace and love. WE ARE AT WAR.**

Additionally, if I wrote a story about 1st century and told a story of a skilled magician, but failed to tell you that the entire land was filled with magicians at the same time, you would think that Elohiym was with us.

Because of Israel violating YAH's laws (**a.k.a. the same laws that brings curses, yet modern religion seeks to destroy**), Israel was dispersed into the four ends of the Earth until the regathering by the Ha'Mashiach at the end of the age. Additionally, YAH states that He would give His glory (meaning chosen people and Earth) to another nation (Gentiles) until the curse period ended (Ha'Mashiach), then YAH would choose Israel and make a new everlasting covenant. Then, YAH would judge the nations. Israel will be saved.

For the last 2,000 (rounding) years during the age of the Gentiles, the church has risen. All their deeds have been criminal, fulfilling prophecy and scriptures. For the last 2,000 (rounding) years, through the 3 main religions of Rome (Christianity, Catholicism, Islam), many have equated calling upon the name of YAH with the name of Yahusha (a.k.a. Jesus), which is an incorrect teaching. YAH is the only name to that can save anyone!

So, let's explore what Rome says of Yahusha (a.k.a. Jesus).

First and foremost, we can say for certain that the person known as Yahusha (a.k.a. Jesus) was an actual person who was born, on Earth, and died, on Earth. The revelation is painfully clear. However, this is one of the most difficult discussions known to man. How can we historically prove Yahusha (a.k.a. Jesus) life and activities? The most famous name on fallen Earth **has little to no evidence other than blind faith** when all other characters and their activities can be confirmed with our physical history and records. Let's also see what historians had to say. The following is a conversation with **Celsus and Origen**.

> When Celsus asks what divine miracles Jesus performed, Origen answers that Jesus' life was indeed full of striking and miraculous events, "but **from what other source can we furnish an answer than from the Gospel narratives?" (Contra Celsum, 2.33)**.
>
> **No one else heard of the Testimonium** - it is never quoted by anyone **until the 4th century** (c. 324), when the notorious Bishop Eusebius begins quoting it.
>
> First says that showing almost any history actually occurred **"is one of the most difficult undertakings that can be attempted and is in some instances an impossibility"** (1.42) and then turns to Josephus' Antiquities of the Jews to offer proof for John the Baptist and James (1.47). But then he adds that (as a Jew) **Josephus**

> **didn't believe Jesus was the Christ** and criticizes him for failing to discuss Jesus in that book! **(Contra Celsum)** (note: Josephus writings have been changed by Christians centuries later)

Yahusha (a.k.a. Jesus) lived during the 1st century and even many centuries later no one had any physical proof of anything concerning what's reported regarding his life. No historian of his time wrote about him. **The only record we have of his life are from the gospels and they were written hundreds of years after his death.** He came, knowing he was going to die, taught, but didn't write any books. Nor did most of his disciples. The most famous story had to wait hundreds of years to be told.

It's also important to note that Josephus, the first century authority Jewish historian, didn't believe in Yahusha (a.k.a. Jesus) as the Ha'Mashiach (a.k.a. Messiah). **Centuries later, Josephus books were all changed to claim acceptance in belief. However, none of Josephus original works held belief that Yahusha (a.k.a. Jesus) was Ha'Mashiach (a.k.a. Messiah).** Josephus reports that a magical man was found in Yahusha (a.k.a. Jesus). This should not be surprising nor a something of authority to proclaim godhood. Many people were magical, and world known during this time. A case in point would be **Simon Magus, one of the greatest magicians of our times. They even thought Simon Magus was the Messiah and that's on historical records.** You can search and discover physical evidence of these claims on Simon Magus, who lived during the times of Yahusha (a.k.a. Jesus) and find them. Many also felt that John the Baptist was the Ha'Mashiach (a.k.a. Messiah).

What saith the Word?

For the Word, I'll reference one of books that Yahusha (a.k.a. Jesus) quotes from a lot. This is the Book of Enoch. A quick background on Enoch: He was the first perfect human born, he was the first to live and not die, he was taken to heaven to learn the secrets of heaven to bring judgement upon the fallen angels (a.k.a. The Watchers or Sons of Elohiym), and he was taken to heaven at pi or 365. Pi is 365.24 and the circumference of a circle. So**, It's a very ancient record that precedes the entire New Testament by many centuries and ALL New Testament writers' quotes from Enoch.** In fact, YAH revealed the plan for the times and seasons of all things. If you understand Enoch, you will understand many mysteries of our times. Because Enoch was the only human to possess the mysteries of heaven and Earth, other than the Son of Elohiym. In short, if Yahusha (a.k.a. Jesus) felt comfortable quoting Enoch, I shall freely share.

By quoting heavily from Enoch, did Yahusha (a.k.a. Jesus) hope that you would study the entire book of Enoch and see the WARNING FROM YAH for the church being ALL CRIMINAL?

Most Christians claim that Yahusha (a.k.a. Jesus) fulfilled Old Testament prophecies regarding what to expect of the Ha'Mashiach (a.k.a. Messiah). All my life, I had conflicts with Christianity. **I would study the Bible, read the prophecies, and could not find a single verse that confirmed that Yahusha (a.k.a. Jesus) was the Ha'Mashiach (a.k.a. Messiah). I reviewed over 500 prophecies claimed in attempts to find a SINGLE SCRIPTURE that Yahusha (a.k.a. Jesus) really fulfilled. Not a blind faith scripture but something very clear and definitive.** I mean we are talking about the Son of Elohiym we're seeking. Shouldn't there be clear maps of revelations. "If" he came, then what's to hide of scriptures? I also could never accept that a Elohiym could be killed and especially by enemies.

Don't worry, I'll share some of the scriptures that Christians use as "confirmations". I encourage you to study this list of scriptures. **What I found is that out of the 500 prophecies/ scriptures, all of them are fulfilled at the end of the age.** The rest are loosely and forcibly twisted and applied. For the record, **IF YOU HAVE A CLEAR SCRIPTURE THAT YAHUSHA (A.K.A. JESUS) FULFILLED, EMAIL ME BECAUSE I HAVE A LIST OF OVER 500 UNFULFILLED.**

Before I share my list, let's look at a few areas for additional context. I'm not a Christian and so this allows me to comfortably discuss the Old Testament AND historical records of facts without quickly or blindly breezing over important details. I find religious people can be haste and like to rush with discussing important details and information, especially when discussing the Old Testament. I find that people avoid uncomfortable subjects regardless of if it's for their benefit (Torah).

Did they steer you away from the Old Testament from realizing that you were being punished?

I encourage you to read this text in entirety.

It is claimed that Yahusha (a.k.a. Jesus) was the Son of Elohiym. Let's see what the book of Enoch states about the Son of Elohiym. Note: the Book of Enoch is much older than the gospels, by many centuries. Note: **most of the New Testament is built off the book of Enoch.**

> 46 At that place, I saw **the One to whom belongs the time before time.** – And his head was white like wool, **and there was with him another individual, whose face was like that of a human being.**" His countenance was full of grace like that of one among the holy angels. • And I asked the one–from among the angels-who was going with me, and who had revealed to me all the secrets regarding **the One who was born of human beings**, "Who is this, and from whence is **he who is going as the prototype of the Before-Time** • And he answered me and said to me, "This is **the Son of Man**, to **whom belongs righteousness**, and with whom righteousness dwells. And he will open all the hidden storerooms; for the Lord of the Spirits has chosen him, and he is destined to be victorious before the Lord of the Spirits in eternal uprightness. •This Son of Man whom you have seen is the One who would **remove the kings and the mighty ones from their comfortable seats and the strong ones from their thrones**. He shall loosen the reins of the strong and crush' the teeth of the sinners. • **He shall depose the kings from their thrones and kingdoms**. For they do not extol and glorify him, and neither do they obey him, the source of their kingship. • The faces of the strong will be slapped and be filled with shame and gloom. Their dwelling places and their beds will be worms. They shall have no hope to rise from their beds, **for they do not extol the name of the Lord of the Spirits (YAH). • (Enoch 46)**
>
> • For this purpose, he became the Chosen One; he was **concealed in the presence of The Lord of the Spirits prior to the creation of the world, and for eternity (Enoch 62)**.
>
> **For the Son of Man' was concealed from the beginning**, and the Most High One **preserved him** in the presence of his power; **then he revealed him to the holy and the elect ones. * (Enoch 62)**
>
> Now, let's see what Ezra/Esdras says about the appearance of the Ha'Mashiach in **4 Ezra/2 Esdras 13:52, 13:26-27, and 7:26-31**:

So, **no one on earth can see my Son** or those who are with him, **except in the time of his day." (4 Ezra/2 Esdras 13:52)**

This is the interpretation of the vision: As for your seeing a man come up from the heart of the sea, •this is **he** whom the **Most High has been keeping for many ages**, who will **himself deliver his creation;** and he will direct those who are left **(4 Ezra/2 Esdras 13:26-27)**

The temporary messianic kingdom and the end of the world

26 "For behold, the time will come, when the signs which I have foretold to you will come to pass; **the city which now is not seen shall appear, and the land which now is hidden shall be disclosed.** •And everyone who has been delivered from the evils that I have foretold shall see my wonders. • For **my son the Messiah shall be revealed** with those who are with him, and those who remain shall rejoice **four hundred years.** • And **after these years my son the Messiah shall die, and all' who draw human breath.** • And **the world shall be turned back to primeval silence for seven days, as it was at the first beginnings; so that no one shall be left.** •And **after seven days** the world, which is not yet awake, shall be roused, and that which is corruptible shall perish and the earth shall give up those that are asleep in it **(4 Ezra/2 Esdras 7:26-31)**.

Ha'Mashiach was concealed and reserved for the end of the age. At the revelation of Ha'Mashiach, He will remove all world rulers and return Earth back to YAH. Then, we all shall be changed along with the resurrection. Then, the regathering of Israel to return to motherland. Then, Ha'Mashiach (a.k.a. Messiah) rules for 400 years. Then, all on Earth die. Then, comes judgement. Then, those saved will awaken to a new heaven and Earth. Hence, this will all happen at the end of the age along with the other 500+ Old Testament prophecies regarding the appearance of Ha'Mashiach on Earth. None of the "salvation" or "savior" prophecies has been fulfilled.

What Christians are guided by is blind faith as there are NO Old Testament scripture prophecies that state that Ha'Mashiach will be revealed more than once. Nor are there any Old Testament scriptures that state that He had to come, die, and be sacrificed for humanity (Jubilees 18:12). I will share the findings of scriptures used by Christians. I encourage you to do the research yourself. See it with your own eyes. They are taking general Old Testament verses and incorrectly applying it to Yahusha (a.k.a. Jesus). Interesting thing about the scriptures many use versus the ones I presented is that the scriptures I present all say the word "Ha'Mashiach" or "Messiah" in the same verse being referenced. **Whereas the verses Christians use ALL are GENERAL statements and extremely loosely they attempt to forcibly apply to Yahusha (a.k.a. Jesus).** I'll list a few. **I personally reviewed over 500 alleged prophecies/scripture, and NONE were fulfilled**. Painstakingly, I took the time to review over 500 scriptures and none were fulfilled by anyone. Again, I challenge you to email me if you can prove, with a scripture as no man on Earth has been able to do this yet for the last 2,000 years!

Some scripture references Christians use (I'll soon have a list of over 400 on my website so you can see for yourself. It's very clear)

Gen 3:15, Gen 5:24, Gen 9:26-27, Gen 14:18, Gen 28:12, Gen 49:10, Ex 12:13, Ex 12:46, Lev 1:2-9, Num 24:17, Deut 18:19, 2 Sam 7:13, 2 Sam 7:14, 2 Sam 7:16, 1 Chron 17:12-13, Job 9:32-33, Psa 2:2, Psa 2:7-9, Psa 9:7-10, Psa 18:2-3, Psa 22:9-10, Psa 22:14, Psa 22:15, Psa 22:18, Psa 22:22, Psa 22, Psa 30:3, Psa. 35:11, Psa. 38:12-13, Psa. 40:6-8, Psa. 45:7-8, Psa. 55:12-14, Psa.89:35-37, Isa. 9:6, Isa 11:1, Isa 11, Isa 22:22, Isa 29:14, Isa 40:3-4, Isa 43:11, Isa 45:21-25, Isa 53:3, Jer 23:5, Jer 31:22, Ez 33:14-15, Dan 2:44-45, Dan 9, Zech 6:12-13, Zech 9, Zech 11, Mal 3:1, Mal 4

In respect of real estate of space in a book, this is an abbreviated list. You can do a search online using key phrase, "What prophecies did Jesus fulfill". Then, read and study the words yourself. You will see **if** you see with your eyes and hear with your ears.

I reviewed hundreds and all point to end of the age. ALL others are EXTREMELY BLIND FAITH. Let's review a few for context. I don't have to list many because you'll see that the trend is the same in that **the name nor word Ha'Mashiach (a.k.a. Messiah) does NOT appear and ALL times when the name Ha'Mashiach (a.k.a. Messiah) appears are ALL END OF THE AGE SCRIPTURES. It doesn't get any simpler than this.**

YAH WROTE THE END FROM THE BEGINNING and revealed it ONLY to His Hebrew Prophets. NO GREEKS or New Testament characters dealt with YAH.

For example, the ENTIRE book of Isaiah reveals YAH's salvation plan. Isaiah literally means **YAH Saves. YAH listed our salvation plan out in Isaiah and all other prophets align with the book of Isaiah. Nothing NEW was added to YAH's salvation plan.** Meaning, **the END is in the BEGINNING.** ALL Isaiah's prophecies were for END OF THE AGE.

So, it's pointless of me listing Isaiah verses because you can read any and see this for yourself. However, as we glance throughout scriptures, we can see how crafty they become. Remember, it's your enemy who hates you and sold you the religion and Elohiym (a.k.a. god) you serve. A Elohiym (a.k.a. god) that is not YAH. An enemy that can only do all criminal, according to scriptures.

1. **Exodus 12:13**, they use this verse to say Christ was the Passover land. Here's the verse. [13] And the blood shall be to you for a token upon the houses where ye are: and when I see the blood, I will pass over you, and the plague shall not be upon you to destroy you, when I smite the land of Egypt. (Keep in mind Jubilees 18:12. YAH provided a lamb already)
    - **Considering space, I shall refer you to search the scriptures. You'll see exactly as this verse. It's taken out of context and does not even mention Ha'Mashiach (a.k.a. Messiah)**

Let's **discuss the virgin birth**. Keep in mind that over 40 pagan gods had virgin births. Why did Yahusha (a.k.a. Jesus) have to have a virgin birth? Before we get into this revelation, let's review what the word really means. This brings up a very important point to highlight. **The original language determines the implied meaning, not the translation**. Therefore, the saying goes, "things get lost in translations". **If only people realized that Adam's very name revealed the color of the original man, dark reddish black and created in the image of YAH.**

There's always a heavenly map to truth. Sometimes, you must study the root meaning of a word or its numerical value. DEEPER ANSWERS are ALWAYS THERE. LOOK.

You must always study the origins and root meaning of words. They all carry priceless value. Case in point. **The Hebrew meaning for the word "virgin" does not mean a**

sexually virgin. The **Hebrew word virgin means "young" or "maid".** Some may say it's a simple mistake when the scribes and priests translated from Greek to English. But let's also cover some additional background to gain better insight. Remember, **whenever any question arises in life, always DO YOUR DUE DILEGENCE AND BE RELENTLESS IN YOUR RESEARCH AND PURSUIT OF TRUTH.**

During the times of Yahusha (a.k.a. Jesus) lived, the world was filled with paganism. A simple description of a pagan is one who worships a Elohiym (a.k.a. God) made of their own hands and imagination or of the hands and mind of another party (For the record a pagan is any Elohiym [a.k.a. God] other than YAH. They do not worship YAH in spirit or truth, and they have no power but in your mind.

It is revealed that even many of Yahusha (a.k.a. Jesus) disciples were former pagans. Let's look at some characteristics of pagan deities. They ALL have the **SAME STORY AS YAHUSHA (a.k.a. Jesus). History reveals over 40 pagan gods with the same story as Yahusha (a.k.a. Jesus) and all were centuries before his life.** Remember the Enoch verse, in that not even the angels were aware of the Son of YAH. This is important because Christians state that Satan knew Yahusha (a.k.a. Jesus) would be born and stole his story. No. Not even Satan knew the Son of YAH.

Also, study the pagan gods in ancient Sumer, Samaria, Babylon, and Mesopotamia. This where all pagan gods come from. This is their beginning. Read the stories and you'll see!

We also find many experienced a virgin birth, born on December 25, did miracles, was crucified, resurrected, and will return to bring judgement. On the surface, this is the story of Yahusha (a.k.a. Jesus). **Would you be surprised to learn that even MANY centuries before Yahusha (a.k.a. Jesus), cultures around the world had this same story for their gods.**

BEFORE Yahusha (a.k.a. Jesus) was BORN, HIS SAME LIFE STORY IS THE SAME STORY as Horus, Mithra, Krishna, Buddha, Pan, Baal, Enki, and Osiris. These stories preceding by centuries and yet Yahusha (a.k.a. Jesus) lived the exact same life, said the same things, and made the same claims. They make it appear

as the same person/story lived OVER AND OVER AND OVER AND OVER through all these different names. How else can their stories be EXACTLY THE SAME?

Sad, when I ask Christians, they say somehow, they stole Jesus' story, thousands of years before it happened! How could this be possible if the Son of YAH was concealed?

Also, if you compare the similarities with the story of Yahusha (a.k.a. Jesus) and the story of Horus (ancient Egypt), you will see an almost identical picture and same story. **The story of Osiris, Isis, and Horus precedes Yahusha (a.k.a. Jesus) by many centuries.** Interestingly, Osiris was an actual man king whose grave has been discovered. There was a King Osiris mentioned in the book of Jubilees during the life of Abraham.

Some other pagan gods that have the same story as Yahusha (a.k.a. Jesus) are Bacchus of Greece, Mithra, Shiva/Krishna, Buddha, Serapis, and Zeus. **Would it also surprise you that even their words/scriptures are very similar and their images? They had the same life, did the same things, and said the same things and looked the same.**

Another interesting note is that the New Testament represents Greeks and were written by Greek writers for a Gentile world perspective and thinking that they could replace Israel by hiding the truth. Keep in mind, we're talking about the same Greeks that completely stole Egyptian history and claimed it as their own by whitewashing lies (see "Stolen Legacy: Greek Philosophy is Stolen Egyptian Philosophy" by George G.M. James). The same Greeks that had a WHITE Serapis image held as Elohiym (a.k.a. God) during the life while Yahusha (a.k.a. Jesus) lived and made the image of Jesus to this same image.

The current world ruler, Rome, is a descendent of this same Greek pagan power. **PAGAN Rome never died.** It was simply reborn and has everyone under their spell and illusion. Why do you think that the pope prays secretly to a Black Madonna (still pagan) and Black Jesus (still pagan), while PUBLICLY selling you a false white Jesus (still pagan)? The same pope that mathematically adds to value 666 and sits on 7 mountains and rules 10 kings as Mystery Babylon.

Rome also preaches a false gospel whereby you can pay a financial price for your sins, and they will be pardoned. This encourages sin. It also builds Rome's financial banks! This is a false teaching. This is not of YAH. The TORAH/LAW NEVER DIES.

I bet Rome makes more money than the biggest S&P 500 company does (APPLE, Microsoft, Google, etc.) just off bribe money to pay off sins, sins which he can't even pardon with heaven.

No worries. Rome is not YAH and is simply a tool being used by YAH. YAH will put all things in order. They won't even be a memory after YAH is done.

I have a simple exercise that will blow your mind. During the time of Yahusha (a.k.a. Jesus), the main religious cults were worshipping Serapis, Apis, Isis, Mithra, Baal, Adonis, Zeus, Olympus, Saturn, etc. **Do a search online and review all the many similarities in their life stories. They are all the same story with different characters and many look exactly the same as Jesus.**

Pagans were ruling and Christianity was on the rise. They needed a way to marriage both and keep the "peace". Having annihilated Jewish religious authority due to the curse of the Gentile world, **they blended all these gods into Yahusha (a.k.a. Jesus). Do the research because you'll see they are all the same stories.**

Side note: Sadly, many celebrate the Gentile world. The world that represents Jacobs Trouble. The Gentile world equals Jacobs Trouble! And The world that hides knowledge of YAH, is all criminal, and kills us! **Lastly, by trusting Gentiles (church), you are trusting the enemies that are used to punish us. You're trusting a source that they themselves cannot even escape being criminal because scriptures proclaim that they would be all criminal and evil. How ironic!**

I want everyone to do a search online. Look at the **picture of Serapis and look at the picture of Yahusha (a.k.a. Jesus).** For the record, the images you see claiming as Jesus are that of Cesare Borgia. His homosexual lover, Leonardi de Vinci has the **world worshipping Cesare as Jesus.** This is the great **CON OF MAN.**

Google all 3 images (Serapis, Jesus, Cesare Borgia). They all look completely identical. MIND YOU, Serapis was around LONG before Yahusha (a.k.a. Jesus) lived.

These are the same images they (Gentiles and Rome) placed into your Bible and sell the world! These same false images are held as sacred. **This is the religious world that you accept and BLINDLY follow.**

I know this may be a mouthful to digest.

I'll recap a few points. **When YAH brings judgement, no man can alter.** What do I mean by this? **Even if you wish to give the benefit of doubt and say that Rome, and it's 3 religions, weren't all secretly evil, your feelings would not be biblical.** You wouldn't be being honest with yourself, your eyes, your ears, or YAH. By legal definition, you will be defined as insane and the living dead. YAH wishes that none should perish, but would repent and follow Torah, so I'll attempt to be thorough and from VARIOUS angles in efforts to assist you in your eternal salvation.

Scriptures clearly state that the church age will be born, do nothing but all criminal, and which would imply all evil. **To deny this would be to deny the Word of YAH.** To deny this would state that man is somehow more powerful than YAH. To deny this would say that the created can overpower the Creator. Why do I emphasis this?

Because scriptures clearly state that Israel was to be punished by way of the age of the Gentiles. As part of this punishment, Israel would be dead to all knowledge of YAH until the Dry Bones awakening, which began when Israel became a nation in 1948 and will consummate at the appearance of Ha'Mashiach.

Furthermore, scriptures declare that a church age would be born and do all criminal acts. So, now you have an evil criminal, a spiritually blinded people, they changed the Bibles and images, they created new religions to capture every region of the world, they recycled the pagan gods and used different names such as Yahusha (a.k.a. Jesus), Maccabees reveals the wars and forced conversions to Christianity, and they forced the world to serve pagan gods disguised as Yahusha (a.k.a. Jesus).

This was all proclaimed to happen and YAH Word never fails void. Additionally, our reawakening and salvation was proclaimed to happen. YAH told Abraham that his children would be enslaved in a foreign land for 400 years and then YAH would send Ha'Mashiach to regather the children of Israel. Let's elaborate historically since we couldn't do it with Yahusha. (a.k.a. Jesus), here's a chance to tie this into real life. American slavery began approximately 1619 when the first Hebrew slaves arrived in the Americas. Those 400 years are up! **Ha'Mashiach will finally appear and save us with mighty wonders**!

Hence, U.S. President Biden and continuation of government has their plane 24/7 in the skies right now! They're living in the air! You heard it here first. The U.S. is running its government from the air, and this was LONG before the Russian crisis. They ONLY do this when they KNOW SOMETHING MAJOR is COMING. They know the DRY BONES ARE AWAKENING (**Ezekiel 37**).

Not to get off topic, but **Ezekiel 37** dry bones is **another major modern mistranslation**. This is not a physical rebirth of the physical dead in these verses. It's the **spiritual awakening of TRUTH TO Black HEBREWS. This was written in scriptures and WILL HAPPEN WORLDWIDE. People will awaken to the TRUTH and the nation of Israel will be born again!** Christians incorrectly teach this is a resurrection of the physical dead. For the resurrection of the physical dead, I refer you to Enoch, Baruch, and Ezra.

YAH is not the author of confusion. Which is why the story of Yahusha (a.k.a. Jesus) presents many unsolved obstacles because **the Word of YAH allows us to confirm things to our real life! We still can't do this with Yahusha (a.k.a. Jesus) 2,000 years later! We have not been able to make sense of Yahusha (a.k.a. Jesus) in our real life. Only in the blind faith of our mind.**

If the enemy can confuse you, they can turn you away from YAH.

Allow me an opportunity to provide additional background and triangulate my thesis. For this, let's visit the books of **Daniel and Maccabees. For the record, I urge EVERYONE to read the books of Maccabees**. This is where you see how evil and wicked the fathers of this "apostle/Gentile" world are. As per the curse and the awakening, many hidden Hebrew books started to resurface when Israel was reborn in 1948. Additionally, YAH ordered many books to be held secret until the last days where they would be revealed.

This was also a time to see how the misinterpretations of scriptures can lead to damaging effects. **Daniel's** prophecies are one of the greatest mysteries of the Bible and centers of great controversy. There are hundreds of books out there about this one area in scripture. Many imply the Antichrist. Some claim the Ha'Mashiach (a.k.a. Messiah). Let's review some scriptures:

> [26] And after threescore and two weeks shall **Messiah be cut off**, but not for himself: and **the people of the prince that shall come shall destroy the city and the sanctuary**; and the end thereof shall be with a flood, and unto the **end of the war desolations** are determined. [27] And **he shall confirm the covenant with many for one week**: and in the **midst of the week**, he shall cause the sacrifice and the oblation to cease, and for the **overspreading of abominations** he shall make it desolate, even until the consummation, and that determined shall be poured upon the desolate (**Daniel 9:26-27**).

Remember, we still discussing the historical and present background of the life and times of Yahusha (a.k.a. Jesus) to provide clarity from many angles of knowledge. The revelation of this verse is so sad because even a lazy person and do a simple search online and you'll see written history confirmed the fulfillment of this scripture. YET, MANY incorrectly claim this is an end day prophecy. **This was the beginnings of Jacobs Trouble.** This already happened.

They have hundreds of books on this subject. Yet, people allow the false narrative than to open the Word of YAH and see how the Word of YAH is confirmed in living history.

In this verse, we are told that the children of Israel will be allowed to rebuild their temple. An agreement will be made to allow this to occur. The Antichrist will break the agreement midway during the seven years. The Antichrist will setup the abomination of desolations. The temple will be destroyed, and the people will be dispersed. These are the events described in **Daniel 9:26-27 (a.k.a. Daniel 70 Weeks). This is how Yahusha (a.k.a. Jesus) KNEW the temple would be destroyed. It's written in scriptures!**

Would it surprise you to learn that this all already happened! AND it happened BEFORE Yahusha (a.k.a. Jesus) was born. Yet, we hear these scriptures being preached as end day prophecies when we can identify clear fulfillments. The fulfillments are revealed in the book of Maccabees. Remember, the Maccabees were written shortly prior to the birth of Yahusha (a.k.a. Jesus). You can also do a simple search and discover this information revealed historically online. Try it out. This will show you how lazy and blind people have become.

During the 1st century, Greek king Antiochus IV fulfilled this scripture by setting up the abomination of desolations. He even sacrificed a pig on the alter. The temple was destroyed. So, if we can stop being lazy and get this from a simple search online. Why are many so blind to follow lies?

Additionally, this brings up another discussion regarding the title "Ha'Mashiach (a.k.a. Messiah)" as this prophecy Daniel 9:26-27 mentions that the Ha'Mashiach (a.k.a. Messiah) will be cutoff. Many know this as Messiah cutoff. Remember also, I told you that the answer for this triangulates in the book of Maccabees. Mighty and conquering Judas Maccabees was the "Ha'Mashiach (a.k.a. Messiah)" that was cutoff when the covenant was violated by Greek king Antiochus IV. If you read the Maccabees, you will see one is can be likened to the conquering of Joshua or King David.

Brings us back to the subject of the title of the name "Ha'Mashiach (a.k.a. Messiah)". This name has been used in scriptures and implied to other characters other than the "end of the age Ha'Mashiach [a.k.a. Messiah]. For example, Moses, Joseph [in Egypt], Joshua, and King David were like prototype Ha'Mashiach (a.k.a. Messiah) characters even though they weren't considered the Son of Elohiym. There are many times this was used in the Old Testament. In those incidences, the Ha'Mashiach character was used by YAH to bring out salvation. The only difference is Ha'Mashiach (a.k.a. Messiah) of Israel will bring salvation, judgement, and the kingdom of YAH at the end of this age.

So, don't get confused when you see this title having been used with others, on a regional level, in the Old Testament. For example, in Daniel 9:26-27, the Ha'Mashiach (a.k.a. Messiah) cutoff applies to Judas Maccabees and not the Ha'Mashiach (a.k.a. Messiah) of Israel and not to the Antichrist. Thus, this is a fulfilled prophecy.

Now that we cleared that up, hopefully you won't have anyone incorrectly selling this as a future unfulfilled prophecy. These scriptures also cannot be used to be applied to Yahusha (a.k.a. Jesus) as they were fulfilled by Judas Maccabees BEFORE the birth of Yahusha (a.k.a. Jesus).

This also provides ADDITIONAL historical background to what was occurring during the life of Yahusha (a.k.a. Jesus). Now, you're gaining additional insight to see how demonically fallen the state of religion and the world was.

They don't teach you this in church, do they? ASK YOUR PASTOR. Show THEM THIS BOOK!

Grab your phone and google search "abominations of desolations". It's so simple and SAD how many simply blindly follow information that NOT BIBLICAL and NOT HISTORICAL.

Let's also remember that Blacks were originally Hebrews who were forced into Christianity during slavery.

As we transition into another phase of Ha'Mashiach, it's a good opportunity to share some research from a fellow Hebrew historian, **Dr. Beneyah Yashar'el**. For the record, I have read hundreds of books, and none are speaking the truth that Dr. Beneyah Yashar'el speaks. I admire her courageous character and her passion to truth. My attempts were to present this volume without quoting any other author and speak directly from YAH. However, after seeing how bad the world is, how dark, how many authors sell us out with misinformation, and the few that speak truth. I owe **my deepest gratitude to Dr. Beneyah Yashar'el. I recommend everyone to purchase and study her books and show her some support. Thank you Dr. Beneyah** for allowing me to feature your research on **The Truth About The New Testament And The Gospels "The Apostles"**. Because her light shines brightly the truth, she is the only author that I quote from in this book.

THE TRUTH ABOUT THE NEW TESTAMENT AND THE GOSPELS WRITTEN BY "THE APOSTLES" (Source: Dr. Beneyah Yashar'el, Hebrew Historian)

As the Israelites continue to awaken to the truth of their identity, they need to understand the great deception that has been perpetrated on them and the entire world by those who have used the Babylonian religions with the Torah to carry out this fraud. Historical records show that the New Testament books are a collection of 27 writings compiled by Christians in the first four hundred years of Christian history. It is defined as the second part of the sacred Scriptures of the Christian church. The first part is called, by contrast, the "Old Testament" or Hebrew Torah and Tanakh. Four "apostles" who wrote the four gospels were claimed by historians to be followers or disciples of Jesus, the Jewish Son of the Highest ELOHIYM born to the Virgin Mary and died, was resurrected so that the world could be saved and redeemed back to him. These New Testament "apostles" included Matthew, Mark, Luke, and John, said to have recorded the life and teachings of Jesus. Followed by the Acts of the Apostles, which chronicles the history of the early Christian missionaries. These are followed by the epistles or letters written by various disciples, most notably Paul, said to be the apostle of the Gentiles. My research shows that these four men or apostles purported to have written the gospels never existed, in the way history claims and the stories recorded do not fulfill the prophecies written in **Jeremiah 31. Therefore, the "new" Testament is not the "new" covenant.** However, **most people are indoctrinated** and believe that what is in these gospels is the infallible word of the Highest. But, in my research, I have found that these documents were made up of pastiches of the Torah and written by the Christians of Rome who wanted to connect to Israel and the Highest ELOHIYM of Abraham, Isaac, and Jacob-Israel.

The Christian church is the Catholic pagan church that began in Rome. They espoused the belief that God is the God of the universe and therefore should not have a chosen people. Thus, the religion was called catholic, meaning universal. When the Roman Empire rose to power in 168 BC, the Hasmonean dynasty of Judea and Jerusalem was still intact. The Hasmoneans had always recognized the latent power of Rome, and their policy had been one of watchful conciliation. And although the relationship with their non-Israelite neighbors was hostile, they remained friendly with Rome and created alliances with them which instructed the rulers to respect the Judean territory. However, Rome did not continue to regard these boundaries. The Judean kingdom became a pawn in Roman politics when they appointed an Edomite king Herod as a client ruler under Roman protection in 37 BC. Antigonus, the last Hasmonean ruler, was removed by Herod's instigation. He made no secret that his sympathies lay with the non-Israelite inhabitants of the kingdom. Once Rome took control, various wars followed, causing the Israelites to be further dispersed and divided into various sects and parties, including the Herodians, Sadducees, Pharisees, and Essenes. These divisions made it easier for Rome to usurp authority over Jerusalem, the Torah, and its teachings.

While in the diaspora, most of the Israelites remained loyal to their traditions. They still had a sense of belonging to a special community. Even when they looked like Greeks, they remained Israelites. They were not Christians and were offended if referred to as such. **They did not believe that the HAMASHIACH of Israel had come because they knew that when he came, they would be delivered from the hand of their enemy, which was Rome.** However, once the Israelites were dispersed, they were exposed, and many fell prey to the Christian philosophy led by some of the Hellenized Israelites. Alexandria was a place where many of the Israelites were in the diaspora and was one of the main centers where the Israelites began to join Christianity. Philo Judaeus's (20 BC-AD 50) influence was enormous on the Israelites who lived there. He was a mystic, a Platonic philosopher, and a loyal Judean, but also loyal to Rome. Like Paul, he aspired to mystical experiences. His soul was "on fire," and his language vibrated with emotion. However, he was Greek to the core in language, education, and manners, and his Bible was the Septuagint (Frend, 1984).

Philosophers like Philo created the ideas in the New Testament, and although they were of the Israelite heritage, they had embraced the doctrines of the Babylonian religions. Philo, along with Plato, understood God as existence apprehensible by the human mind as abstract Perfection. Yet God was also the Creator, creating the universe out of Non-being and stamping upon it the pattern of order and rationality, his Reason or Logos. The Logos was interpreted in Platonic terms as "the Idea of Ideas," the first begotten Son of God, pattern, and mediator of Creation, and "Second God." Scripture was the word of the Logos to be understood by the same mystical process as that by which the human mind approached the Logos himself. **Therefore, the Bible (New Testament) implies that humanity was eventually destined for deification, representing harmony and conformity with the Divine.** These are the same ideas espoused in the **Gospel of John** and taught in the **New-Age religions** today and were considered new when the New Testament was compiled in the **late fourth century**.

According to historians, a flood of gospels and other literature forced Christians to make selections in their estimation of authoritative Christian literature during the second century.

However, the **earliest reference to the current collection of books of the New Testament appeared in 367AD** in the letter of Athanasius, bishop of Alexandria. History shows that in Alexandria, Egypt, where Israelites were dispersed in huge numbers, Christianity which had already been established in Rome, was **forced** upon them. **The story of Jesus was not written until both the northern ten tribes of Israel and the Judeans had been in the diaspora for centuries. Jesus/Yahusha was not connected to the Hebrews. He is the Indo-Aryan god Mithra mixed with the other pagan gods of Egypt and Greco-Rome. The Judeans would never tolerate this Jesus, and why they were still being hunted down and killed by Rome until the late 17th century.** However, suppose the New Testament was indeed a continuation of the history of the Israelites. Why did it not onect the story to the Hasmonean dynasty, the last Israelite dynasty to rule in Judea and Jerusalem? The Edomite Romans removed the historical books of the Maccabees from the Torah and called them Deuterocanon, or second books. And have completely excluded them from the Protestant bible. The books of the Maccabees should at least attest to this Messiah Jesus's coming.

Moreover, the Roman authority compiled a new set of books, including the four Gospels and the writings of Paul, called the New Testament. **They insist that these books are not an accumulation of historical facts but rather documents of faith and, as such, are primarily concerned with the theological implications of the life and death of Jesus.** Although there is **no evidence** as to who wrote these accounts, historians generally assume that after the death of Jesus, some of his disciples recorded his sayings before they were forgotten. **The group of documents is called Q** (from the German word Quelle, meaning "source"). They further assume that the Q documents, although overall authentic, were colored by presuppositions and included sayings mistakenly ascribed to Jesus.

Additionally, they noted that the Gospel writers Matthew and Luke are assumed to have used a lot of material from the Q documents. However, despite whether these assumptions are correct, two conclusions remain undisputed: **that Jesus himself wrote nothing and that the content of the Gospels suggests or implies two sources.** One is a record of sayings ascribed to Jesus, and the other is contemporary opinion reflecting the understanding of early Christians. In principle, they are not reliable. **Therefore, it can be concluded that these writings are not the infallible word of the Highest YAHUAH and have no foundation in the Hebrew Scriptures. If they were, some of the**

other prophets of Israel would mention Jesus by name or at least by characteristics. And, **since the entire story is made up, it could also be assumed that there were no twelve apostles.**

However, suppose there are apostles, Biblical historians are unsure about who wrote the gospel of Matthew. The early church fathers hold that Matthew, one of the 12 Apostles, was the author of this Gospel. However, the results of modern critical studies stress that Matthew depended on the Gospel writer Mark for a substantial part of his Gospel and have caused the Biblical scholars to abandon Matthean authorship. Other historians claim that an unknown Christian wrote the Gospel of Matthew from Antioch in Syria around 90 AD. Yet, tradition has attributed this Gospel to Jesus' disciple, the tax collector of this name (**but called Levi in the parallel texts in Mark and Luke**). The Gospel of Mark is never identified in the historical record; however, the early church tradition associated the book with John Mark, a companion of St. Peter, who would have learned what he reported about Jesus from him. He was said to have accurately preserved this material. The conclusion drawn from the tradition is that the Gospel of Mark largely consists of the preaching of Peter arranged and shaped by John Mark.

In the Gospel of Luke, the author's name does not appear anywhere in the text. However, it is believed to be a companion book to Acts because the language and structure of these two books indicate that the same person wrote them. And certain sections in Acts use the pronoun "we," indicating that the author was with Paul when the events described in these passages took place. Based on Luke's association with Paul, it is believed that he also wrote this book in Antioch of Syria, where he is believed to have been born. Historians believed that he was a Gentile by birth, well educated in the Greek culture, a physician by profession, and Paul's companion at various times during the second missionary journey. John, the fourth gospel, was believed to be authored by the apostle John, the disciple of Jesus. However, late second-century tradition claimed Ephesus as this Gospel's place of origin. But it is not easy to confirm. Textual evidence, however, suggests it was written in the final decade of the first century. Historians agree that although the unnamed author was anciently thought to be Jesus' disciple John, the son of Zebedee, this was questioned by Origen and others as early as the third century. They conclude that it is more likely, to have been written by the disciples of John living in a community he founded.

When these Gospels are compared to the writings of the Hebrew text and the historical background knowledge of the Israelites, there is no doubt they were not spoken by the Highest or divinely inspired by anyone connected to him. Like all the other books of the New Testament, these gospels are pastiches of the Torah and Tanakh mixed with the pagan ideologies of Greco-Rome to make a universal religion known as Catholicism.

Edom-Rome needed to create a new religion that would include Esau's descendants in Jacob's blessings. They wanted to negate the plan and purpose the Highest designed for his chosen Jacob-Israel and replace him with Jesus, their savior god. They are still attempting to create this new world order with a one-world religion using the various Babylonian religions described as the "New Age."

Furthermore, there is no record that Jesus left that was written by himself that connects him to the Highest. The Highest told Moses how to identify and determine whether the prophets that rose in Israel would be speaking his word. He informed him that the prophets raised in Israel would be like him from among the Israelites. The Christian church applied this prophecy to Jesus, but the Highest referred to any prophet that came out of Israel, including Isaiah, Jeremiah, Ezekiel, etc. "Then YAHUAH replied to me: "They are right in what they have said. I will raise for them a prophet like you from among their people; I will put my words in the mouth of the prophet, who shall speak to them everything that I command. Anyone who does not heed the words that the prophet shall speak in my name, I will hold accountable. **But any prophet who speaks in the name of other gods or presumes to speak in my name a word that I have not commanded the prophet to speak that prophet shall die" (Deuteronomy 18:17-20)**. The Israelites would be able to recognize if the word was of the Highest by whether the word he spoke proved to be the truth.

Moses established the model used by the prophets who would mediate the Highest YAHUAH to his people. The prophet, like the king, would be from among Israel, and they should recognize that the prophet's oracles do not originate from other deities, from spirits, from skilled manipulation of objects, or from the prophet's own reflection. However, these are all practices used in the Christian church. **For example, they pray to "the Holy Spirit" and Jesus, another deity.** They use the **cross** as an object of worship to bring about certain results, and they practice the art of meditation and reflection. But the law in Israel only provides two criteria to distinguish a true or false prophecy. **The first is that the prophet should speak exclusively on behalf of ELOHIYM and report only ELOHIYM's words, and the second makes the fulfillment of a prophet's oracle the measure of the truth.**

The Highest YAHUAH's teachings are not complicated and not mysterious like the mystical religion of Christianity written in the New Testament and the other Babylonian religions. He says what he means and means what he says. The least among the Israelites would be able to understand. The Christian church rejected the Law of the Highest through its New Testament and all it stood for. They criticized the Torah and Tanakh and called it the Old Testament. They interpreted Christianity as a religion of insight and personal assurance of salvation through Christ Jesus. The idea that God was to be feared and that the believer would fall easy prey to temptation if he were not threatened with punishment was dismissed. Although they could not deny that the Hebrew scripture held some sway, their prophets like Tertullian declared, "Listen, you sinners," and any of you not yet so, that you may be able to become so. A better god has been discovered, one who is neither offended nor angry nor inflicts punishments, who has no fire warming in hell, no gnashing of teeth in the outer darkness" (Tertullian Marcion I. 27). He confirmed that to worship an unknown God, sending Christ as a "healthful" Spirit swooping down from heaven" on an alien world to guide humankind, **was to make Christianity into another mystery religion with no roots in the past.** (Ibid., I. 19.2).

As Tertullian states, Christianity is indeed another of the mystery religions of Babylon. It does not fulfill the prophecy written by the prophet Jeremiah. Christianity does not produce a new covenant, but it is a new religion created by Rome with a new God. It has no relationship to the Highest God of Abraham, Isaac, and Jacob. The storyline is not confirmed by Jeremiah's prophecy and therefore was not fulfilled by the Israelites or those who claim to be Christian. The prophet Jeremiah wrote the direct words of the Highest as he spoke to hi'; **"Behold the days come saith YAHUAH, that I will make a new covenant with the house of Israel**, and with the house of Judah: Not according to the covenant that I made with their fathers in the day that I took them by the hand, to bring them out of the land of Egypt; Which my covenant they brake, although I was a husband unto them, saith YAHUAH: But this shall be the covenant that I will make with the house of Israel; After those days, saith YAHUAH, I will **put**

my law in their inward parts, and write it in their hearts; and will be their ELOHIYM, and they shall be my people. And they shall teach no more every man his brother, saying, Know YAHUAH: for they shall all know me, From the least unto the greatest of them, saith YAHUAH: For I will forgive their iniquity, and I will remember their sin no more" (**Jeremiah 31:31-34**).

The covenant was made with the Israelites in the wilderness and will be made with Israel and Judah after they fulfill their punishment and the wicked people their wickedness because YAHUAH cannot change. The prophecy is yet in the future. However, if there is a new covenant, why is a universal religion claiming that everyone who receives Jesus is now grafted in when it said the covenant would be made with Judah and Israel? Why are the preachers still preaching if the new covenant is in effect? Why do the Israelites remain in the diaspora living as gentiles under the curses of Deuteronomy 28? Why do they continue to sin if the law is written on their hearts and inward parts? Why do they still need to be taught to know YAHUAH? If Jeremiah is a true prophet of the Highest, why are the things he predicted not fulfilled? **Those who say that Jesus came to save the world and has already done so by his death and resurrection need to answer these questions.**

The world will be at peace when this prophecy is fulfilled in Israel, and sickness and death will no longer have power over the living. **However, the prophet Jeremiah also confirmed that it is the Israelites who the Highest will redeem, not the gentile nations of this world. These nations that have engaged in the slaughter of the Israelites will be punished, and many will go to the place of condemnation prepared for Satan and his demons.**

Therefore, the Highest at this same time makes it known through the prophet Jeremiah who his people are and reveals why they could never be replaced. "Thus, saith YAHUAH, which giveth the sun for a light by day, And the ordinances of the moon and the stars by night, Which divideth the sea when the waves thereof roar; **YAHUAH of hosts is his name**: If those ordinances depart from before me, saith YAHUAH, then the seed of Israel also shall cease from being a nation before me forever. Thus, saith YAHUAH; if heaven above can be measured, And the foundations of the earth searched out beneath, I will also cast off all the seed of Israel For all they have done, saith YAHUAH" (**Jeremiah 31:35-37**).

Based on this prophecy, Israel cannot be removed from being the chosen people of the Highest because as long as the sun rises in the east and sets in the west, Israel remains the chosen. They are his children, and no one or nothing will be able to pluck them from his hand, including the false Babylonian teachings written in the New Testament by the so-called apostles of Jesus.

SHALOM!

SOURCES: CEPHER Bible (2017). Library of Congress-in-Publications Data, Cepher Publishing Group.

Frend, W.H.C. (1984). The Rise of Christianity. Philadelphia: Fortress Press.

Nigosian, S. A. (2000). World Religions. Hampshire and London: PALGRAVE.

The New Oxford Annotated Bible with Apocrypha 3rd Ed.

The Herdman's Bible Dictionary, Edited by Allen C. Myers.

Zondervan Compact Dictionary.

Zondervan King James Study Bible

THE TRUTH ABOUT THE NEW TESTAMENT AND THE GOSPELS WRITTEN BY "THE APOSTLES" (Source: Dr. Beneyah Yashar'el, Hebrew Historian)

As we have revealed throughout this study, and the information provided by Dr. Beneyah Yashar'el, the Deuteronomy curses, the deep sleep of Israel curse (Isaiah 29:10), Enoch 93 Apocalypse of Weeks, Daniel 70 weeks and desolation of abominations, the unfulfilled new covenant Jeremiah 31 prophecy that comes at the end of the age, ALL the information presented in the books of the New Testament are not divine inspired, nor are they credible or reliable, nor are they authentic and genuine, nor are they historical facts, and ALL the books of the New Testament created a new and false gospel that's mixed with paganism and not of YAH. **The New Testament does away with the Law of Moses (a.k.a. Torah Law) and they falsely preach salvation through blind faith in a deity other than YAH.**

This revelation presents many challenges for one that has been nurtured by the religions of Rome (Christianity, Islam, Catholicism). Growing up in a Christian family, when I first was awakening, I realized the many complex layers of false indoctrinations were prevalent amongst those of faith. I didn't have an issue accepting Ha'Mashiach would be black, as I felt this my entire life. In the beginning of my awakening, my difficulties stemmed from trying to combine and mix the Hebrew books (Old Testament) with the Greek books (New Testament) as it's presented in one full volume in the Cepher Millennial Edition. My research has revealed, based upon scriptures, YAH never dealt with any other nation or people. YAH chose Israel and only dealt with Israel. YAH only spoke with Hebrew prophets and YAH revealed the end from the beginning so nothing new was required to be written. The New Testament creates a new Elohiym (a.k.a. God) other than YAH.

My research has revealed that you cannot mix the Hebrew books with the Greek books. Additionally, my research has revealed that the Greeks stole their information from the Hebrew books and mixed the New Testament writings with paganism. If you study the writers of the New Testament, you will find that the book of Enoch is quoted heavily by all writers, especially the (red) words of Yahusha (a.k.a. Jesus).

Speaking on Yahusha (a.k.a. Jesus), I have studied his words, extensively, my entire life. I can recite them by heart. When you're reading the New Testament, they put the words that Yahusha (a.k.a. Jesus) spoke himself in the color of red. When you open your Bible, you will find that Yahusha (a.k.a. Jesus) spoke approximately 31,426 words. For the record, there are approximately 179,011 words in the New Testament books combined. Additionally, Yahusha (a.k.a. Jesus) never authored any books himself.

If you study, the words that Yahusha (a.k.a. Jesus) spoke himself, he **NEVER CALLED HIMSELF ELOHIYM (A.K.A. GOD). NOT ONE SINGLE TIME.** When asked if you were Elohiym (a.k.a. God) or the Ha'Mashiach (a.k.a. Messiah), he never confirmed and said yes. He may have thought he was, but he never made the claim.

Additionally, Yahusha (a.k.a. Jesus) prayed to the Father, said he can only do the will of the Father and not his own will, he wept, he doubted YAH when he felt forsaken, and he even killed a fig tree. When I think about Yahusha (a.k.a. Jesus) killing a fig tree and said it wouldn't live again. I can't help to think about how Israel is symbolized by a FIG TREE. Was Yahusha (a.k.a. Jesus) sending a silent message that's he's killing Israel?

Many lay claims that Yahusha (a.k.a. Jesus) did many miracles, such as raising the dead. Did you ever read **2 Kings** and how Elijah and Elisha raised the dead, centuries before Yahusha (a.k.a. Jesus)? Did you know that Elisha parted the waters like Moses did? Did you know that Elijah didn't die and was taken right to heaven? On a historical perspective, did you know that many people did magic during the times of Yahusha (a.k.a. Jesus)? Do a simple search online and this will reveal this. For example, Simon Magus was a very famous magician. Did you forget about the sorcerers and magicians from Egypt? The same Egypt that it's said that Yahusha (a.k.a. Jesus) went when he was a child. Ever wonder why there's so many missing years of Yahusha (a.k.a. Jesus) is because he was in Egypt learning magic. Ever wonder how pagans like Buddha and Krishna speaks of Yahusha (a.k.a. Jesus), is because they all attended the same secret magic schools from Egypt. They all were instructed by the mystery schools based in Egypt. This is where they learned magic, divination, astronomy, mathematics, geometry, physics, electromagnetic energy, secret sciences, chanting, and meditation amongst other things. And the secrets of breathing.

One of the interesting stories about Yahusha (a.k.a. Jesus) is his resurrection story. I can't help but thinking about mystery Egypt and mystery Babylon when I study the resurrection story of Yahusha (a.k.a. Jesus), I'll tell you why. In the mystery religions, they focus on your chakra energy, and they learn the secrets arts of meditation and breathing. The pagan gods of mystery religions are in the land of the dead, the underworld. To connect with this realm of the dead, they seek to imitate a death-like process or appearance. Some, when in deep meditation, even appear as dead. **They look lifeless. Sometimes, even breathing stops and returns.** They must closely resemble a dead corpse and death process. **In mystery Egypt and mystery Babylon, some even bury themselves alive in coffins!** Yes, they do secret society rituals imitating a funeral. Therefore, Egyptians call it, "The Book of the Dead" or "The Book of the Gates". **When I study the story of Lazarus, I think of this process of appearing dead.** Lazarus was trained in the secret sciences. Perhaps, he was too deep in sleep and needed a more skilled magician to bring him back and that's where Yahusha (a.k.a. Jesus) comes in.

And, when I return to the resurrection story of Yahusha (a.k.a. Jesus), I notice something that many people miss. I notice that they give him a wet sponge (perhaps with secret medicine) and his body was taken by a rich man and the oils and supplies that were taken to his burial. Did they him back from appearing as sleep? Did he survive the crucifixion? Is this how his message ended up in remote places like China and India? Did he travel and spread his message there after his "death"? Remember he only preached for 2.5 years. Yet, he's known all over the world. Unfortunately, There are more questions about Yahusha (a.k.a. Jesus) life than answers.

Yahusha (a.k.a. Jesus) spent many years being trained in secret magic. Another aspect of the mystery magic is that they work off Earth's energy grid system of electromagnetic energy. Many people don't know this, but the Jordan river is somewhat magical. As well as the land of Israel. Remember, this is the same Jordan river that it's reported John the Baptist did his ministry and Yahusha (a.k.a. Jesus) was baptized. The Jordan River is located on a major Faultline on Earth. The elite are skilled in manipulation of energy. Yahusha (a.k.a. Jesus) knew how to manipulate energy to do magic.

Speaking on energy, we can share this discourse in a metaphysical manner. Perhaps, some of you new agers may be enlightened. This will also allow for a moment to understand the Son of YAH and his role, speaking on energy. **Keep in mind, when I reference the Son of YAH, I'm not referring to Yahusha (a.k.a. Jesus). Additionally, I will retain the frame of mind that all scriptures that conform to the Torah and Tanakh are good for the edification of the spirit. Thus, you will find some scriptures from the New Testament quoted. Remember, they stole from Hebrew writers. However, I'm speaking of the coming Son of YAH, Ha'Mashiach and not Yahusha (a.k.a. Jesus).**

Bible Secret Unlocked: The Right Hand of YAH, The Son of Elohiym, The Mysterious Ha'Mashiach of Israel and World

In the beginning, **YAHUAH Elohiym created the heavens and the earth**. And the **earth was without form and void**, and **darkness** was upon the **face of the deep**. And the **Spirit of YAHUAH Elohiym** moved upon **the face of the waters** (**Genesis 1:1-2**) and **YAHUAH Elohiym** said, **Let there be Light** (**Genesis 1:3-4**).

46 At that place, I saw **the One to whom belongs the time before time**. – And his head was white like wool, **and there was with him another individual, whose face was like that of a human being**." His countenance was full of grace like that of one among the holy angels. • And I asked the one–from among the angels-who was going with me, and who had revealed to me all the secrets regarding **the One who was born of human beings**, "Who is this, and from whence is **he who is going as the prototype of the Before-Time** • And he answered me and said to me, "This is **the Son of Man**, to **whom belongs righteousness**, and with whom righteousness dwells. And he will open all the hidden storerooms; for the Lord of the Spirits has chosen him, and he is destined to be victorious before the Lord of the Spirits in eternal uprightness. •This Son of Man whom you have seen is the One who would **remove the kings and the mighty ones from their comfortable seats and the strong ones from their thrones**. He shall loosen the reins of the strong and crush' the teeth of the sinners. • **He shall depose the kings from their thrones and kingdoms**. For they do not extol and glorify him, and neither do they obey him, the source of their kingship. • The faces of the strong will be slapped and be filled with shame and gloom. Their dwelling places and their beds will be worms. They shall have no hope to rise from their beds, **for they do not extol the name of the Lord of the Spirits (YAH)**. • (**Enoch 46**)

- **For this purpose, he became the Chosen One; he was concealed in the presence of The Lord of the Spirits prior to the creation of the world, and for eternity (Enoch 62).**

For the Son of Man' was concealed from the beginning, and the Most High One **preserved him** in the presence of his power; **then he revealed him to the holy and the elect ones**. * (**Enoch 62**)

Hebrews 12:29 teaches that **YAHUAH Elohiym is a consuming fire. Deuteronomy 32:4** teaches us that **YAHUAH Elohiym is a Elohiym of Righteousness. Yahuah Elohiym is the Elohiym of the living** (**Matthew 16:15-16**).

Because of man's fallen state and **in Adam we all died,** due to the first sin and **DNA passes down from the Father to child** (**1 Corinthians 15:22**), one must be purified to be in YAH's presence. If you study the books of Enoch, it also reveals that even many angels never seen YAH.

Therefore, YAH coming to Earth destroys Earth and all due to our fallen states. By lighting up your darkness. Your DARKNESS IS DESTORYED BY HIS BRIGHT LIGHT.

Just as the sun is too bright, so is the Father. That's why governments attempt to cover the sun with fake clouds and chemtrails. The man of sin fears the sun and any bright natural light. Fact remains, the sun cannot destroy the righteous! Only those fake suns!

Earth is too dark because of sin. This is the reason for the veil between heaven and Earth. The Creator must separate from His creation because of the darkness of your sin.

The fact is, beyond the veil (the firmament) is Yahuah Elohiym on the throne with earth as His footstool (Isaiah 66:1-2). YAH is on top of His flat-Earth dome and flat concentric circle all at Pi, 365.24.

Just because your human eye with our fallen level of senses cannot perceive it, it doesn't mean YAH ceases to exist. YAH is simply in a higher level of density/dimension that is visible at higher levels of righteousness, consciousness, and vibrational frequencies. You must have a pure heart to see Yahuah Elohiym (Matthew 5:8).

Many humans are limited to the use of five senses. The pure in heart sees the Father, YAHUAH Elohiym and the Son, Ha'Mashiach. The Father and the Son are One (John 1:1-3). The Son is not YAH and is not another Elohiym.

Therefore, YAH uses an earthly vessel/superhuman avatar (seed of a woman – Genesis 3:15, John 3:16) to communicate and to pave the path for reconciliation back to YAH where YAH will once again reside with His children after the Millennial Kingdom – 4 Ezra/2 Esdras 7:26-31). Yahuah Elohiym will be their King and Elohiym, and the land will be protected and at peace forever. This will be the job of Ha'Mashiach, Son of Yahuah Elohiym.

Unlocking Bible Mysteries and Hidden Secrets Revealed
HUMAN SACRIFCES FOR FINANCIAL GAINS
Salvation is a free gift to Israel. Israel will be saved. Read Isaiah (YAH SAVES)
Yahusha (a.k.a. Jesus) didn't purchase it and he wasn't the lamb of YAH. YAH provided a replacement for Abraham (see Jubilees 18:12). No man can take away another man's sins.
Salvation is free to Israel and no human sacrifice could ever buy this.
ALL Freemasons engage actively and aggressively and secretly in human blood sacrifices. Most FRATS.
Ever want to mathematically prove a human sacrifice? DO THE MATH. Start at the year of death. Add 3 years for the Resurrection [Payoff – life change]. For example, if someone died in 2019, the payoff would be this year, 2022. Seldomly, it is slightly extended or manipulated for an illusion. This math led me to consider hip hop's KW as another false prophet. Remember, there are many false prophets.
This is not just celebrities. It's the entire public including your own families. Celebrities provide the clues. For an easy way to prove this start with any celebrity. OR start at a year of a life change (ex. New business, job, car, home, a new record, etc.) and subtract 3 years to see who died that year.
Do this with your family too. Sadly, many Christian pastors sacrifice the living loved ones for Satan. Do the math in your life to see who sacrificed a human, even family and loved ones.
GUARANTEE you will find at least one or LOTS! They also payoff through fabricated lawsuits.
Be mindful who and when people receive any settlement money even if they're seeing a doctor and even if they really were injured. Especially

those who work in prisons as they always receive settlements to keep Israel in jail!
Unfortunately, It's all a game to get paid. Doctors and lawyers are in on it too. Even the insurance companies. Everyone makes money. WHY? Because Frats don't allow you to accumulate any wealth. Especially in your own name. You must be a consumer and immediately spend that money, that you sold your soul for, like a sinful nigger heading on the highway to eternal hell. That's your FAST MONEY! That's BLOOD SACRIFICES FOR EARTHLY POSSESSIONS.
IT WILL BLOW YOUR MIND! WE ARE WORST THAN THE DAYS OF NOAH AND LOT. The entire Earth has fallen and there are so few left that are not demon possessed and controlled. They are EXTREMELY GOOD AT HIDING THIS. NUMBERS CANNOT LIE. FEW have not engaged in a human blood sacrifice. Many are being sacrificed daily. Follow the numbers!
You WILL NEVER LOOK AT LIFE THE SAME WHEN YOU DO THE MATH. NUMBERS NEVER LIE.
The numbers are DISGUSTING. The Freemason god is a letter G and it stands for Geometry. Everything that they do has numerical value. When your number comes up, it's time for you to DIE. This is how celebrities are killed and sacrificed to their hidden demonic god. That's why people like MJ and KB had to murdered. You are KILLED when the NUMBERS makes more sense for DEATH than LIFE. That's how biggie puffed it up after death and Black Panther!

What everyone hides and doesn't teach is that we are at the end of the Great Tribulation, Jacobs Trouble (70 Weeks of Daniel) and the "Times of the Gentiles". We experienced all the signs and actions of prophecies concerning our punishment, slavery ended 400 years ago, and we lost 2/3rds Israel. Everyone spiritually died.

Currently, we are at the end of the Gentile world and completed Jacobs Trouble (as we already experienced the fire of 2/3rds Israel killed. We are the remnant.)

YAH set forth a plan of 6,000 years of sin, to perfect the creation 7,000 years, and to reside with creation forever into infinity (8). That's why the number 8 represents infinity. See Daniel 9.

Unlocking Bible Mysteries and Hidden Secrets Revealed
NUMBERS
The number **6 means sin**. The number **7 means completion or perfection**. Sin (6) is made to an end at 7/Ha'Mashiach 13 = 6+7. Ha'Mashiach comes to end sin and bring us into infinity (8) with perfection (7). The number **8 means infinity**

The end was planned from the beginning (Isaiah 46:10). The numbers were SET on a FIXED TIME OF YAH on a FIXED UNMOVABLE FLAT EARTH (Psalms 104:5). No man can change YAH's time nor understand or perceive it! Time created before man. The created will never understand the Creator, YAHUAH Elohiym (Romans 1:20).

Unlocking Bible Mysteries and Hidden Secrets Revealed
IN ADAM ALL DIE
DNA passes down from the father to the children
Because of the sin of our forefather, Adam, we are all born to die and become devils' food. That's why Ha'Mashiach must come in order that we may live again.
Every new birth has the fallen seed of Adam
We all must be born again in the spirit of YAH through Ha'Mashiach. All must complete this spiritual rebirth to see YAH

Most of the atom is empty space. The rest consists of a positively charged nucleus of protons and neutrons surrounded by a cloud of negatively charged elections. Protons, neutrons, and elections seeking to exist and constantly attracting itself to one another in perpetuity.

For human life to occur, it takes a sperm and an egg to come together to light the spark of life and generate kinetic energy that undulates magnetically to create life.

The spiritual energy of a male needs a female human womb to manifest physical life (also keeping in mind that Eve, the first mother, was the first to sin and cause Adam to fall into eternal deadly sin. Adam fell and sinned. He is the father of sinners. Eve is the mother of sinners, which is why **the Son, Ha'Mashiach was created as a prototype before the world was created and concealed.**

YAH made sure that Adam's DNA is not in Ha'Mashiach. Ha'Mashiach is the only person without the DNA of Adam. Therefore, the Father sends the Son to save you. Technically YAH is in heaven (Isaiah 66:1)! YAH will also never birth Himself as a human to be under the laws of a human body and nature. The Creator will never be subject to His creation.

The Father, Yahuah Elohiym simply implanted His spiritual energy seed to the Son of YAH to manifest the fullest connection to Yahuah Elohiym on Earth, therefore Ha'Mashiach is called Elohiym with us [**Isaiah 9:6**].

During the creation of life and birth, the spirit of the father passes on to the child through the womb of a mother. Every human birth has **the seed of fallen Adam. We all do! Everyone except Ha'Mashiach.**

Thus, DNA and its traits, personalities, characteristics, behaviors, etc. passes from Father to child. **The life and sins of the father passes on to the child through the birthing process**. Therefore, the atom always exists and is duplicated into perpetuity. The father lives through the child (so on and so on into eternity/perpetuity).

The spirit of Adam (fallen 1st father) lives on through each new human birth except Ha'Mashiach birth (He was born in heaven and manifested on earth and the only one).

Every time that a human is born, the spiritually fallen state of man is birthed into the world. Therefore, in Adam all die (**1 Corinthians 15:22**). You are born to die.

In a sense, without Ha'Mashiach, you are born just to die (just like Esau), being subjected to a life of sin whereas the wages of sin are death (Romans 6:23). We must all repent and obey Torah (**Matthew 3:2**), so don't go plucking the sore on Esau's eye, when you have a cloud over your own (**Matthew 7:1-5**)!

The Kingdom of Heaven is not made for all. Heaven is made for a few and (**Matthew 7:13-14**) and only the pure in heart shall see Yahuah Elohiym (**Matthew 5:8**).

Being born to die. That's why, Adam and Eve had to be removed from the Garden of Eden and the Tree of Life to avoid conviction into eternal damnation and hell. The Tree of Life will return in the New Kingdom once sin is eliminated.

Speaking electromagnetically, it takes the positive energy and negative energy to come together, "mate" or "know each other", and create balance. The balance, or flat line, is what appears materially and regulates life (Medically speaking, when you flat line, you die or "you see Yahuah Elohiym" as energy is designed to stay in constant motion along a straight endless line {string theory, mathematics, and quantum physics reveals some clues. However, no man will ever solve the mystery of Yahuah Elohiym, let alone Pi}).

We live on a flat Earth. We live on the flat baseline of Earth's electromagnetic energy grid. We are children of the limitless Creator trapped inside a firmament creating life of the flesh (sin).

Unlocking Bible Mysteries and Hidden Secrets Exposed
DNA MANIPULATION OF 5G
Did you know that 5G technology allows scientific access to your DNA? Your DNA is the computer code of your life. It controls everything about you.
By illegally using technology, they seek to remove the image of the Creator, Yahuah Elohiym and artificially produce humans using Artificial Technology (AI to replace nature) with all your lustful and pride-filled personal images, just to your blind liking of low vibrational frequencies!
Keep in mind, there's nothing new under the sun. They have tried this before and failed. They will fail again just as prophecy claims.
It all **starts with an electronic device, such as a cell phone, tablet, or computer and at the drop of a silent and secret button and**

you're changed not even realizing it. Locked into technology. Do you want to live in a computerized environment? Locked in technology forever? Your own Metaverse?
Ever wonder why everyone is giving away 5G phones so freely on massive levels? Free $400- $2,000 smart phones!
Ever wonder why the rich is spending trillions on Metaverse? Buying Real Estate in Artificial Technology! Pouring their wealth into a fake computerized environment! Why is everyone transferring to digital electronic currency?
WHY DO YOU LIVE IN ELECTRONICS AND NOT YAH???

Positive and negative energies produce life. It takes male and female, masculine and feminine to "know each other".

To be clear, Ha'Mashiach is not some alien from outer space, which doesn't even exist. **He was born in heaven and will manifest on Earth as a human, being Elohiym with us and not replacing YAH and not YAH coming flesh.**

Unlocking Bible Mysteries and Hidden Secrets Revealed
Melchizedek
A fun fact to study in this series of works is the mysterious Melchizedek, which sets the heavenly Priesthood. There's no biblical record of his birth or death. The Bible/Cepher is silent about many things concerning him. He was the one who blessed Abraham. He's claimed to be immortal.
Was this a code for Seth? Enoch – the first perfect human? A hidden character?
Stay tuned in this series

Let's examine Ha'Mashiach on another level.

In the beginning, **Yahuah Elohiym created the heavens and the earth**. And the **earth was without form and void**, and **darkness** was upon the **face of the deep**. And the **Spirit of Yahuah Elohiym** moved upon **the face of the waters (Genesis 1:1-2)**.

Because of the fall of man, no man can see Yahuah Elohiym face and live (Exodus 33:20). The light would have to perish to see the darkness within. The light is the Spirit of Yahuah Elohiym.

The spirit is like a light whose switch is turned on. It has an electromagnetic silent illuminating shining of energy and a thought vibrational frequency. The stronger the connection, the brighter the light shines. You ever hear the saying, "it takes a mass of amount of darkness to bring forth the light"? The more darkness, the brighter the light when it shines and illuminates the darkness within.

Unlocking Bible Mysteries and Hidden Secrets Revealed
I AM
I AM THAT I AM A child of darkness Thought so much Became light Birthed in the seas of eternity Journeying the galaxy as Stars Thoughts morphed into matter **I am the Word** Prophetic Thoughts **Product of the original thought form** **Creatures of darkness** **Shining as light forms** Spectacles of light Star Dust Breaking forth from the darkness

Emerging
Into the seas of space

Consciousness
Illuminated thoughts
Having the crystallized experience of life

The illustrations of the voice within

If the darkness
Seized to think
Would the light fail to shine?

Through darkness
Came forth light

Light is the illumination of darkness
The darkness within

I AM THAT I AM
Because the darkness thought
Gian Michael Simmons

Devils are fallen angels in the spirit realm. They see things concerning the spirit. They, too, are light and can see light. They are creatures of illuminating degrees of darkness. **They are a darker form of light, a lower vibrational frequency, further away from the source of light and the original power source (YAH),** the darkness of the face of the deep waters. They are a form of light that is further removed from the Father, YAHUAH ELOHIYM.

Light can always see the light, as well as the darkness within, to an extent as **it is the light that clothes the darkness in form and likeness** (YAH made Adam and Eve **"coats of skin"** after they were **cursed** and **removed** from the Garden of Eden).

The stronger the connection to the power source, the brighter the light shines. This is how **devils (dark faded light**) was able to recognizes the righteous of YAH. Remember, Job was perfect in righteousness. Yet, Satan noticed him. The more righteous, the brighter the light. The devil sees the light and launches an attack to extinguish the light as the darkness seeks to control the light.

It **Matthew 5:14**, **Yahusha challenges us to let our lights shine brightly.** Keeping in mind, devils will perceive you because, being so dark, they will see the light.

Remember in the first chapter of the book of **Job** and the story on Sarah, revealed that **Satan is not locked away in hell (not yet at least his day is coming).** Satan is always busy searching the Earth for the righteous of YAH. He's always on the prowl for his next victim to **TEMPT.**

The devil always seeks to mimic the Creator, Yahuah Elohiym. That's why you must study your Torah and put on the full armor of YAHUAH Elohiym (**Ephesians 6:11**)

Unlocking Bible Mysteries and Hidden Secrets Revealed
THE DEVIL
(a.k.a. Satan, Baphomet, Baal, Enki, Lucifer, Shiva, Christian JESUS, Allah, Krishna, Set, Pan, Saturn, Pope, Mystery Spiritualism YOU, etc.)
There is only one Elohiym and that is YAHUAH Elohiym.
The devil is not an equal to the Creator, Yahuah Elohiym. The devil is not a creator and is subject to the Creator, Yahuah Elohiym (see the **book of Job**) and to the creation.
The devil is not an equal adversary to YAH. Yahuah Elohiym creates the good and the evil.
The devil is a tool used by Yahuah Elohiym. The **devil is not a god and is a fallen angel created by YAH.**
The devil has no power except what YAH allows and what you (the light) give/unplug.
NEVER FEAR THE DEVIL. HE HAS NO POWER!
The only power of the Devil is to TEMP YOU
SHINE THE LIGHT OF YAH ON THE DEVIL
For more about the mystery of the devil and more, stay tuned in this series.

By seeking to mimic the Creator, Yahuah Elohiym, the devil diminishes his light and brings you another form of light to appear as the darkness of the Father (Lucifer, "Light-Bearer", etc.). Thus, **the devil is but a negative light form of darkness**, a lesser form of energy further away from the source, a lower vibrational frequency, an evil and darker form of darkness.

Whereas the darkness of the Creator is love and balanced by the Light of the World, Ha'Mashiach. There is no light source to balance the darkness of the devil's dark faded light. **The devil's light can never be love.**

<u>This may be a very difficult concept to accept and believe or follow.</u> **Which is why faith is the substance of things hoped for and the evidence of things not seen (Hebrews 11:1). John 1:18 teaches us that no man has seen the Father except the Son. No man has seen the Darkness (Genesis 1:1-2) except the Light the Darkness Spoke (Genesis 1:3).** They are one **and the same. Light is the Illuminating WORD of the Darkness (John 1:1-3**).

The following is very important to repeat to study and overstand:

> **Hebrews 12:29** teaches that **Yahuah Elohiym is a consuming fire. Deuteronomy 32:4** teaches us that **Yahuah Elohiym is a Elohiym of Righteousness (PURE LIGHT).**
>
> **Yahuah Elohiym is the Elohiym of the living (Matthew 16:15-16).** Yahuah is patient, not wanting anyone to perish, but everyone to come to repentance **(2 Peter 3).**

Because of man's fallen state and **in Adam we all died,** due to the first sin and DNA passes down from the Father to child (**1 Corinthians 15:22**), one must be purified to be in YAH's presence (**therefore YAH coming to Earth destroys Earth due to fallen states, which is why YAH uses an earthly vessel/avatar (seed of a woman – Genesis 3:15, John 3:16), someone subject to the same law, to communicate and to pave the path for reconciliation back to YAH and to do His Works on Earth**), which is why **YAH set aside the Levites** to be **purified** for **high priestly service to Him**. <u>That's why he chose Ha'Mashiach as His Only Son to be YAH's PURE LIGHT on Earth. He never replaces YAH.</u>

Simply put, if you were to be in YAH's presence in your sinful state, you would die and cease to exist for YAH's righteousness is too bright for darkness.

This helps to explain why you don't see YAH. Seeing Him, in sin, will kill you! You must be born again (John 3:1-21), the Torah (Deuteronomy 28), and only the PURE LIGHT (pure in heart) see's YAH (Matthew 5:8)!

Right now, YAH has us in a protected enclosed incubator. He's still watching our every move!

Death is the only portal to Yahuah Elohiym, even to sight one must kill the flesh and spirit to see Yahuah Elohiym. Which is why **we must be born again of the spirit of YAH (John 2:1-21**).

How can the darkness perceive darkness? Light is but the illumination of the darkness within the darkness that spoke in the beginning. Light is the illuminated thought crystalized.

He is also the **Chief Cornerstone of creation** (**Psalms 118:22**) and without YAH, there is no light (life) as the darkness needs the light for the (darkness) thought (life) to shine and manifest creation.

Light was the first act of creation (**Genesis 1:3**). Once the thought spoke, naturally came forth the Light. **The act of thought and the creation of Light go hand and hand.**

Another way of looking at it is **Darkness is clothed by Light**. This is the natural order unless it's artificially created by computerized programming (Artificial Intelligence).

Unlocking Bible Mysteries and Hidden Secrets Revealed
MYTH OF OVERPOPULATION
Did you know that YAH created the Earth for Israel and not Israel for the Earth? YAH provides all that we need for earthly life. We can never overpopulate Earth, just as we can never deplete Earth's unlimited FREE ENERGY. Population control is another false teaching of Mystery Babylon. We barely inhabit the planet!
YAH did say, BE FRUITFUL AND MULTIPLY!
Earth was made for MANY. Heaven made for a FEW

Unlocking Bible Mysteries and Hidden Secrets Revealed
The EYES
Sight is very complex to understand. We have 2 outer eyes which has little to do with our physical sight other than taking in physical light. It is our brain that tells us what that light looks like.
Inside of everyone's center forehead is the Pineal Gland (spiritual eye/ 3rd eye). This is where all sight is generated/takes place. The light is absorbed by your 2 outer eyes or what I call 2 "black holes". **The blackness in the center of your eye is a magnet that pulls in light.** That's why it's black, just like a magnet. The magnet absorbs the light spectrum, and the perception of that light is synthesized in the Pineal Gland and not by your outer eyes.
All sight occurs with your spiritual eyes. (That's why blind people can still see!) Your pineal gland, then, tells your brain's computer how to perceive (intake) the reception of light. This forms or reveals the images of that light as sight.
That's how I feel a way that demons travel from human to human just by looking at someone, using magnetic energy. They travel by eyesight from black hole (eye) to black hole (eye) from soul to soul from magnet to magnet based upon the vibrational frequencies of the host recipient. So, keep your vibrations high with love and YAH.
This is also why devils don't look into the eyes of righteousness lest they be healed.
EVER WANT TO HEAL A DEMON? IF YOU HAVE A PURE HEART, LOOK INTO THEIR EYES WITH LOVE
Be careful who you look at if you don't have the heart of repentance!

Close your eyes. It's dark when you first close your eyes. It's a dark sea of darkness. It's the spirit of darkness on the face of the deep (Genesis 1:1-3).

Difficult to form a perception until you imagine a thought (**Genesis 1:3**). However, **once you think or an idea pop into your head, it naturally creates light. Let there be Light**. This is an automatic instant event.

The act of thinking creates a form of light. This happens because when you think, you create a light vibration. This is what manifests creation, the manifestation and creation of your thought. **Without a thought, there is no light. Without light, there is no life.**

The illumination of light is called life.

There is no light as light is the illumination of thought. That's why Light was the first act of creation and will always be.

This is also why the Father (Primordial Darkness/Thought) and Son (Light/Thought in Creation) are One (Illumination of Thought). **The light is the thought that clothes and expresses the darkness.** All are one and the same reflection. **Thus, Ha'Mashiach is One with YAHUAH Elohiym, The Father and Son are One (John 10:30).**

Unlocking Bible Mysteries and Hidden Secrets Revealed
AI – ARTIFICIAL TECHNOLOGY
The enemy is trying to outsmart the Creator. **They seek to replace the Creator (Yahuah Elohiym), with Artificial Technology (Science) and replace your brain computer (Ha'Mashiach/TORAH) with programmed algorithms (Mathematics).**

Think about the Matrix movies, which were all written by a black woman (Unlocking Bible Mysteries and Hidden Secrets Revealed).

To do this, they must stop you from thinking. That's why scientist and governments have been studying you and learning everything there is to know about you. They get educated by you with things such as technology, social media, financial accounts, emails, interviewing, records, questionnaires, studying habits, personality, your track record, paying off your loved ones, and surveys, and more. They keep you busy and distracted by oppressing you.

Unlocking Bible Mysteries and Hidden Secrets Revealed
ILLEGAL – SECRET HUMAN IMPLANTS
Did you know? The majority all people are already government implanted with a rice sized computer chip. The government knows where you are, what you are doing, and what you are always saying.

All medical professionals take a medical oath of secrecy by penalty of death. All FRATS and Freemasons take this very same secret oath to hide the identity of the Children of YAH and Creator, Yahuah Elohiym.
All educators and elected officials take this same oath of secrecy on penalty of death. That's why every black leader, teacher, and celebrity has sold us out. That's why YAH must get us HIMSELF!
Because they get paid to hide your history and Creator for instant gratification and they throw it in your face with things such as Hip Hop and Entertainment behind extremely coded language! And YOU BUY THE SINFUL SHAME! BLASPHEMY
Freemason Secret: They have been building inside our hollow flat-Earth since the Noah flood. **They have entire cities underground. THIS PROVES A FLAT EARTH.** (this is work every member must do) and they feel they can hide from YAH. They can get anywhere underground from all over the world within minutes with hidden free energy sciences. Some misinterpret this verse to be an unfulfilled prophecy.
WHY DO WE PAY FOR FREE ENERGY USING ELECTRICTY FOR ENERGY WHEN EARTH GIVES UNLIMITED IT FREE?
Ever wonder why a black man named NIKOLA TESLA was MURDERED. Robbed by JP Morgan and Trump ancestors. Science stolen by Thomas Edison! The BLACK Albert EINSTEIN! Is TESLA BLACK TOO?
THE EARTH PROVIDES UNLIMITED FREE ENERGY
WE ARE ILLEGALLY GETTING ROBBED and DESTROYING EARTH with ELECTRICITY and OIL/FUEL

Unlocking Bible Mysteries and Hidden Secrets Revealed
MOST MEDICINE IS SECRETLY SNAKE VENOM
Remember, Yahusha warns against taking oaths from man in **James 5:12**. Prime example are those in the **medical industry who secretly pledge to a demonic deity/serpent god. This is the mystery behind the Caudex medical sign of Hermes. Their LOGO, a snake around an electromagnetic pole! They show you a demon in your face every time you visit a medical facility or professional.** It's on their chest AND IN THEIR LOGO.

An extremely hidden horrible secret is that all medicine originated from ancient mystery Egypt. They worshipped the snake. MEDICINE IS nothing but SNAKE VENOM.
This is an extremely hidden secret that no one will tell you. They are manipulating snake venom in medicine in worship to their snake serpent god.
That's why cancer drugs will never cure you. That's why no one ever gets cured from sickness. You spend a lifetime taking the seed of the devil through medicine.
They don't even use nature for drugs/medicine. Nature will heal you naturally.
NO MAN DRUG/NO MAN MEDICINE WILL OR CAN EVER CURE YOU. ONLY NATURE and YAH
DID YOU KNOW THAT FASTING HEALS MORE THAN DRUGS, including CANCER!
If you take care of your health, you can never get sick!
ALL VACCINES KILL AND CHANGE DNA CODE
ANOTHER MARK OF THE BEAST (VACCINES)
Aside from this. **They secretly chip every person on the planet with rice-sized and very difficult to detect, computers. You don't even feel it because it's so small, microscopic.**
They even have access to remotely read your mind as you THINK AND CHANGE YOUR THOUGHTS instantly in REAL TIME.
Basically, they can turn you into a robot and you don't even notice it. Research Edward Snowden and whistleblowers. This is above top-secret information.
Revelations from the Highest, Yahuah Elohiym

They know more about you than you know about yourself. They have been preparing an artificial reality for you. They want to artificially replace your perceived thoughts with computer trapped minds. **They want to stop you from thinking and to accept their programmed thoughts without thinking.**

They must stop you from thinking for the deception to be successful and seamless string theorizing in quantum sciences trying to be Pi.

<u>They want to replace "YOU' with a "computerized you" and they need to clone (duplicate/replica) the system (thoughts and natural life) so you won't even notice the change or swap (into technology/computerized life).</u>

This is the science behind stopping you from thinking.

The thinking naturally meditates upon the astral Father (Primordial Darkness of YAH), which naturally produces Ha'Mashiach the Light of the World and First Act of Creation (Gen 1:3) a.k.a. Salvation.

They want to replace the Father Creator, Yahuah Elohiym. To do that, they must replace the Son, Ha'Mashiach. That's why they need you to reject Ha'Mashiach and Torah.

Rejecting the Son, Light of the World, Ha'Mashiach is the same as rejecting the Father Creator, Yahuah Elohiym as the Father and Son are One. That's like rejecting and denying yourself and your only salvation!

They seek to have the AntiMashiach (Pope and Technology) replace the Son, Ha'Mashiach, backed by artificially intelligent created humans' technology (**Transhumanism**).

That's why they flood us with technology. They must get you used to **being locked away in technology and lost in time**. They want you comfortable living in an **artificially computer programmed reality without thinking (Think about the game Sims).**

That's why we live on our phones and electronic devices. The money god has you. Now, **the computer has become your god.**

You spend more time out of life (stuck in technology) than you do in life (with Yahuah Elohiym and Ha'Mashiach/ the Torah).

We spend little to no real time with the Creator of Life, Yahuah Elohiym (Genesis 1:26, Genesis 2:7) in fasting and prayers. Which is why we spend no time creating the things of YAH. But we're constantly being created by artificial intelligence and the devil.

This is the real reason why social media was created as it wasn't created for your benefit. That's why Facebook, Apple, and Microsoft were financed by the big global banks. **The same banks that hide free energy and secret sciences**. Watch what these big banks do! Because **society creates an artificial culture that elevates their artificially controlled puppet human celebrities**.

In secret societies, they sell you the concept of becoming as a god. Then, they create a name, brand, and image of that celebrity. They create a god personage. Then, they launch their attacks on you to steal your energy and resources. They indoctrinate you into their false religion, masked by their shine. Then, they teach you their word and law (products), which means you must closely follow, become a consumer, a missionary brand ambassador, recruit, and elevate a false god by spreading the "go-spell". Then, you mimic them!

Even your "mega-church" bishop or pastor, that's an image of a created god that they are selling you. Bishops are from Mystery Babylon not Israel. Another false prophet. They are all FREEMASONS; the ENTIRE CHURCH was started by Freemasons (C.O.G.I.C.)! And, we know Freemasons are backed by the Illuminati, the same Illuminati that started the NAACP and Nation of Islam. All headquartered in Rome.

So, now you have a **false prophet**. Their products and merchandise become your **"mark of the beast". Mystery Babylon is secretly involved in all aspects and activities of daily life and in every industry.**

Secretly, many celebrities and world leaders are possessed by demons and have "handlers" to control their puppets.

Black celebrities don't even control their wealth or anything they say or do. It's all for imagery to sell a myth and an agenda. They are ALL BROKE and CONTROLLED BY THEIR MASTER SATAN.

Why don't you think they never came together to save us? Why do think Civil Rights sold us out from going back to Africa, when we were united as a people and free? It's Because that's the nature of the beast even though you've made a god out of them and spent your livelihood financing your fallen gods ("Celebritics"). They can never be Ha'Mashiach and save you. **They are always spiritually and financially broke, regardless of what FORBES says, and in league with Satan.**

That's why they're always human blood sacrificing. **BLOOD THIRSTY SAVAGES always on the prowl, like Satan, constantly stealing energy!**

They always need a recharge of energy because they can't even hold water. That's why you can **NEVER TRUST a DEVIL!**

STOP LETTING RIVERS OF LIFE RUN DRY!

Now, The West rapper is your fallen god that throws your history in your face just as if he's a child of Esau-Rome that silenced a loving mother for a demonic payday, chasing a white devil, for fashion and fame, like many of you.

HEY, has you dying to be unacceptable white chasing your white devil in a red dress! If you're that desperate for lyrics, I can give you some **uplifting** free hot lines directly **from and for heaven**, in silence. I'll only speak to you. YAH has something for your "**Strange Fruits**". Maybe that's why Jesus Walks.

It won't even be funny! **Always remember, how you're destroying our own Black youth and blasphemy! Just like every Black so-called- leader out of "kill a black "and "sellout" Chicago! Repent**

Even the BLACK MUSLIMS KNOW WE ARE ISRAEL, and they HIDE YOU BEHIND FALSE ISLAM, WHICH IS ROME and MYSTERY BABYLON! Same with EGYPTIAN MYSTERY SCHOOLS AND MAGIC. ALL MYSTERY BABYLON. Why do you think they killed Malcolm? He figured it out!

The only reason I call poetically is to get you to repent for violating Israel! Give you a chance to repent before YAH COMES. That's how I LOVE TO GIVE A CHANCE TO BE SAVED. That's why I must search out your sins, in love and righteousness with the spirit of truth. So, you can REPENT.

Hey, You are not Esau and Esau cannot save you and will never accept you. Esau will only deceive you! For Salvation is free with YAH if you REPENT. OBEY TORAH. DEPART FROM EVIL. Return to LOVE. LET MY PEOPLE GO TO YAH.

They use celebrities, entertainers, educators, leaders, power, and religion to blindly usher you into a fallen matrix computer programmed and controlled by **artificial intelligence and a demon. They have created a beast that they can't even control. Many are AFRAID OF WHAT they tapped into! Even demons crying for YAH, it's that bad!**

They need you to forget about the true source, YAHUAH Elohiym. The only way to manifest this is by getting you to stop thinking and to reject the Ha'Mashiach and Torah.. Which is silly because salvation is free in Ha'Mashiach, IF YOU REPENT, DEPART FROM EVIL, OBEY TORAH/LAW = ETERNAL LIFE/ FREE SALVATION FROM THE CREATOR, YAHUAH Elohiym Courtesy of Ha'Mashiach

Unlocking Bible Mysteries and Hidden Secrets Revealed
FASTING and MEDITATION ON THE WORD OF YAH
There is POWER in fasting, reading the Torah, and meditating on YAH's Word.
FASTING CURES MORE THAN MAN's MEDICINE
FASTING CAN CURE CANCER and ALL DISEASES!
FASTING OPENS SPIRITUAL EYES to YAH
When you close your eyes and connect, in like-minded thought (righteousness), with the Father in silence (natural darkness), you bring forth Ha'Mashiach (The Torah and Light of the World and Salvation). You connect with POWER!
That's why Christians don't want you meditating or thinking. **That's why they keep you busy all day chasing sin.**

They don't want you to know YAH. They need you to blindly accept their demon god, white Jesus, or some other fallen deity.
BEGIN TO FAST ON YOUR HEALING AND CALL YAH

The enemy's final act of deception is an attempt to lock you away, in technology, and throw away the keys, artificial technology/quantum physics controlled by demons.

This is one of the secrets behind COVID and 5G, their last attempt to_rewrite your DNA code. Their attempt at the **"Great Reset"** before the 2nd Exodus and Coming of Ha'Mashiach. That's why they are distracting the world with the Russian crisis and whatever else they can produce through their Hollywood-like secret government show called life. **Most importantly, they are trying to play out the false book of Revelations.** These are not accurate to Hebrews. If anyone would like a good research study on the Book of Revelations and its deceptions, read "The Apocalypse Deception" by Fred Harding. He does a good job summing up the research. Any one of Dr. Beneyah Yashar'el books will enlighten you. Even Moses Farrar, Hebrew historian. Or any Tanakh book.

This is another reason why they built a culture and LAWS based upon feminine homosexual energy and chaos. Think about the NBA or NFL back in the 70s and 80s. Nowadays, professional athletes look prettier than models and all the males are built to have a homosexual physical appearance. They want you looking up to gays, feeling like they're equals, idolizing, and wanting to be like them. That's why gays run the world. That's why they made Hip Hop GAY! EVERY RAPPER HAS DONE SOMETHING GAY! HEY! REPENT.

Here's what people do for the cost of fashion and fame: **All secret societies must do secret gay rituals. That's why Hip Hop is so gay.**

They sell you a fake hard image and they're soft in the real streets. They are **married to beards (female imposters as wives),** have **fake families** for **appearance sakes of scripted reality TV playing in real life**, and they are **closet case homosexuals living lives as demons. This is in many industries in life and all industries that have high income earnings. This may shock you.** Demons in human bodies. Possessed. Gays are how TP got a tranny ma dea.

Unlocking Bible Mysteries and Hidden Secrets Revealed
DANIEL PROPECHY – DANIEL 2,3,9
Daniel prayed to YAH to reveal YAH's plan for salvation to Israel. He had several visions and revelations. He had an image of a statue revealing the 4 kingdoms that would rule before the coming of YAH's Kingdom on Earth.
We are living with the 4th beast, which is the last beast, which is Esau-Rome. Prophecy also states the feet of the statue are mixed with **iron (Esau-Rome)** and **clay (Israel) at this time (last 2,000 years).**
That's why many of Israel have sold out to the enemy. However, because **iron and clay don't mix, the statue will fall.**
CLAY represent the FATHER/Potter and IRON is the DEVIL
PROPHECY PROCLAIMS THE END FROM THE BEGINNING
ISRAEL MUST COME OUT OF MYSTERY BABYLON
Ezekiel 37 Great Hebrew Awakening

Sadly, for Israel, most successful blacks you see either perform secret homosexual rituals, human-blood sacrifices, child trafficking, child slavery, cannibalism, or bestiality. They are doing horrible things. **They make a deal with Satan for instant gratification.**

Many black Hollywood entertainers are active human cannibals and blood thirsty. They kill and eat human babies for the energy a baby releases. They even eat human brains and hearts!

If you ever want to blow your mind, google a picture of the pope. Look how blood thirsty he looks. Look into his eyes and see Satan.

This is the artificially controlled world they want to create, a demonic world of hell, that you don't even notice you're at war. You confuse war for peace. **Nowadays, we call war peace because the governments have been silently and secretively at war against us for centuries.**

They still want the ability to manifest a creation. They don't want to die. They require some form of "life". They still need to manifest some form of creation. They just want to get rid of the Natural Light.

Ha'Mashiach is the Light of the World. Ha'Mashiach is also the Torah/Law of Yahuah Elohiym a.k.a. Salvation.

By studying your Torah, you bring the Creator to life.

This is the job of the Son to **return the hearts of the children to their Father Creator, Yahuah Elohiym (Malachi 4:6).**

<u>This will be events like you never seen or heard of before.</u> **The 2nd Exodus. IT'S FREEDOM TIME. HEAVEN ON EARTH WITH YAH.**

THE DAY OF ATONEMENT, when Earth RETURNS to its OWNER! Our Day of Atonement this year is October 4, 2022, watch closely! Don't just watch, get Saved Now and REPENT. Learn and Obey Torah. COME OUT OF MYSTERY BABYLON.

Read about the coming of Ha'Mashiach in the books of Isaiah, Ezra, Enoch, Ezekiel, Jeremiah, Enoch, Jubilees, Torah, Malachi, Zechariah, and Baruch.

I'll leave you with a few scriptures: 2 Chronicles 7:14, Isaiah 52:15, Isaiah 58:1, Isaiah 61

Section closing

The great mystery of man is solved. The man named Yahusha (a.k.a. Jesus) was an actual person that came and focused his ministries on the dispersed Hebrews. The Hebrews were suffering Deuteronomy curses and living during the birth of the church age, a church that was all criminal and not the ways of YAH (Enoch 93). Furthermore, Israel was experiencing the curse of deep sleep (Isaiah 29:10) and this curse ends at the coming of the Ha'Mashiach (Enoch 93). If you study the words of Yahusha (a.k.a. Jesus), you will discover that he only spoke to the lost tribe of Israel (Matthew 15:24). Rome killed him and made a Elohiym (a.k.a. God) of him. Twisting his teachings. Yahusa (Jesus) wouldn't even accept Christianity!

Although one can argue that Yahusha (a.k.a. Jesus) did the works that was expected of Ha'Mashiach (a.k.a. Messiah), Yahusha (a.k.a. Jesus) never admitted or claimed that he was Ha'Mashiach (a.k.a. Messiah) or Son of YAH. In fact, when asked the question, he always reverted it back to another party to answer rather than answering himself with a simple confirmation of an affirmative yes. We revealed that Yahusha (a.k.a. Jesus) lived during a time of many magicians and Yahusha (a.k.a. Jesus) was trained in Egypt, in magic at the same Egyptian mystery magic schools as all pagans. Furthermore, we revealed that the story of Yahusha (a.k.a. Jesus) is the same life story as many other pagans' centuries before his birth. Additionally, we revealed that the cult of Serapis, Zeus, Adonis, Baal, Mithra, Krishna, Hesus, Horus, etc. were all merged into the cult of Yahusha (a.k.a. Jesus).

Lastly, we revealed that YAH spoke the end from the beginning and YAH only dealt with Hebrew prophets. The Jeremiah new covenant was never sanctioned by YAH and this prophecy remains unfulfilled despite what Rome and Christians claim. The New Testament are a combination of forgery of Old Testament writers and a mixture of paganism (Mystery Babylon). The New Testament is a false prophet that preaches a new gospel which claims that Yahusha (a.k.a. Jesus) is Elohiym (a.k.a. God), that the name of Yahusha (a.k.a. Jesus) is one with YAH and saves, and that people could do away with the Moses Torah Law and gain salvation. These are all false teachings and a contradiction to the Torah Law of YAH and Old Testament Hebrew writers.

Yahusha (a.k.a. Jesus) taught a ministry. Yet, he did not author any books. Many, if not all, his sayings were from Hebrew writers such as Enoch, Daniel, and Isaiah. During the life of Yahusha (a.k.a. Jesus), many experienced deaths by crucifixion. Yahusha (a.k.a. Jesus) dying by the cross was no different than the many Hebrews who died by the cross of Rome. Yahusha (a.k.a. Jesus) charge was for the claims of him being the Son of YAH. A claim that **few** made, and he never confirmed nor denied. He may have thought that he was the Ha'Mashiach, but he never received any confirmation from YAH that he was Ha'Mashiach. Therefore, at the cross, Yahusha says, Father why have thou forsaken me (**Matthew 27:46**). A person whose mission was alleged to come to die, must've known that he was going to die, yet he felt YAH had forsaken him. Why is that? **Deuteronomy 18:17-20** provides the answer.

> **But any prophet who speaks in the name of other gods or presumes to speak in my name a word that I have not commanded the prophet to speak that prophet shall die" (Deuteronomy 18:17-20).**

Yahusha (a.k.a. Jesus) was not Ha'Mashiach (a.k.a. Messiah), nor was he the Son of YAH. After Yahusha (a.k.a. Jesus) death, there remained over 500 unfulfilled prophecies regarding Ha'Mashiach (a.k.a. Messiah).

As we revealed in **Enoch 62**, the Son of YAH (Ha'Mashiach) was created before the foundations of the world, concealed to protect the holy seed (**Gen 3:15**), and will appear at the end of the Gentile world to bring about eternal judgment and the Kingdom of YAH on Earth. Ha'Mashiach will also fulfill **Jeremiah 31 new covenant prophecy.**

Thus, bringing us back to my **mystery challenge** that I stated in the beginning of this discourse. Fact remains, we are at the end of the Gentile world, and nothing remains to hinder the coming of Ha'Mashiach. Sin has reached its fulfillment and only eternal judgement remains. YAH has spoken. We know that Ha'Mashiach will be born of the seed of a woman (**Gen 3:15**) and a Hebrew virgin (young maid).

We know that he would be all righteousness as he was created before this fallen world of sin and the keeper of righteousness (**Enoch 62**). By being born of a woman, we know that he would be born under the same laws of a human body. Additionally, we know that he would be a suffering servant being bruised for the iniquities, chastisements, infirmities, and sins of Israel. We know that he would suffer because of his righteousness. He would experience the sins of Israel which are contrary to his righteousness. A person of perfect righteousness that would be forced to carry the sins of Israel. He would be forced to experience all levels and aspects of human life. To save Israel, he would have to wear their sins in order to show them how to remove them.

We know that he would be forced away from the land of the living (meaning social world and not physical world Christians' claim). We know that friends, family, and society will turn their backs on him. We know that he will be betrayed by a best friend. We also know that he would suffer a wound on his side. He would be bruised, and it would be pleasing to YAH. We also know that YAH would personally keep his creature and no weapon formed against him could prosper. We know that he will be in the world and the world will perceive him not.

A suffering servant that's hidden in our midst, in the world that perceives him not. We know that when the trumpets sound, the powers of heaven were shaken as the Ha'Mashiach treads the winepress alone. The Ha'Mashiach broke the chains and read the books that were sealed in the heavens. The Ha'Mashiach prophesizes over the spiritual valley of Israel's dry bones and revives a dead nation. The nation of Israel is reawakened by the true knowledge of YAH and the 12 Tribes of Israel are regathered and taken back to the Promised Land for the kingdom of YAH on Earth. This suffering servant that rises to destroy the kings of the land and return all things back to YAH.

This is **not** Yahusha (a.k.a. Jesus). This is the coming of Ha'Mashiach. In the next section, we will learn what Ha'Mashiach will do at his coming.

Unlocking Bible Mysteries and Hidden Secrets Revealed
THE SACRIFICE OF YAHUSHA (A.K.A. JESUS)
If you haven't come to understand by now, Yahusha (a.k.a. Jesus) was not the Son of YAH or the Ha'Mashiach. Additionally, ALL SCRIPTURES pertaining to the COMING OF HAMASHIACH are for END OF THIS AGE. Yahusha (a.k.a. Jesus) was not the sacrificial lamb of YAH. In Jubilees 18:12. YAH provided a replacement for Abraham to fulfill the requirements. Yahusha (a.k.a. Jesus) was a man that they turned into a Elohiym (a.k.a. God). There was NO NEED for a sacrifice to be made for Israel as ALL ISRAEL WILL BE SAVED PER SCRIPTURES. Which reveals ANOTHER FALSE TEACHING OF CHRISTIANITY. You cannot be saved by believing in Yahusha (a.k.a. Jesus). By doing so, you will die just as Yahusha (a.k.a. Jesus). Yahusha (a.k.a. Jesus) is another pagan god that cannot save you. Also, be careful of speaking in tongues as Elijah nor Elisha spoke in tongues and they both had the Ruach Ha'Qodesh (a.k.a. Holy Ghost) long before the New Testament.
Israel will be saved for Abraham sakes, and the TORAH LAW will be written in our inner parts to fulfill the Jeremiah 31 prophecy.

SOMETIMES

Life creates for you a double
If you don't study
Closely
There can be trouble

To know is to love
Difficult loving what you don't understand
Leaving us with many questions
Who is this man?

To some
He's good
To others
He's bad

Conflicting views
You been had

That's like
When I die
Them making a god of me
Free you from Christianity

Just because
You stop thinking
Doesn't mean
It's not there

Drying
Wet Thoughts
To abandon fear

Escaping the truth
Are you really thinking clear?

Never stop thinking
Even when you fear

THE TRUTH

Ha'Mashiach of Israel (a.k.a. Messiah)

UNLOCKING SECRETS OF COMING OF HA'MASHIACH

Unlocking Bible Mysteries and Hidden Secrets Revealed
REMAINING PROPHECIES - 2ND EXODUS REVIEW
(print for your knowledge of today's times – what to expect)
Did you know? The Ha'Mashiach's role is to reconquer Earth and bring the children of Israel back to the Promised Land, with a Mighty Hand, for "heaven on Earth" while we're still alive (This means our generation. US!). To establish Yahuah Elohiym's Kingdom of heaven on Earth (not some Mystery Babylon teaching of a heaven in the sky).
This will be the Second Exodus and will be unlike any event ever in our history!
The 12 Tribes of Israel will be gathered from the four corners of Earth for one final Exodus back to the Promised Land. Israel will rule the entire world again.
The world will serve Yahuah Elohiym and pay reparations. Non-Israelites who repent and walk in righteousness can be saved. All will submit to Israel, who will submit to Yahuah Elohiym.
All nations that commit(ted) against Israel and those who don't submit will perish. Babylon will fall!
This is the only true "last days Bible prophecy" that Esau-Rome Mystery Babylon (Christianity, Catholicism, Islam, Spiritualists, etc.) doesn't want you to know!
This is Scriptures Confirming Scriptures for the Full Image of Yahuah Elohiym's Salvation Plan from the foundation of the world.
For the 2nd Exodus, some of the miracles of YAH will be:
• Take the world by surprise, as no one would see it coming nor expect the appearance of Ha'Mashiach (Remember the "Days of Noah" and "Days of Lot" are warning signs for the Coming of Mashiach
• Regather the children of Israel from every dispersed land "Egypt-bondage houses all around Earth" (black, brown, and yellow)

• Smite the waters (dry the waters) and produce walkways on the waters, leading from every continent back to the Promised Land. (think Red Sea)
• The Vial and Bowl Judgements of Revelations (see Revelations 16: 2-21) AND SIGNS AND WONDERS
The Book of Revelations can only be understood within the additional context of the Torah (Isaiah, Esdras, Daniel, Enoch, Jubilees, Baruch, etc.) whereas the Word of YAH is confirmed out the mouths of 2-3 witnesses (2 Corinthians 13:1). Furthermore, no prophecy ever hinges upon a sole prophet, whereas each prophet has a piece of the story and never the entire story except the Son of Elohiym. You must piece the puzzle together, from different witnesses (Bible books) to see the entire picture
As a standalone "last day" prophecy, Revelations becomes a mystery teaching from Mystery Babylon to reproduce a Tribulation that has already been fulfilled for the last 2,000 years.
You already have the Mark of the Beast and don't even realize it. It's called Christianity, Islam, Catholicism – All the products of Esau-Rome, The Antichrist Pope
Study the books of Isaiah, Ezekiel, all the books of Esdras and Baruch. Stay tuned in this series! Become a free member at www.gianmichaelsimmons.com
Fast and pray and Use your Third Eye!
CALL ON YAH

COMING OF HA'MASHIACH SCRIPTURE REFERENCES

ENOCH 104:10-13

104:10 "And now I know this mystery: For they the **sinners shall alter** the just verdict and many sinners will take it to heart; **they will speak evil words and lie**, and **they will invent fictitious stories and write out my Scriptures on the basis of their own words.**"

104:11 "And would that they had written down all the words truthfully on the basis of their own speech, and neither alter nor take away from my words, all of which I testify to them from the beginning!"

104:12 "Again know **another mystery! That to the righteous and the wise shall be given the Scriptures of joy, for truth and great wisdom.**"

104:13 "So to them shall be given the Scriptures; and they shall believe them and be glad in them; and all the righteous ones who learn from them the Ways of Truth shall rejoice. **(Enoch 104:10-13)**

30 And it shall come to pass after these things, **when the time of the advent of Ha'Mashiach is fulfilled, that he shall return in glory.** 2 Then all who have fallen asleep in hope of him shall rise again. And it shall come to pass at that time that the treasuries will be opened in which is preserved the number of the souls of the righteous, and they shall come forth, and a multitude of souls shall be seen together in one assemblage of one thought, and the first shall rejoice and the last shall not be grieved. 3 For they know that the time has come of which it is said that it is the consummation of the times. 4 But the souls of the wicked, when they behold all these things, shall then waste away **(2 Baruch 30-1:4)**

32 But as for you, if ye prepare your hearts, so as to sow in them the fruits of the Torah, it shall protect you in that time in which El Elohiym is to shake the whole creation **(2 Baruch 32).**

74 And it shall come to pass in those days that the reapers shall not grow weary, nor those that build be toil worn; for the works shall of themselves speedily advance together with those who do them in much tranquility. For that time is the consummation of that which is corruptible, and the beginning of that which is not corruptible. 3 Therefore, those things which were predicted shall belong to it: therefore, it is far away from evils, and near to those things which do not die. 4 This is the bright lightning which came after the last dark waters **(2 Baruch 74:1-3).**

19 And after these things I heard a great voice of much people in heaven, saying, Alleluia; Salvation, and glory, and honour, and power, unto YAHUAH Elohiym:

[2] For true and righteous are his judgments: for he hath judged the great whore, which did corrupt the earth with her fornication, and hath avenged the blood of his servants at her hand **(Revelations 19:1-2**).

[11] And I saw heaven opened and behold a white horse; and he that sat upon him was called Faithful and True, and in righteousness he doth judge and make war.

[12] His eyes were as a flame of fire, and on his head were many crowns; and he had a name written, that no man knew, but he himself.

[13] And he was clothed with a vesture dipped in blood: and his name is called The Word of YAHUAH Elohiym.

[14] And the armies which were in heaven followed him upon white horses, clothed in fine linen, white and clean.

[15] And out of his mouth goeth a sharp sword, that with it he should smite the nations: and he shall rule them with a rod of iron: and he treadeth the winepress of the fierceness and wrath of YAHUAH Elohiym.

[16] And he hath on his vesture and on his thigh a name written, King Of Kings, And Elohiym of Elohiym **(Revelations 19:11 -16).**

25 This is the meaning of the vision: Whereas you saw a man coming up from the midst of the sea: 26 The same is he whom El Elyon has kept a great season, which by his own self shall deliver his creature: and he shall order them that are left behind. 27 And whereas you saw, that out of his mouth there came as a blast of wind, and fire, and storm; 28 And that he held neither sword, nor any instrument of war, but that the rushing in of him destroyed the whole multitude that came to subdue him; this is the interpretation: 29 Behold, the days come, when El Elyon will begin to deliver them that are upon the earth. 30 And he shall come to the astonishment of them that dwell on the earth. 31 And one shall undertake to fight against another, one city against another, one place against another, one people against another, and one realm against another. 32 And the time shall be when these things shall come to pass, and the signs shall happen which I showed you before, and then shall my Son be declared, whom you saw as a man ascending **(4 Ezra/2 Esdras 13:26-32).**

[17] But Israel shall be saved in the Lord with an everlasting salvation: ye shall not be ashamed nor confounded world without end (**Isaiah 45:17**).

[11] I, even I, am the Lord; and beside me there is no saviour (**Isaiah 43:11**).

[9] Thou whom I have taken from the ends of the earth, and called thee from the chief men thereof, and said unto thee, Thou art my servant; I have chosen thee, and not cast thee away (**Isaiah 41:9**).

14 For the Lord will have mercy on Jacob, and will yet choose Israel, and set them in their own land: and the strangers shall be joined with them, and they shall cleave to the house of Jacob.

[2] And the people shall take them, and bring them to their place: and the house of Israel shall possess them in the land of the Lord for servants and handmaids: and they shall take them captives, whose captives they were; and they shall rule over their oppressors.

[3] And it shall come to pass in the day that the Lord shall give thee rest from thy sorrow, and from thy fear, and from the hard bondage wherein thou wast made to serve,

[4] That thou shalt take up this proverb against the king of Babylon, and say, How hath the oppressor ceased! the golden city ceased!

[5] The Lord hath broken the staff of the wicked, and the sceptre of the rulers.

[6] He who smote the people in wrath with a continual stroke, he that ruled the nations in anger, is persecuted, and none hindereth.

[7] The whole earth is at rest, and is quiet: they break forth into singing (**Isaiah 14:1-7**).

[11] For thus saith the Lord God; Behold, I, even I, will both search my sheep, and seek them out (**Ezekiel 34:11**).

3 Behold, I will send my messenger, and he shall prepare the way before me: and the Lord, whom ye seek, shall suddenly come to his temple, even the messenger of the covenant, whom ye delight in: behold, he shall come, saith the Lord of hosts.

[2] But who may abide the day of his coming? and who shall stand when he appeareth? for he is like a refiner's fire, and like fullers' soap:

[3] And he shall sit as a refiner and purifier of silver: and he shall purify the sons of Levi, and purge them as gold and silver, that they may offer unto the Lord an offering in righteousness.

[4] Then shall the offering of Judah and Jerusalem be pleasant unto the Lord, as in the days of old, and as in former years.

[5] And I will come near to you to judgment; and I will be a swift witness against the sorcerers, and against the adulterers, and against false swearers, and against those that oppress the hireling in his wages, the widow, and the fatherless, and that turn aside the stranger from his right, and fear not me, saith the Lord of hosts.

[6] For I am the Lord, I change not; therefore ye sons of Jacob are not consumed (**Malachi 3:1-6**).

The hand of the Lord was upon me, and carried me out in the spirit of the Lord, and set me down in the midst of the valley which was full of bones,

[2] And caused me to pass by them round about: and, behold, there were very many in the open valley; and, lo, they were very dry.

[3] And he said unto me, Son of man, can these bones live? And I answered, O Lord God, thou knowest.

[4] Again he said unto me, Prophesy upon these bones, and say unto them, O ye dry bones, hear the word of the Lord.

[5] Thus saith the Lord God unto these bones; Behold, I will cause breath to enter into you, and ye shall live:

[6] And I will lay sinews upon you, and will bring up flesh upon you, and cover you with skin, and put breath in you, and ye shall live; and ye shall know that I am the Lord.

[7] So I prophesied as I was commanded: and as I prophesied, there was a noise, and behold a shaking, and the bones came together, bone to his bone.

[8] And when I beheld, lo, the sinews and the flesh came up upon them, and the skin covered them above: but there was no breath in them.

[9] Then said he unto me, Prophesy unto the wind, prophesy, son of man, and say to the wind, Thus saith the Lord God; Come from the four winds, O breath, and breathe upon these slain, that they may live.

[10] So I prophesied as he commanded me, and the breath came into them, and they lived, and stood up upon their feet, an exceeding great army.

[11] Then he said unto me, Son of man, these bones are the whole house of Israel: behold, they say, Our bones are dried, and our hope is lost: we are cut off for our parts.

[12] Therefore prophesy and say unto them, Thus saith the Lord God; Behold, O my people, I will open your graves, and cause you to come up out of your graves, and bring you into the land of Israel.

[13] And ye shall know that I am the Lord, when I have opened your graves, O my people, and brought you up out of your graves,

[14] And shall put my spirit in you, and ye shall live, and I shall place you in your own land: then shall ye know that I the Lord have spoken it, and performed it, saith the Lord.

[15] The word of the Lord came again unto me, saying,

[16] Moreover, thou son of man, take thee one stick, and write upon it, For Judah, and for the children of Israel his companions: then take another stick, and write upon it, For Joseph, the stick of Ephraim and for all the house of Israel his companions:

[17] And join them one to another into one stick; and they shall become one in thine hand.

[18] And when the children of thy people shall speak unto thee, saying, Wilt thou not shew us what thou meanest by these?

[19] Say unto them, Thus saith the Lord God; Behold, I will take the stick of Joseph, which is in the hand of Ephraim, and the tribes of Israel his fellows, and will put them with him, even with the stick of Judah, and make them one stick, and they shall be one in mine hand.

[20] And the sticks whereon thou writest shall be in thine hand before their eyes.

[21] And say unto them, Thus saith the Lord God; Behold, I will take the children of Israel from among the heathen, whither they be gone, and will gather them on every side, and bring them into their own land:

[22] And I will make them one nation in the land upon the mountains of Israel; and one king shall be king to them all: and they shall be no more two nations, neither shall they be divided into two kingdoms any more at all.

[23] Neither shall they defile themselves any more with their idols, nor with their detestable things, nor with any of their transgressions: but I will save them out of all their dwellingplaces, wherein they have sinned, and will cleanse them: so shall they be my people, and I will be their God.

[24] And David my servant shall be king over them; and they all shall have one shepherd: they shall also walk in my judgments, and observe my statutes, and do them.

[25] And they shall dwell in the land that I have given unto Jacob my servant, wherein your fathers have dwelt; and they shall dwell therein, even they, and their children, and their children's children for ever: and my servant David shall be their prince for ever.

[26] Moreover I will make a covenant of peace with them; it shall be an everlasting covenant with them: and I will place them, and multiply them, and will set my sanctuary in the midst of them for evermore.

[27] My tabernacle also shall be with them: yea, I will be their God, and they shall be my people.

[28] And the heathen shall know that I the Lord do sanctify Israel, when my sanctuary shall be in the midst of them for evermore (**Ezekiel 37**).

50 hear this word and with one. the remembrance of your heart all that you shall learn. 2 **For the earth shall then assuredly restore the dead**, which it now receives, in order to preserve them. It shall make no change in their form, but as it has received so shall it restore them, and as I delivered them unto it, so also shall it raise them. 3 For then it will be necessary to show to the living that the dead have come to life again, and that those who had departed have returned again (**2 Baruch 50:1-3**).

[12] And it shall come to pass in that day, that the Lord shall beat off from the channel of the river unto the stream of Egypt, and ye shall be gathered one by one, O ye children of Israel.

[13] And it shall come to pass in that day, that the great trumpet shall be blown, and they shall come which were ready to perish in the land of Assyria, and the outcasts in the land of Egypt, and shall worship the Lord in the holy mount at Jerusalem **(Isaiah 27:12-13)**.

[10] And the devil that deceived them was cast into the lake of fire and brimstone, where the beast and the false prophet are, and shall be tormented day and night for ever and ever.

[11] And I saw a great white throne, and him that sat on it, from whose face the earth and the heaven fled away; and there was found no place for them.

[12] And I saw the dead, small and great, stand before YAHUAH Elohiym; and the books were opened: and another book was opened, which is the book of life: and the dead were judged out of those things which were written in the books, according to their works.

[13] And the sea gave up the dead which were in it; and death and hell delivered up the dead which were in them: and they were judged every man according to their works.

[14] And death and hell were cast into the lake of fire. **This is the second death.**

[15] And whosoever was not found written in the book of life was cast into the lake of fire **(Revelations 20:10-15).**

Then, after this matter, on the tenth week in the seventh part, there shall be the eternal judgment; and it shall be executed by the angels of the eternal heaven- the great judgment which emanates from all of the angels. The first heaven shall depart and pass away; a new heaven shall appear; and all the powers of heaven shall shine forever sevenfold. Then after that there shall be many weeks without number forever; it shall be (a time) of goodness and righteousness, and sin shall no more be heard of forever.

"Now I shall speak unto you, my children, and show you the ways of righteousness and the ways of wickedness. Moreover, I shall make a revelation to you so that you may know that which is going to take place. •Now listen to me, my children, and walk in the way of righteousness, and do not walk in the way of wickedness, for all those who walk in the ways of injustice shall perish (**Enoch 91:15-19**)

29 After these years shall **my Son Mashiach die, and all men that have life. 30 And the world shall be turned into the old silence seven days, like as in the former judgments: so that no man shall remain.** 31 And **after seven days the world, that yet awakens not, shall be raised up, and that shall die that is corrupt.** 32 And the earth shall restore those that are asleep in her, and so shall the dust those that dwell in silence, and the secret places shall deliver those souls that were committed unto them. 33 And **El Elyon shall appear upon the seat of judgment**, and misery shall pass away, and the longsuffering shall have an end: 34 But judgment only shall remain, truth shall stand, and faith shall wax strong **(Esdras 7:29 -33):**

[6] And he said unto me, These sayings are faithful and true: and the YAHUAH Elohiym of the holy prophets sent his angel to shew unto his servants the things which must shortly be done.

[7] Behold, I come quickly: blessed is he that keepeth the sayings of the prophecy of this book **(Revelations 22:6-7).**

REMEMBER TO STAY TUNED TO THE SERIES.

Unlocking Bible Mysteries and Hidden Secrets Revealed
LOVE AND SHARE
The job of all believers is to spread the message of the Good News, Forgiveness of Sin Ha'Mashiach by repenting and obeying the TORAH and follow YAH
Everyone that you know and don't know must have a copy of this book. Follow the projects of works
Be sure to tell everyone to get their copy wherever books are sold
LOVE AND SHARE A TREE
REPENT. OBEY TORAH
COME OUT OF MYSTERY BABYLON
WOE!
CALL ON YAH
Become a free member at www.gianmichaelsimmons.com

TORAH LAW - 10 COMMANDMENTS - REPENT

- **I am the Yahuah your Yahuah Elohiym. You shall not have strange Elohiym before me. You shall not make to thyself any graven thing; nor the likeness of anything that is in heaven above, or in the earth beneath, nor of those things that are in the waters under the earth. You shall not adore them nor serve them.**
- **You shall not take the name of the Yahuah your Elohiym in vain.**
- **Remember to keep holy the Sabbath day.**
- **Honor your father and your mother.**
- **You shall not kill.**
- **You shall not commit adultery.**
- **You shall not steal.**
- **You shall not bear false witness against your neighbor.**
- **You shall not covet your neighbor's wife.**
- **You shall not covet your neighbor's goods.**

EXODUS 20

(also review Deuteronomy curses and blessings)

Note: Moses did reveal additional laws and commandments. **A commandment is a law of YAH that all must comply with or be cursed. I encourage you to study the complete laws of YAH.** There are 613 laws, not all are for everyone. The 10 commandments are the general summary laws all must obey.

HOLY DAYS AND TORAH CALENDAR

Lunar month = 29.53 days

Lunar year = 354.36 days (11 days shorter than solar year)

Solar year = 365.24 days (also the **circumference of a circle 365.24**)

The Bible using the **Lunar Calendar** for all events of Israel that will have an impact on the world. The **Solar Calendar** is used for all "local" events of Israel. **You must use both calendars in synchronization FOR A 13TH MONTH!**

THE MESSIANIC NUMBER OF HA'MASHIACH, 13 RECONCILES THE HOLY CALENDAR TO BALANCE THE SOLAR AND THE LUNAR CALENDARS!

Spring Feasts:

1. Passover
2. Unleavened Bread
3. First fruits
4. Feast of Weeks (Pentecost)

Fall Feasts

5. Feast of the Trumpets (Rosh Hashanah)
6. Day of Atonement (Yom Kippur)
7. Feast of Tabernacles (Sukkoth)

2022 Feast Dates (according to Cepher.net)

• **Passover**	**April 14th**
• **Unleavened Bread**	**April 15th- 21st**
• **First Fruits**	**April 17th**
• **Feast of weeks (Pentecost)**	**June 5th**

- **Feast of Trumpets (Rosh Hashanah)** **September 25th**
- **Day of Atonement (Yom Kippur)** **October 4th**
- **Feast of Tabernacles (Sukkoth)** **October 9-16**

COME OUT OF MYSTERY BABYLON

Mystery Babylon =
Christianity, Islam, Catholicism,
Spiritualism, Witchcraft, Sorcery, ETC. Pagans/
Atheism, FREEMASONS = Esau-Rome

- **After reading this book of works, your eyes should be opened to see the reality about Mystery Babylon. She hides in all things. Any religion or noun (person, place, or thing) that teaches things that contradicts the Word of YAH and is not YAH is Mystery Babylon. These are the works of the Anti Ha'Mashiach and are blasphemy. They will only lead you to eternal hell and damnation, right along with them.**
- **ALL RELIGIONS ARE MYSTERY BABYLON FREEMASONS**
- **It's blasphemy to claim a white Jesus or any other false images**
- **ISLAM, CHRISTIANITY, and CATHOLICS know exactly WHO ISRAEL is and they TARGET YOU with FALSE TEACHINGS. They were all started by Freemasons.**
- **The Sabbath was changed to Sundays for sun worship of serpents**
- **Yahusha (a.k.a. Jesus) was born in September, which is the 7th month to Hebrews. He was not born in December.**
- **Yahusha birth date was changed to worship serpents and nature**
- **It's blasphemy to celebrate Christmas, Easter, and most holidays as they all have pagan origins and secret meanings.**
- **There's no scriptural teaching of any birthday celebrations.**
- **All Mystery Babylon was involved with slavery and genocide of Black Hebrews, even this day!**
- **They attempt to replace Israel. Everyone Is involved, including some Israelites (the mixed feet of the Daniel Prophecy)**
- **Daniel sets forth 4 kingdoms to rule Earth before YAH comes. Esau-Rome is the last, 4th beast. They represent the feet of Daniel where we have clay mixed with iron. The clay is Israel. The iron is Esau-Rome. The two are working together as sell-outs. Just as this is not a solid foundation, once truth gets out, the feet breaks and the statue falls. You're**

coming out of Mystery Babylon is already written in prophecy. Don't feel bad. It's written by YAH.

- **They sell false interpretations of the Bible/Cepher**
- **They hid Hebrew books for centuries (ex. Jasher, Jubilees, Maccabees, Enoch, Baruch, Esdras). Books that prove our identity and YAH's plan for salvation.**
- **They all have pagan teachings, customs, and traditions**
- **THEY ARE ALL FREEMASONS**
- **SATAN SERPENT WORSHIP**
- **They all use witchcraft, sorcery, divination, and magic**
- **They teach things against YAH**
- **All in league with SCIENCE WHICH IS AGAINST YAH**
- **You CANNOT "Christianize" HEBREWS**
- **You CANNOT hide in fallen ISLAM**
- **ROME IS THE ENEMY and MYSTERY BABYLON**

Unlocking Bible Mysteries and Hidden Secrets Revealed
GENDER
In the beginning, YAH made both male and female to represent the human family to produce life. After YAH made ADAM (male and female), YAH rested and said that everything is all good.
The law of nature requires both male and female to produce life naturally. It's the combing of positive and negative that creates life and carries energy. Think of a battery, you have two polar opposites of energy along the same line. A battery has both positive and negative to produce energy or life. Each gender has their role. YAH created male and female
The enemy attacked the family structure, removed the man out of the household, so females are raising children alone. The system matrix is designed for the male to be systematically incarcerated in a public institution, such as prison. That's why there's more Blacks in prisons than in any educational institution.
They involve in secret sciences of manipulating Earth's electromagnetic energy. That's how they flood you with feminine energy and homosexuality. Lust. Pride. Temptations of the flesh. You cannot choose your gender!
Honor the creation from the Creator, YAH
SEX CHANGE IS AN ABOMINATION OF YAH
PLAY YOUR ROLE

RETURN THE HEARTS OF CHILDEN TO THE FATHER

I leave you with this. Softly, YAH is calling you home!

A Father had allowed his children to go to a playground. They were there playing while the Father was observing and watching. The children were playing so long. They thought that they were having a good time. They were fooled. They were ignorant that the Father had a conversation with the parent of the other children that were playing with the Father's children. The other parent had taken his children AND the Father's children. He took them off the playground and took them to his playground.

The children were taken as young babies. **As children, they were raised by the parent that stole them. They were ignorant of this as they were young and could only remember the thief as their father. They had forgotten their real Father.** The thief raised them to believe that they were his children. **The thief removed their identity. Gave them his own.** He colored them. Not realizing that black cannot be colored. Black thought that they were a color. He trained them to conform to his demonic ways and hidden it behind fake religions, customs, holidays, traditions, rules, culture, laws, and life. He even gave them a new calendar. **A new way to see time**.

So, the children are raised not knowing who they really are. They have a false identity. They even praise the thief. The thief gave them his false education, false way of life, false way of thinking, false way of acting, false way of talking, false way of loving, and false god to praise and pray to.

Let's fast forward. The children are now older. The children are wise. The children are waking up to realize that they have been stolen. The children realize that they are not the children of their thief. The Father remembered the conversation that he had with the thief. So, the Father is searching for the ends of the Earth for His children. The children are searching for the depths of their soul for their Father. The magnet of Love. The magnet of YAH, The Father, is attracting the children to come together. The thief had no power to hold the children any longer. The spells have been removed. The tricks no longer work. The truth has been revealed. **Ezekiel 37** dry bones are coming to life!

Will you go back home with your REAL FATHER, or will you stay with a lying thief?

Come Home to YAHUAH Elohiym. The ONLY TRUE Elohiym. I LOVE YOU. I pray that you listen, love, pray, and overstand. YAHUAH Elohiym be ALL THE GLORY, HONOR, PRAISE.

Unlocking Bible Mysteries and Hidden Secrets Revealed
The Book of Revelations Signs and Wonders
The Book of Revelations is an extremely coded text and cannot be interpreted literally alone. **John**, using allegories and symbolism is communicating visions that he is receiving, in the order of him receiving the visions, and not necessarily in the order of sequence of events. To understand the context, one would need to turn scriptures to the books of **Esdras** and **Baruch** to confirm a **triangulation** of **facts, Jubilees**.
Did you know that no event remains to bring forth Ha'Mashiach? Some examples of fulfilled prophecies include 2/3rds Israel lost through the fire, 1/3 Israel remains to be saved, wars, signs in nature, and mass falling away of saints. The horseman has ridden. The fallen stars are already on Earth. **Heaven has been shaken! The sealed book has been opened by the White Horse. The Anti-Mashiach and False Prophet are here. All religions end at Rome, with the Pope – Anti Mashiach. Esau-Rome false religions of Christianity, Islam, Catholicism, all Marks of Mystery Babylon, COVID vaccine, are all MARKS OF THE BEAST.** This has been the last 2,000 years completing Jacobs Trouble representing the Gentile world.
WORMWOOD PROPHECY FULFILLED
Majority of our drinking water is already poisoned with unsafe chemicals. That's why we're forced buy water when it's free from our sinks. Also, many water animals perish due to man's pursuit of robbing Earth's resources. The amount of oil and waste in our waters is eliminating species of fish. Even drinking water kills as blood!
Did you know? FLOURIDE KILLS
The WORD OF YAH has PROVEN AUTHENTICITY
Revelations, Unlocking Bible Mysteries and Hidden Secrets Revealed

THE PRAYER OF MANASSEH

1 O Yahuah El Shaddai of our fathers, Avraham (Abraham), Yitschaq (Isaac), and Ya' agov (Jacob), and of their righteous seed; 2 who have made heaven and earth, with all the ornament thereof; 3 who have bound the sea by the word of your commandment; who have shut up the deep, and sealed it by your terrible and glorious name; 4 whom all men fear and tremble before your power; 5 for the majesty of your glory cannot be borne; and your angry threatening toward sinners importable:

6 But your merciful promise is unmeasurable and unsearchable; 7 for you are El Elyon, of great compassion, longsuffering, very merciful, and repent of the evils of men. You, O Yahuah, according to your great goodness, have promised repentance and forgiveness to them that have sinned against you; And of your infinite mercies have appointed repentance unto sinners that they might be saved.

7 for you are El Elyon, of great compassion, longsuffering, very merciful, and repent of the evils of men. You, O Yahuah, according to your great goodness, have promised repentance and forgiveness to them that have sinned against you: And of your infinite mercies have appointed repentance unto sinners that they might be saved. 8 You therefore, O Yahuah, that are the Elohiym of the just, as to Avraham, and Yitschaq, and Ya'aqov, which have not sinned against you; 9 but you have appointed repentance unto me that am a sinner: For I have sinned above the number of the sands of the sea.

10 My transgressions, O Yahuah, are multiplied: My transgressions are multiplied, and I am not worthy to behold to see the height of heaven for the multitude of my Torahless deeds. I am bowed down with many iron bands that I cannot lift up my head, neither have any release: For I have provoked your wrath and done evil before you: I did not do your will, nelther kept I your commandments: I have set up abominations and multiplied offences. 11 Now therefore I bow the knee of my heart, beseeching you of grace. 12 I have sinned, O Yahuah, I have sinned, and I acknowledge my Torahless ways;

13 Wherefore I humbly beseech, forgive me, O Yahuah, forgive me, and destroy me not with my iniquities. Be not angry with me forever by reserving evil for me; neither condemn

me to the lower parts of the earth. 14 For you are the Elohiym, even the Elohiym of them that repent; and in me you will show all your goodness: for you will save me that am unworthy according to your great mercy. Therefore I will praise you forever all the days of my life: for all the powers of the heavens do praise you, and yours is the glory forever and ever. Amein.

CONCLUSION

In **Matthew 5:8**, we are taught that only the pure in heart shall see YAHUAH Elohiym. I have seen YAH. I have travelled the vastness of darkness in efforts to speak life and love to prepare the hearts of the children to return to their Father, YAHUAH Elohiym and I solely used the Word of YAH.

I have spoken light to the vast seas of darkness with the fearless faith of Elijah and with the **Ruach Ha'Qodesh**. I shined the light on sin.

My desire was to not leave any stone unturned in order that you may receive the stone that the builder's rejected, which has become the chief cornerstone. That cornerstone is Ha'Mashiach, the Son of YAHUAH Elohiym.

We reviewed the cornerstone of a wonderful story from creation to reconciliation back to YAH. YAH created all things. The first act of creation was the Light of the World, Ha'Mashiach.

All things are subject to YAH. We know that YAH created the heavens and earth. We know that the first Adam and Eve sinned and subjected man to the veil between heaven and Earth.

YAH is a Elohiym of consuming fire. Because of the veil, YAH uses His Son, Ha'Mashiach to bring all things to reconcile back to the Father, YAHUAH Elohiym.

In the division of nations, we are made aware that YAH chose the children of Israel as His chosen people and seed. Furthermore, we were made aware that the entire Bible/Cepher is the history of Israel and YAH's salvation plan.

We identified the 12 Tribes of Israel to be your modern-day Africans in the Americas, blacks, browns, and yellow, a.k.a. African Americans, etc. The 10 tribes will join from their secret hiding place.

We are made aware that Ha'Mashiach and the Father are one in righteousness and YAH is the only one that can save you. Additionally, we learn that Ha'Mashiach is of the color of a garnet crystal stone, which is of a dark reddish-black color. We also learn this is the color of Adam and Eve, and of YAH. Keep in mind, YAH is a spirit.

Unlocking Bible Mysteries and Hidden Secrets Revealed
THE ROSE
Did you know? **The red rose is a secret symbol of Ha'Mashiach because of the color and the fact that it's immortal. The pomegranate is another symbol.**
That's how poetic YAH is. There's always loving multi-layered meaning
YAH LOVES FOREVER

Ha'Mashiach is set to appear at any moment to usher in the kingdom of heaven on Earth. **The time to repent is now to be saved. I highly suggest that you over-study this book and be sure that everyone you know has a copy.** You may also become a free member of my online community at www.gianmichaelsimmons.com and follow me on social media @GianMichaelSimmons.

ALL PRAISES TO YAHUAH Elohiym (a.k.a. YAHWEH).

REPENT - SEEK THE KINGDOM OF HEAVEN ON EARTH

YAH is a Elohiym of Righteousness. Only the pure in heart shall see YAH and the Kingdom of Heaven on Earth. No man knows the hour of the coming of Ha'Mashiach.

We are at the End of the Gentile World. **Scriptures are clear that Only Judgement Remains.**

With this said, **the coming of Ha'Mashiach will be to bring judgement on this world and to usher in the Kingdom of Heaven on Earth. As well as to regather Israel back to the Promised Land.**

He is not coming to preach, teach, or produce miracles to impress you. Ha'Mashiach is coming to bring **Immediate Judgement on ALL THINGS UNDER THE SUN.**

WOE TO ALL SINNERS. YOU MUST REPENT.

WOE TO THOSE WITH MARKS OF THE BEAST.

WOE MYSTERY BABYLON.

Ha'Mashiach is coming to send sinners to eternal hell and those saved into eternal heaven. Thus, THE TIME TO BE SAVED IS NOW.

Ha'Mashiach is the ONLY JUDGE OF THIS WORLD and HEAVEN. HE is THE ONLY WAY TO BE SAVED.

SALVATION IS A FREE GIFT IF YOU REPENT AND OBEY THE TORAH LAW OF YAH.

ALL SINNERS WHO DO NOT REPENT WILL GO TO ETERNAL HELL AND NEVER LIVE AGAIN.

The DEVIL WILL BE DEFEATED AND LOCKED AWAY IN BURNING HELL FOREVER.

Those who are saved will experience HEAVEN ON EARTH WITH YAH, FOREVER.

SCRIPTURES ARE CLEAR THAT WE ALL MUST BE BORN AGAIN. This is a SPIRITUAL REBIRTH to KILL THE FLESH

(some examples: Religion, Lust, Pride, Damnation, Jealousy, Evilness, Witchcraft, Sorcery, Blasphemy, Murder, Theft, Lying, Stealing, Cheaters, Adultery, Homosexuality, Bestiality, Demonism, Spiritualism, Mystery Babylon, Child Abuse, Paganism, Haters, Discrimination, Racism, Prejudice, Violence, The Flesh and Abominations of YAH, ETC.)

Aside from the young children, **we will ALL FACE JUDGEMENT DAY ALONE WITH YAH.**

No man can pray you into heaven. No man can buy you into heaven. No money and no one can save you. No job title can save you. Clergy cannot save you. No sin will escape punishment.

All sins will be accounted for as th**e BOOK OF LIFE will be opened to reveal your LIFE CHOICES, ACTIONS, and INACTIONS. NOTHING CAN HIDE.**

Only the things of YAH will SAVE YOU.

YAH forgives if you repent and obey TORAH LAW.

Scriptures reveal many beautiful stories about the FORIVENESS OF SIN. Some examples:

- **Moses committed murder, defending a Hebrew, at a young age. YAH Forgave him and Moses went on to be the Lawgiver of Israel after leading**

the 12 Tribes of Israel from the Exodus of Egypt. Moses is credited with writing the Torah.

- **King David sinned. His lust of women, had him to take a wife that YAH forbade. This was the secret motivation behind one of his missions that wasn't divinely inspired. YAH forgave him and King David went on to becoming another "Abraham-like" significant character of Israel. Ha'Mashiach is in his lineage.**

ASIDE FROM BEING AN ENEMY OF YAH. NO MATTER WHAT YOU ARE DOING OR HAVE DONE, YOU CAN TURN FROM EVIL, FOLLOW YAH, AND BE SAVED.

There are 2 MAIN INGREDIANTS to BEING BORN AGAIN (SPIRITUALLY)

1. **Baptism of Repentance**
    a. **This is the message that Noah and Elijah preached as one that cries in the wilderness to set the path for YAH. It's a purification process of righteousness. He will send Elijah for Elijah represents FEARLESS REPENTANCE. You MUST REPENT TO SEE YAH. To be saved, you can't be afraid or have fears.**

    The first step to being born again is to depart from evil and REPENT. The spirit of Elijah also brings complete **FEARLESS FAITH IN YAH.** Read and Study about Elijah and (**Books of Kings**).

    You are preparing holy grounds for YAH.

    b. **Those who walk with YAH are new creations. ALL THINGS OLD PERISH. This is when you LET GO OF SIN. All things require WORK, which is why FAITH WITHOUT WORKS IS DEAD. Study TORAH Daily.**

    Make an active decision to **LET GO ALL THINGS THAT ARE NOT OF YAH.** Let GO ALL THINGS OF THIS WORLD.

Those that are friends of this world are enemies of YAH.

Take ALL THINGS to YAH in PRAYERS. Bring YAH all your struggles. YAH will GUIDE YOU. YAH will lead you beside the still waters for HIS NAME'S SAKE. Though that you walk through the valleys of the shadows of darkness, **FEAR NO EVIL. YAH will be with you**. YAH will prepare a table before your enemies for HIS NAME'S SAKE.

DON'T GIVE UP THE FIGHT FOR YOUR LIFE. Even the youth may faint and be weary. Young men shall utterly fall. Wait upon YAH. You'll mount upon wings just as eagles. You will run and not faint. Weeping may endure for a night, but JOY will come with YAH.

You must obtain a Torah and begin to study the Word of YAH. Say the prayer of Manasseh. Ask YAH to forgive you. STOP DOING THE THINGS THAT KILL THE SPIRIT OF YAH. Read 2 Chronicles 7:14.

Learn YAH's LAW and OBEY. Fast and pray, often. Learn the Holy feast days. **Honor the Sabbath, which is Saturday and not Sunday.**

Stop pagan traditions and holidays. Come out of Mystery Babylon.

Learn and obey the Torah Law, the 10 commandments. We are to LOVE EACH OTHER AND YAH.

2. **Baptism of the Ruach Ha'Qodesh (a.k.a. Holy Spirit of YAH)**

The Ruach Ha'Qodesh is the spirit of YAH that abides in the hearts of all believers and those that follow TORAH Law.

No man has seen the Father, YAHUAH Elohiym, except the Son, Ha'Mashiach. For YAH so loved the Israelites, YAH created Earth, and the coming heaven on Earth, and YAH gave His Son, Ha'Mashiach so that whosoever believe in YAH shall not perish but shall have eternal life.

The Ruach Ha'Qodesh is the spirit power of YAH.
YAH is the only name that conquers all things, including your devils and sin.

We must begin to call on the name of YAH. Ask for YAH's Ruach Ha'Qodesh to abide in the tabernacles of your heart. The baptism of repentance will prepare the place before you enemies and purify the grounds for YAH's holy presence to enter beyond the VEIL.

Elijah was a mighty man of fearless faith. He went on to be one of the greatest of prophets. He even started a prophet school for Hebrews. He walked with YAH. He was raptured and didn't die.

They represent the spirit of repentance for you need fearless faith to walk with YAH. You need to be equipped and prepare your holy ground.

The baptism of repentance sets the stage for the baptism of the Ruach Ha'Qodesh, which is the Spirit of YAH abiding in the tabernacles and temple of your soul. You carry the ARK OF YAH.

Once you have the baptism of repentance and the baptism of Ruach Ha'Qodesh, you have the keys to BEING BORN AGAIN. You walk with YAH.

Those who walk with YAH are new creations and old things pass away. You are now a new man or woman in YAH in righteousness.

Scriptures also teach us that we fight not against flesh but against spirits and princes, therefore we MUST PUT ON THE FULL ARMOR OF YAH.

There's no greater joy than what YAH will give to you and forever.

The Coming of Ha'Mashiach is to BRING IMMEDIATE JUDGEMENT ON THIS WORLD AND EVERYTHING IN IT.

THE TIME TO BE SAVED IS NOW.

It's important to note, these are NOT TEMPORARY JUDGEMENTS COMING. The JUDGEMENTS COMING are ETERNAL. Meaning, they will last FOREVER.

In eternal heaven, on Earth, will be YAH and all the children of YAH. In eternal hell will be the devil and all those that sin.

Giving credence to the spirit of repentance, fearless faith, and the spirit of the Ruach Ha'Qodesh, it was my hope that I left no stone unturned to present an opportunity for you to see the errors in your ways and to have an opportunity to be born again in the spirit of YAH. Secure the stone that the builders rejected for King of Kings is the cornerstone and the only way to be saved is YAH.

I pray that this message is consigned throughout the four winds of the Earth, all the lands and seas, the inner-Earth and the outer/surface Earth, the dark caves and mountains, and the depths of your soul. May the children of Israel and those that cleave, seek the kingdom of heaven and LOVE. Seek YAH.

The most sacred place in the whole wide world is in the Arms of YAH. There's no place that I'd rather be than in the Arms of YAH, our Elohiym and King of Kings and Elohiym of Elohiym.

Judgement Day is Coming. Seek The Kingdom of Heaven

ABOUT THE AUTHOR

Gian Michael Simmons

YAH Bless

The movement has begun! **Silence Speaks Love Liberates. Now, REVELATIONS UNLOCKING BIBLE MYSTERIES AND HIDDEN SECRETS REVEALED**

Amazon Author Page: www.amazon.com/author/gianmichaelsimmons

www.gianmichaelsimmons.com

Repent. Seek ye the kingdom of heaven is at hand

YAH holds the keys to salvation

Gian is a man of YAH and walks with YAH in all his ways. He is a single father to Isaiah. Seven months ago, Gian retired from a 19-year Wall Street career to focus on the works of YAH.

Gian attained his bachelor's degree from the State University of New York at Albany, where he served as a student president for over three years.

Gian was the first college graduate in his family. He was proud of the opportunity to encourage others. He was a very active student-leader and he served as President for three consecutive years and received the President's Undergraduate Leadership Award, the highest prestigious recognition, for each of those years. During Gian's freshman year, he wrote and directed a play and filled the audience. He donated the proceeds to a local charity. This would become the event that would land Gian the office of presidency. During his leadership at Albany, Gian galvanized the students and leaders, had many landmark events, and left a historical lasting impact felt throughout generations of students, past and current. Gian always committed his life's mission to developing relationships, creativity, leadership, diversity and equality, community service, philanthropy, and being a seeker of the kingdom of heaven.

During Gian's leadership years at the University at Albany, he represented the students with leaders such as the Late- Coretta Scott King, the- Late Betty Shabazz, Hillary Clinton, the Late-Congressman John Lewis, the Late- Maya Angelou, Dr. Sonia Sanchez, Saul Williams, Chuck D, Professor Griff, Tommy Hilfiger, the Late- Dr. Carson Carr Jr., Dr. Marcia Sutherland, Dr. James Turner, Cornel West, Jay Z, Diddy, Wyclef Jean, just to name a few. Gian is very talented, loves to create, and rise in leadership. In college, Gian planned many events. One event that he's most proud about is founding the first Capital District Hip Hop Conference attended by many from all over the world. Gian wrote the blueprint for the 3-day conference, which included several events such as workshops, keynote speakers, panel discussions, poetry event, hip hop show and party, dinners, and fashion show. Gian enjoys being a leader and providing opportunities of progressive growth for man and equal opportunity.

Gian has always remained an active member in his community. In his spare time, he enjoys reading and writing. He also loves to cook. At a young age, Gian would ask his mother to buy him books instead of toys. His favorite book was the Bible and dictionary and he loved to learn new words daily. Gian has been writing from a very young age and enjoys exercising various writing styles. His dream is to write movies. Gian enjoys being a student of the engagements of words and characters. Writing has always been a hobby for Gian. Gian is a student of wisdom, knowledge, and a seeker of higher truths. Gian enjoys maintaining an intimate relationship with YAH through His Son, Ha'Mashiach. Gian enjoys reading the Holy Bible and Cepher, studying text and verses, learning from the parables and stories, the threshing floor of prayers, learning obedience and the laws of YAH, studying the prophets, the promise of YAH and allowing the text to clothe himself as coats of skin and armor of protection. Gian has always heard the calling and enjoys walking with YAH.

Since discovering the identity of the Children of YAH, Gian has a deep passion to educate others of true knowledge of YAH. Gian is a voice crying in the wilderness to reveal the errors in our ways to get us to repent. He wishes for none of us to perish, but for each of us to examine ourselves, depart from evil, and turn to YAH. Turn your hearts to the Father Creator, YAH.

Gian is also excited to announce the start the foundations of his non-profit organization called **"Love Liberates Inc. Nonprofit"**. A portion of this book's proceeds will go to help start this charitable project that he's very excited about. The mission of Love Liberates is to restore the hopes and joys of life, to motivate and encourage others, to foster mentorship, meditation group, inner city community services, and homeless outreach.

Gian also created a social media website with full-service features for a safe place for people to fellowship, join groups and network, learn new things, expand in wisdom and understanding, be entertained with engaging writings, blogs, and podcasts, shop with free worldwide shipping, and more. Keep in mind that if you see the name Jesus mentioned, it is reference to Yahusha and to target Hebrews list in Christianity. It's usage does not indicate the false character of Esau-Rome's Jesus.

You may find **Gian Michael Simmons Productions** and **Love Liberates Non-Profit** at www.gianmichaelsimmons.com and follow Gian's social media pages for updates. Gian can be found @GianMichaelSimmons on Facebook, LinkedIn, Instagram, WordPress and @GianMSimmons on Twitter. Stay tuned!

Bookmark and Become a Free Member

WWW.GIANMICHAELSIMMONS.COM

Amazon Author Page: www.amazon.com/author/gianmichaelsimmons

For more information on **Gian Michael Simmons Productions**, projects, groups, writing and poetry samples, and **Love Liberates Inc. Nonprofit**. Also on the website, over 200 products including clothing, coats, face masks, posters, hats, bags, and more! Member Reward Program for points on spending, member coupons, and **Free Worldwide Shipping. By joining, you receive a one-time use 20% off coupon to use for online shopping.**

Gian is also working on a subscription-based podcast channel, newsletter, and expanding social media groups and podcasts. Everything from faith, poetry, music, teaching essential skills, financial literacy, events, networking, and more. Stay tuned.

You may **become a member** of my personal website for exclusive-member content and **download the free Spaces by Wix app** for a personalized experience.

JOIN ME ON FACEBOOK AND MY SOCIAL MEDIA WEBSITE

Transforming my Facebook group page. The page is currently called "Silence Speaks Jesus Saves" currently 2,000 members. Search in Facebook groups. The name of Jesus is being used to target **Hebrews lost in Christianity and its usage implies the actual character of Ha'Mashiach. I will be updating the name in the future.** I will also be updating my page for Hebrews.

Welcome to Silence Speaks Jesus Saves Facebook Group. My personal website is www.gianmichaelsimmons.com. I am a professional Hebrew Author and leader. The only true living YAH. For all YAH lovers, share your favorite Bible scriptures, prayers, lessons, songs, and stories. If you need prayer, share your prayer request. If you are a pastor, share your ministry. If you are a Hebrew author or artist, share your works. Share your testimonies to bear witness to the power of YAH. All positive vibes for Hebrews.

I encourage active participation on my Facebook group. All can submit posts. All can add new members. Share the love. Bear with me as I clean up my page and update.

All can add new members, share posts, post, comment, and network. Follow @ GianMichaelSimmons on LinkedIn, Facebook, Facebook page, Instagram, WordHub and @GianMSimmons on Twitter. Over 100,000 Followers and Growing.

Published author www.gianmichaelsimmons.com

Gian Michael Simmons Productions
www.GIANMICHAELSIMMONS.com
Amazon Author Page: www.amazon.com/author/gianmichaelsimmons

Silence Speaks and Love Liberates Media Kit

The purpose of me establishing the ***Silence Speaks and Love Liberates Media Kit*** is to share some love, recognize your leadership, commitment to the service of the works of YAH, and **to solicit your support behind this major movement of YAH: Silence Speaks and Love Liberates.**

Thank you for your love, service, and dedication. I admire your generosity for service to the works of YAH. The examples from your leadership helped to inspire me to join in solidarity and oneness as we seek to do the work of YAH.

As a fellow leader for the progression of man, I would like to solicit your support on this exciting project and movement of love. The current crisis on Earth and the magnitude of this message warrants the call for higher levels of leadership and representation. This is a heavenly message for man in our desperate time of need.

The journey begins with a major movement: businesses and writing projects and accumulates into my nonprofit, community service, online businesses, and various projects to prepare the youth of today and to speak to the hearts of all generations of man.

It brings me great pleasure to introduce myself and announce **Gian Michael Simmons Productions**, a professional business conglomerate doing the works of YAH. I will be writing books, movies, series, novels, music, and other forms of expression. I also built a social media website and app to include all functions as any social media site for the public. I also have a motivational and financial empowerment blog, newsletter, and full podcast lineup.

My movements are called Silence Speaks and Love Liberates

1. Have you ever sought a higher truth in YAH?
2. Have you ever wondered why am I here, on Earth?

3. Have you ever wondered if the Earth were a sphere or flat?
4. Have you ever questioned what you were taught and believe?
5. Are you struggling with issues stemming from the flesh?
6. Do you seek a higher purpose and a reason to live greater than yourself?
7. Have you ever wondered how you can connect with YAH?

The Time Has Come To Seek A Higher Truth Other Than Faith
Faith Without Works Is Dead

The movement has begun! **Silence Speaks Love Liberates and now Revelations, Unlocking Bible Mysteries and Hidden Secrets Revealed.**

Silence Speaks and **Love Liberates** are movements combined with business projects and followed by a Multi-Book-Volume Series, over 100 pages in each volume, to connect you with YAH.

The series are designed for one to read in any order, as each multi-dimensional book has a different focus matter of discussion and flows with the overall theme of Silence Speaks and Love Liberates. For committed and advanced readers, you may read the series in the order as follows as each following volume presents a journey to God and additional aroma to the **feature books, which are highlight books for all readers. The feature book for Gian Michael Simmons Productions is "Revelations, Unlocking Bible Mysteries and Hidden Secrets Revealed.** I would highly suggest that all to read this volume. Again, all books may be read in any order. The focus and contents of each book may be found in each book description. Additionally, all projects are described in mission statements.

Repent. Seek ye the kingdom of heaven is at hand
YAH holds the keys to salvation

Available on Amazon books, Apple Books, Barnes and Nobles on Paperback and E-Book versions. E-Books also on my website

Revelations, Unlocking Bible Mysteries and Hidden Secrets Revealed - FEATURE

Amazon Author Page: www.amazon.com/author/gianmichaelsimmons
Website: www.gianmichaelsimmons.com

Gian Michael Simmons walks with YAH and is a seeker of higher knowledge, truth, and love.

HOW YOU CAN SUPPORT

- **All Books are priced in a manner to allow one to purchase the entire set of public works. I am a self-publisher who retired, invested my resources, fighting the system to save you!**
- **SPREAD THE WORD. MAKE SURE EVERYONE BUYS A BOOK**

- **All volumes are available for purchase on Amazon books, Apple books, Barnes and Nobles, and by directly on my website. I am also selling autographed copies of all volumes. I accept CashApp, Zelle, and PayPal. Secured payments.**
- **Leave book reviews on Amazon books, Apple books, and www.GianMichaelSimmons.com**
- **Post pictures with books and share my posts/videos and your picture posts on social**

MEDIA

- **JOIN GROUPS ON MY SOCIAL MEDIA WEBSITE – www.gianmichaelsimmons.com**
- **Be sure to SHOP! - Join for rewards and coupons**

Click the "Shopping link" at www.GIANMICHAELSIMMONS.COM

1. Join and be an active site member and help grow the site. New members receive 20% off coupon single-use and reward points for every dollar spent.

To prepare you for the journey of Silence Speaks and Love Liberates, I added over 200 products on my website in conjunction with my projects. Men's, women's, kids clothing, and other products with free worldwide shopping. Face Masks, Hats, hoodies, shirts, tees, bathing suits, bags, posters, baby clothing, home products, phone cases, and more. All kids clothing has been discounted. **All proceeds will go to help fund my Love Liberates Inc. Nonprofit. Also, all new members receive a new member discount and coupons.**

Love Liberates Inc. Nonprofit will focus on youth mentorship, leadership, and homeless outreach. More information to follow. Stay Tuned!

Also, blog, nonprofit, music, and podcast lineup coming soon. **Download the Spaces by Wix app and become a member for a personalized experience**

- **Visit www.GIANMICHAELSIMMONS.com**
- **Buy your copy wherever books are sold. Gian can be found on LinkedIn, Facebook, Facebook Group, Instagram@ GianMichaelSimmons and @GMSimmons on Twitter. My personal website is: www. GianMichaelSimmons.com**

Featured on my website will be poetry, clothing and apparel, merchandise, accessories with free worldwide shipping. I will also have blogs: motivation, personal development, teaching of essential skills, and financial wellness. I will also be adding a subscription-based podcast lineup. As a member, you can interact with the site as any social media platform with an app and website versions. You may create profiles, posts, comments, and more.

I also started **Love Liberates Non-Profit,** which will also be featured on my website. Love Liberates Inc. will focus on youth mentorship to prepare the youth, ages 16-21, for personal and career development. We will also do homeless outreach. I will have a podcast, teaching of YAH, essential skills, scholarships, and monthly newsletter coming soon.

- I am currently looking for board members and mentors

· I am also looking for professionals, from various industries, to host podcasts teaching essential skills and having important conversations. I paid the expenses of the platform and am offering you a chance to have a free channel. It can also be good exposure to your brand. I currently have over 100,000 social media followers and growing.

- **If you're interested in becoming a board member, hosting a podcast, being a mentor, or purchasing a book directly through my self-publishing company, feel free to contact me by email, at gian@gianmichaelsimmons.com**
- **I am also interested in interviews, podcasts, events, programming, and any positive synergies to collaborate. I'm interested in bringing this to radio, podcasts, and developing music, video, and audiobooks. This is a message that needs to be heard around the planet and rejoiced in the heavens.**

It would be an honor to receive your support and to visit my website to learn more about myself and this very important mission. Join my website as a free member and set up your profile today. As a businessperson, we all are aware of the metrics that companies assess us with on social media, such as comments, likes, shares. Trust me, I do not do this for personal attention and/or fame. I have enough of that to pass around. So, **be sure to be visible and active in your support.** If you're not capable of supporting personally, perhaps you may refer me to one who does support the works of YAH. As children of YAH, we must also display an example to encourage others. I appreciate all your love and support. I do this for YOU. My life is to do the work of YAH. SPREAD THE GOSPEL OF THE GOOD NEWS! YAH FORGIVES AND SAVES! REPENT.

I appreciate your time and attention. I look forward to your support.

Have a pleasant day

Gian Michael Simmons
Gian Michael Simmons Productions
Website: www.gianmichaelsimmons.com
Email: gian@gianmichaelsimmons.com
Amazon Author Page: www.amazon.com/author/gianmichaelsimmons